MUSLIMS AND INDIAN NATIONALISM

Muslims and Indian Nationalism

The Emergence of the Demand for India's Partition 1928-1940

UMA KAURA

MANOHAR
2025

First published 1977
Reprinted 2021, 2022, 2023, 2025

ISBN 978-81-944962-9-8

Published by
Ajay Kumar Jain *for*
Manohar Publishers & Distributors
4753/23 Ansari Road, Daryaganj
New Delhi 110 002

Printed at
Replika Press Pvt. Ltd.

Contents

Preface

The present book is an attempt to discuss the attitude of the Muslims towards Indian nationalism between 1928 and 1940. The outstanding political development in India during this period was the widening of the gulf between the Congress and the Muslim League, and the emergence of the demand for India's partition as embodied in the famous Lahore resolution of the Muslim League adopted in March 1940.

It is not generally realized that this demand had not emerged all of a sudden but was the end result of a process which had begun in 1928 with the failure of the All Parties Convention to satisfy the moderate section of the Muslim League led by Muhammad Ali Jinnah. In between came the emergence of the Muslim All Parties Conference, formulation of Jinnah's Fourteen Points, the Round Table Conferences, the elections of 1937, the failure of the Congress-League coalition proposals, the general Muslim reaction to Congress ministries during 1937-39, the intensification of separatist feelings among the Muslim elite and the encouragement of these feelings by the British, particularly after the outbreak of the Second World War. So far no serious effort has been made to analyse in depth the background and the nature of these developments.

This study is based on the official records of the Government of India, both published and unpublished, and the collection of private papers deposited at the various libraries in New Delhi and London. The records of the All-India Muslim League and other collections of private papers have been deposited at the Karachi University and are not accessible to an Indian scholar. It was, however, possible to find the published records of the Muslim League and brochures and memoranda issued by it and the private papers of some Muslim leaders in New Delhi. Use has been made of the relevant Urdu sources also.

I would like to convey my sincere thanks to Professor Bimal Prasad, of the School of International Studies, Jawaharlal Nehru University for his constant encouragement and guidance ever since I started working on the subject. My acknowledgments are also due to the staff of Nehru Memorial Museum and Library, National Archives of India, Gandhi Smarak Nidhi Library, Jamia Millia Islamia Library, Jawaharlal Nehru University Library and Sapru House Library in New Delhi; and India Office Library and British Museum in London.

New Delhi Uma Kaura

1

The Historical Background

With the decline of the Mughal Empire and the loss of political power to the British, the Hindus and the Muslims started drifting away from each other. The Muslims grew apprehensive of Hindu domination and resented the tenacity with which the Hindus had advanced themselves in various spheres. The fears they entertained in relation to the Hindus greatly influenced the role they were to play in future. In spite of a common history of a thousand years, the two communities could not present themselves as a single political entity. All efforts of the Indian National Congress to achieve this objective failed miserably and, although the Congress always had some Muslims in its ranks and a few of them even occupied the highest positions in it, by and large they preferred to organize themselves separately in order to protect and advance their political rights and interests.

An overwhelmingly predominant view of Hindu-Muslim relations in the nineteenth and twentieth centuries is that the Hindus were more advanced than the Muslims; they had moved ahead of the latter by taking more enthusiastically to Western education and government employment. Many books written on the subject have laid stress on Muslim backwardness as being the main cause for the development of Muslim separatism in India.[1]

1. See, for example, Wilfred Cantwell Smith, *Modern Islam in India: A Social Analysis* (London, 1946), p. 163. He observes :

Some recent historians, however, do not support the hypothesis of Muslim backwardness in all the provinces.[2] On the contrary they argue that the Muslims of North-Western Provinces and Oudh (U.P.) were more advanced than the Hindus and constituted an administrative and cultural elite. Indeed, according to this view the Muslims of U.P. played a major role in the origin and development of Muslim separatism in India because they were a privileged minority and their leaders were determined to maintain their privileges. That province had been a centre of Muslim power since the end of twelfth century. A large proportion of the community lived in towns and they as well as those who lived in the countryside were mainly landlords.[3] The British policy of keeping Persian and then Urdu as the language of administration and the recruitment of subordinates from the traditional Muslim bureaucratic elite of Persian origin also benefited the U.P. Muslims. Their language dominated in the courts and primary schools of the province.[4] They were educationally ahead of Hindus. The Director of Public Instruction of Oudh pointed out in 1874-75 that there were more English schools in Muslim towns than in Hindu towns like Ayodhya. The Muslims were not backward in higher education either. The percentage of Muslims to the total population of U.P. was 14.1 but the percentage of Muslim students in colleges was 18.6 in 1896-97, 19.7 in 1901-2

> . . .Communalism would not have been so effective a divisive force, nor could the upper class Muslims have been so effectively repressed, had the Muslim and Hindu section of the classes concerned been at the same economic level. But they were not. Economic development within the British imperialist system benefited a group of Indians of whom a larger proportion were Hindus than Muslims.

2. On this point see, Anil Seal, *The Emergence af Indian Nationalism: Competition and Collaboration in the late Nineteenth Century* (London, 1968); Peter Hardy, The *Muslims of British India* (London, 1972); Aparna Basu, *The Growth of Education and Political Development in India, 1898-1920* (Delhi, 1974); Prabha Dixit, *Communalism in India: A Struggle for Power* (Delhi, 1974) and Paul R. Brass, "Muslim Separatism in U.P. : Social Context and Political Strategy Before Partition", *Economic and Political Weekly* (Bombay), vol. 5, January-May 1970.
3. Brass, n. 2, p. 167.
4. Seal, n. 2, p. 306.

and 20.8 in 1916-17.[5] In government employment also, the Muslims continued to be ahead of the Hindus till 1931. Despite increasing Hindu competition, Muslims held more than 45 per cent of all the uncovenanted executive and judicial posts in the provinces in 1880s. In fact they held much more than what was due to them as their share. As C.J. Lyall noted in 1882, "...The Muhammadans as a class belong to the middle and higher strata, [they] possess much more than the share of Government employment which their mere numbers would give them, and are comparatively a thriving and energetic element in society."[6]

The fact is that the establishment of the British rule in India affected the different classes of Muslims differently and the nature of the response of the Muslims to the British rule also assumed different forms in different provinces. There were certain Muslims who gained by collaboration with the British. Peter Hardy, who repudiates the popular belief that Muslims as such suffered discriminatory treatment, has explained it by pointing out that after 1857 "there was a shift in landholding within the Muslim community itself, with those having a Mughal past losing to those with a British future." Such Muslim loyalists as Mahmud Ali Khan of Chhatari, Faiz Ahmad Khan, Abdul Shakur Khan, Inayat Allah Khan of Aligarh and Imdad Ali of Mathura district were typical of those for whom British rule was a blessing and who were prepared to follow Sir Syed in promoting Western education among the Muslims. "As the Punjabi Muslim was loyal to the British", adds Hardly, "he gained in grants of land and in so far as the Bengali Muslim was standing aloof from British education he continued to suffer exclusion from official employment."[7]

In Bengal the position of the Muslims was exactly the opposite of that in U.P. Here they were backward—both economically and educationally. They were also hit by the British rule. The administrative reforms of Cornwallis had reserved higher executive posts for Englishmen and they, were therefore, excluded from them. The Permanent Settlement had elevated

5. Basu, n. 2, p. 150.
6. Seal, n. 2, pp. 305-6.
7. Hardy, n. 2, pp. 78-9.

the Hindu collectors to the position of landlords and had given them the opportunity to amass wealth which otherwise would have fallen to the share of Muslims. The Muslims were also hit by the dropping of Persian as the official language in 1837.[8]

It was Hunter, who publicized the conditions of Muslims in Bengal in 1871 and established the myth that they were backward everywhere. He argued that Muslims had kept aloof from English education because it was "opposed to the traditions, unsuited to the requirements and hateful to the religion."[9] The Hunter Education Commission Report of 1882 also observed that because of pride of race, a feeling of superiority, and religious fears, the Muslims had kept aloof from English education.[10] There is no doubt that the Muslims found it very difficult to tear themselves away from the past. Though they had ceased to be the governing class in India, they were still so much obsessed with their vanished glory and privileged status that they considered themselves as composing the aristocratic class of the country. Sir Syed also pointed to this tendency among Muslims when he wrote from England in 1869 that "...the fatal shroud of complacent self-esteem is wrapt around the Muhammadan community; they remember the old tales of their ancestors and think there are none like themselves. The fatal shroud which is around them has blinded them to the beautiful flowered garden which lies before them."[11] This complex among the Muslims deterred them from taking to English education in large numbers. But another factor responsible for the educational backwardness of Muslims was that even though the upper classes among them showed some keenness to acquire English education, they did not have enough opportunities of doing so. The first schools and colleges were opened in Calcutta where the Hindus predominated. The Muslim districts of East and North Bengal were neglected by the government. Here 85 per cent of the Muslims were agriculturists and it

8. Basu, n. 2, p. 148.
9. W.W. Hunter, *The Indian Mussulmans* (Lahore, 1964), p. 125.
10. Basu, n. 2, p. 151.
11. Syed Rais Ahmad Jafri, ed., *Rare Documents* (Lahore, 1967, pp. 85-6.

was not within their means to afford English education. And because they were cultivators, this education was neither useful nor necessary for them. In the provinces where they were engaged in trade and commerce as in Bombay or in the professions as in U.P., they showed keenness to go for it. But in Bengal, the Muslims lagged behind the Hindus in higher and professional education.[12]

Hunter's arguments, however, were used to characterize the condition of Muslims in all the provinces and were soon exploited by Muslim leaders to wring concessions from the government and later in the appeals made to their community to keep aloof from the Congress. These were the arguments used, for instance, in the famous Memorial of the National Muhammadan Association presented to Ripon in 1882. The Memorial of the Association asked for preferential treatment for Muslims because "no measure of reform adopted within the community would have any appreciable effect in arresting the progress of decay. . . ."[13] Among its demands were reservation of a proportion of jobs for the Muslims, less emphasis on university education as a qualification for office, no simultaneous examinations for the civil services and provision for the special educational requirements of the Muslim community.[14]

Sir Syed also put forward the same argument when he urged the Muslims to concentrate on English education. His plea was that if they did not do so "they would not only remain a backward community but would sink lower and lower."[15] His main concern was for the spread of English education among the Muslims. With this end in view he worked hard for a reconciliation between the British Government and the Muslim upper middle class. After the formation of Indian National Congress in 1885, the efforts made by its leaders to induce the Muslims to join it infuriated Sir Syed.[16] "To his

12. Basu, n. 2, p. 155.
13. Memorial of the National Muhammadan Association, 6 February 1882, *Muslim Selection*, Part 3, p. 237; cited in Seal, n. 2, p. 312,
14. *Ibid*, p. 312.
15. Theodore de Bary, *et al.*, *Sources of Indian Tradition* (New York, 1958), p. 744.
16. A counter-movement in favour of Congress was started by

co-religionists", he said very bluntly that if they joined the Congress "nothing but national disaster lay in store for them."[17] According to him, the object of the promotion of the Congress was that "the Government of India should be English in name only, and that the internal rule of the country should be entirely in their own hands."[18] What antagonized Sir Syed was not the Congress and its leaders but the demands made by the Congress—its clamour for a system of representative institutions and facilities to Indians to compete for the civil service.

In his famous Lucknow speech of 1887, he laid bare the reasons: "whatever system of elections be adopted there will be four times as many Hindus as Mahomedans and all their demands will be gratified." Moreever he feared that since the larger community would override the interests of the smaller community, "the ignorant public would hold government responsible for introducing measures which might make the differences of race and creed more violent than ever."[19] He therefore, advocated that the power of appointing members to local boards and district councils should be held by the government which would maintain that "due and just balance in the representation of the various sections of the Indian population which the system of elections pure and simple would fail to achieve."[20]

Sir Syed really despised the institution of democracy and the attempts at democratization by the Congress mainly because of his feudalistic outlook. The main strategy adopted

the Deoband Muslims. The Deoband leadership differed fundamentally from Sir Syed. In 1885 a 'Fatwa' was issued declaring that in worldly matters co-operation with Hindus was permissible. Maulana Gangohi, the successor of Maulana Nanawtawi (the founder of Deoband School) warned the Muslims not to co-operate with the activities of Sir Syed. A. Faruqi, *The Deoband School and the Demand for Partition* (Bombay, 1963), p. 43.

17. Rafiq Zakaria, *Rise of Muslims in Indian Politics* (Bombay, 1970), p. 53.
18. *Ibid.*, p. 57.
19. *Ibid.*, p. 121.
20. *Ibid.*

at this time by him and his colleagues,[21] who all belonged to the aristocracy, was to decrease the effectiveness of Bengal Hindus (who were most prosperous at that time) and to preserve their own privileged status as a minority. That was the main reason why Sir Syed consistently warned the Muslims against accepting the Western representative system in India which could mean their reduction to a position of permanent minority. In U.P. which was backward in the spread of English education, the most coveted and best-paid jobs in the public service were not occupied by those who were schooled in English. By 1886, only 18 per cent of the executive and judicial officers in the uncovenanted services had passed the University entrance examination. As competitive examination and a university degree were to be essential requirements for holding office, the local population was bound to be hit hard. Graduates from Aligarh, Muir or Canning Colleges were not numerous and what they dreaded was that graduates from outside the province, Bengalis in particular, would get the jobs.[22]

Sir Syed's speeches on all the points at dispute with the Congress reflect his bias against democratic institutions. The tenor of his arguments was that since the Muslims were historically more important and influential, their rights should be granted on that basis. Speaking on the question of representation in the councils by election and the holding of civil service examination in India he said:

> Will the members of noble families in our country like it that a person of lower class or lower status, even if he has taken the B.A. or M.A. degree and possesses the necessary ability, should govern them and dispose of their wealth, property and honour? Never. Not one of them will like it. The seat of the counsellor of the Government is a place of honour. Government cannot give it to anybody except a man of high social status. Neither can the Viceroy address him as "My colleague" or "My honourable

21. Not only Sir Syed but his colleagues also believed in complete subservience to the British. Chief among them were Nawab Mohsin-ul-Mulk, Muhammad Salimullah Khan, Khawaja Altaf Husain Hali, Maulvi Nazir Ahmad and Maulvi Zakaullah.
22. Seal, n. 2, p. 321.

colleague", nor can he be invited to royal levees which are attended by dukes, earls and other men of high rank. So Government can never be blamed if it nominates men of noble families.[23]

Badruddin Tyabji, the president of the Third Congress, was a Muslim. He made efforts to persuade his coreligionists to participate in the national mainstream by joining the Congress, as he very strongly felt that Muslims should make a common cause with their fellow-countrymen on issues which concerned the whole country. In his presidential address he appealed to the Muslims not to distrust the Congress : "...So far as general political questions are concerned, I, for one am utterly at a loss to understand why Mussalmans should not work shoulder to shoulder with their fellow-countrymen or other races and creeds for the common benefit of all."[24] In order to obviate the suspicions lurking in the minds of the Muslims that the Hindus, being numerically stronger, might pass a resolution in Congress, hostile to Muslim interests, he had requested the Standing Congress Committee to consider a proposition that a rule should be passed to drop any subject or any resolution in the case of Muslim delegates unanimously objecting to it. This proposition was duly adopted.[25]

Tyabji approached Sir Syed also in order to win him over to the Congress, but the latter refused to "run a race with persons with whom we have no chance of success." He also objected to the term "National Congress" and observed: "... I do not understand what the words 'National Congress' mean. Is it supposed that the different castes and creeds living in India belong to one nation or can become nation, and their aims and aspirations be one and the same?" His own contention was that it was "quite impossible" and he asserted that there could be "no such thing as a National Congress nor can it be of equal benefit to all people." He regarded it as

23. S. Abid Husain, *The Destiny of Indian Muslims* (Bombay, 1965), p. 36.
24. Badruddin Tyabji's Presidential Address to the Third Indian National Congress held in Madras in 1887, Appendix II in A.G. Noorani, *Badruddin Tyabji* (New Delhi, 1969), p. 150.
25. *Ibid.*, Appendix IV, p. 197.

"not only injurious to our own community but also to India at large."[26]

Tyabji's reply to Sir Syed is noteworthy. He argued that Muslims should not only advance the cause of India but also safeguard their own interests. He assured Sir Syed that it was within the power of the Muslims to oppose such measures of the Congress which they thought were harmful to them:

> ...It is in our power, by firm and resolute action, to divert the course the Congress shall take and my strong conviction is that the Mussalmans can by united action confine the Congress to such topics only as they may deem desirable or safe for discussion. . . . If the Mussalmans as a body do not like that the members should be elected, they could easily modify the proposals so as to suit their own interests. My policy, therefore, would be to act from within rather than from without. I would say to all Mussalmans 'act with your Hindu fellow subjects in all matters in which you are agreed but oppose them as strongly as you can if they bring forward any propositions that you may deem prejudicial to yourselves'.[27]

The British statesmen and officials were ready to treat the Muslims as a distinct political group in India. They were nominated to serve on the Imperial Legislative Council and on the Education and Public Service Commissions. Before the introduction of the elective principle into the constitution of rural local governments as a result of Ripon's Reforms (1883), the Muslims were officially nominated to such bodies. The Education Commission of 1882 conceded that the backwardness of Muslims, as shown in the educational statistics, except in college education, had been exaggerated. Nevertheless, the Commission advocated "a leaning towards generosity in the treatment of Muslims", recommending the recognition of Hindustani in primary and middle schools as the Muslim vernacular, (which in the Punjab, Madras or Bengal

26. *Source Material for a History of the Freedom Movement in India : Collected from Bombay Government Records*, vol. II,1885-1920, p. 70.
27. *Ibid.*, p. 71.

it was not), the teaching of Persian and Hindustani in middle and upper schools, the encouragement of higher education for Muslims and a special section on Muslim education in the annual official reports on public instruction. Going outside its terms of reference the Commission also recommended that provincial governments should be asked to appoint, by patronage, a proportion of Muslim public servants.[28] Confusing the aspirations of upper class Muslims with those of the lower sections of society, the Commission spoke of the Muslims as a class who "have fallen behind in the race of life under British rule."[29] The Government of India resolutions of 23 October 1884 (which spoke of it being desirable to give Muslims exceptional assistance in some respects) and of 15 July 1885 (which assumed that the Muhammadans' as such aspired to rival Hindus in State employment) "helped to endow the Muslims with a separate social as well as religious personality, which needed to be recognized in British policy".[30]

The Indian Council Act of 1892 accepted many demands of the Congress such as enlargement of councils, discussion of financial statements and right of interpellation. The Muslims felt that the Government had succumbed to Congress pressure. They became more firm in their conviction that unless their interests were protected by the government, they would be completely wiped out. Hence they felt that they must devise measures to secure their full share in the constitutional reforms.[31] In despair, the fight against the introduction of representative element in the legislature was given up. A draft scheme was prepared by Sir Syed and other leaders in December 1896 which dealt with Muslim representation in the legislative councils and municipalities and was presented to the Government by the Muhammadan Anglo-Oriental Defence Association. The idea conveyed in the scheme was that the Hindus and the Muslims should get

28. Education Commission Report (1882), pp. 505-7, quoted in Hardy, n. 2, p. 121-2.
29. *Ibid.*, p. 6. Quoted in Hardy, p. 122.
30. Quoted in Hardy, p. 122.
31. Zakaria, n. 17, p. 138.

equal number of seats in the legislative councils because if the Hindus had "numerical superiority", the latter's "historical position" was equally important. The second suggestion was that in the towns where the Muslims comprised one-fourth or more of the population they should be given equal number of seats with the Hindus because "the importance of a section of population depends not only on its numbers but on other considerations".[32]

These arguments were made more convincing as a result of the poor showing of Muslims in elections, particularly to local boards and municipalities. In the elections to the Poona City Municipality held in 1895, the Muslims boycotted the elections as they were sure of not getting even one candidate elected.[33] In the legislative councils, including that of Bengal, which had the largest Muslim population in India, the Hindus had almost double the Muslim representation. "Less in number than the Hindus, those Muslims in the legislative councils were also not representative of Sir Syed and his group, which undoubtedly had a large Muslim following among the upper and educated classes particularly in North India."[34]

It was during this time that there emerged a Hindu revivalist movement in order to arouse the enthusiasm of the masses for political action. The aggressive Hinduism of Tilak and his colleagues especially during the annual Ganpati and Shivaji celebrations, made the politically conscious Muslims feel even more insecure and apprehensive of their future. The ascendancy of the Arya Samaj in the Punjab reinforced the aggressive Hindu image and strengthened the Muslim suspicion because most of the active members of the Punjab Congress were supplied by the Arya Samaj. This was interpreted by Muslims as foreshadowing the "virtual establishment of a Hindu raj" in India once the British relinquished their power.[35]

32. *Ibid.*, p. 140
33. *Ibid.*, p. 142
34. *Ibid.*
35. K.W. Jones, "Communalism in the Punjab: The Arya Samaj Contribution", *Journal of Asian Studies*, vol. 27, November 1968, p. 59.

Meanwhile efforts were made through the Muslim reform movements of the nineteenth century to transform Muslim attitude towards the Hindus. These movements were generally based on a rejection of medieval Islam in India in favour of the early Islam in Arabia. For they preached against the customs which so many Muslims had acquired together with the Hindus—intercession at the tombs of saints, consultation of Brahmins, even vegetarianism and aversion to the remarriage of widows.[36]

By the beginning of the twentieth century, there was a growing realization among the Muslims that they had to have a political organization of their own. The partition of Bengal (1905) also gave some fillip to the growing political consciousness among the Muslims because in the new province they wouid have much greater share in its control and administration. The general basis of participation by Muslims in the Swadeshi movement (started against the partition of Bengal) also deserves emphasis. Most sections of the Muslim society remained loyal to the British Government. An article in *Islam Prachark* in 1905 stated that "under British Rule we are undeniably dwelling in great peace and happiness."[37] Similarily the Muslim press denounced the Swadeshi movement. Another article in *Islam Pracharak* in 1907 rejoiced over the failure of this perverse Hindu Swadeshi movement which "survives in name alone in newspaper propaganda and the dry orations of wordspinners. Otherwise, it is now quite dead."[38]

Despite this professed loyalty of the Muslims towords the British and their strong dislike for the Swadeshi movement, ever since the death of Sir Syed they were not as critical of the Congress as they used to be before. The Muslim press also became quite mild and there were occasional demands from some Muslim leaders for Hindu-Muslim unity and Congress-Muslim co-operation. An article in *Naba Nur* in 1905 reveals the political opinion of a section of educated Muslim society.

36. Hardy, n. 2, p. 59.
37. Quoted in M. Nurul Islam, *Bengali Muslim Public Opinion as Reflected in the Bengali Press, 1901-1930* (Dacca, 1973), p. 47.
38. *Ibid.*, p. 50.

> The British are reluctant to fulfil the aspirations they have aroused in the hearts of the educated of this country by disseminating political ideas from time to time and by spreading English education . . . . It is a travesty of truth to say that these political agitations are confined merely to Hindus. With the spread of education, the desire to ameliorate the motherland is spreading throughout the whole country . . . . For a whole decade the Muslims stood aloof from political agitations. . . . But what good has it done them?[39]

In fact the younger generation among the Muslims had even started thinking in terms of throwing in their lot with the Congress.[40] As regards the nature of a political organization, some Muslims like Nawab Mehdi Hussain of Lucknow wanted to make common cause with the Hindus. Others like Mohsinul-Mulk, Secretary of the Aligarh College and his colleagues cherished the old idea of reviving the Grand Council of chosen leaders to take care of Muslim interests. Some orthodox Muslims also advocated friendship with the Congress on the ground that Muslims were to encounter two kinds of *Jehad* : (1) *Jehad-e-Asgar* (small struggle), in defence of religious rights and liberty, and (2) *Jehad-e-Akbar* (big struggle), involving representation to the rulers for the redress of grievances and the suffering of the subjects. The Congress, they claimed could expect the support of all Muslims in regard to *Jehad-e-Akbar*. As a result of this change in attitude among a substantial section of Muslims there were 50 Muslim delegates at the Twenty-second Congress (1906) including prominent youngmen like Wazir Hasan, M.A. Jinnah and Abbas Tyabjee. It was at this Congress that Jinnah moved an amendment for the deletion of the clause which had made provision for the reservation of seats in the legislatures and services for the educationally backward classes.[41]

The Muslim leadership, however, was still in the hands of landholders and members of the upper middle class. The

39. *Ibid.*, pp. 57-9.
40. Zakaria, n. 17, p. 102.
41. *Ibid.*, p. 103.

government was forced to take note of the growing uneasiness among a community which had been intensely loyal to them and which had never resorted to the methods of agitation to safeguard their interests. Lord Minto, who was appointed Viceroy in 1905, was particularly well disposed towards the Muslims and wanted to give full consideration to their interests. He has very often been accused of exploiting the political consciousness of the Muslims and thus diverting it towards communalistic channels. It has been asserted that the Muslim Deputation was engineered by the Government to offer resistance to nationalist activities and that W.A. Archbold, Principal of the Aligarh College, was its originator. But these charges have been repudiated by some recent historians.[42] Their unanimous view is that Archbold was acting on behalf of and under instructions from Mohsin-ul-Mulk and not vice versa. It was in reply to the letter dated 4 August 1906 that he wrote his letter of 10 August 1906,[43] which has been repeatedly quoted to prove that the British aroused the Muslims as a counterpoise to Hindus.[44] Mohsin-ul-Mulk had written to Archbold on 10 August 1906 illustrating the trend of Muslim thought and the apprehensions of the

42. S.R. Wasti, *Lord Minto and the Indian National Movement*, 1905 to 1910 (London, 1964); M.N. Das, *India under Morley and Minto : Politics behind Revolution, Repression and Reforms* (London, 1964); Matiur Rahman, *From Co-operation to Confrontation* (London, 1970).

43. Archbold had written to Mohsin-ul-Mulk : "the Viceroy agrees to receive a deputation of Muslims. The address to be presented to the Viceroy should be signed by important Muslim leaders of all provinces. While expressing gratefulness for the new policy, it should represent that the system of nomination and not election should be adopted. . . .It is necessary that the opinion of zamindars should be given due weight. Time is short, and if we want to build up a movement, we must hurry up."
Quoted in Ram Gopal, *Indian Muslims* (Bombay, 1959), p. 97.

44. See A. Patwardhan and Asoka Mehta, *The Communal Triangle* (Allahabad, 1942); G.N. Singh, *Landmarks in Indian Constitutional and National Development* (Delhi, 1950); B.M. Chaudhri, *Muslim Politics* (Calcutta, 1946); Ram Gopal, *Indian Muslims* (Bombay, 1959) M. Noman, *Muslim India* (Allahabad, 1942) ; Lal Bahadur, *The Muslim League*, 1954.

Muslims that they might be neglected in any increase of representation on the Legislative Council. He wrote :

> You are aware that the Mohammedans already feel a little disappointed and young educated Mohammedans seem to have a sympathy for the "Congress". . . . There is still a general complaint on their part that we (Aligarh people) take no part in politics, and do not safeguard the political rights of Mohammedans, they say that we do not suggest any plans for preserving their rights. . . I have got several letters drawing attention particularly to the new proposal of "elected representatives" in the Legislative Councils. They say that the existing rules confer no rights on Mohammedans; and no Mohammedans get into the Council by election. . . .[45]

There is, however, no doubt that the British welcomed Mohsin-ul-Mulk's initiative and did everything possible to encourage it. The latter's letter was presented to Minto by Dunlop Smith, his private secretary. On 15 August Minto wrote to Morley about the Muslim apprehensions : "I have always had great hopes of the Mohammedan population. . . and now that they are becoming somewhat alarmed at what they consider Bengali success, the justice of our safeguarding their interests will become all the more apparent."[46] On 1 October 1906 Minto received the Muslim Deputation composed of Muslim nobles, jagirdars, zamindars, taluqdars, lawyers, merchants and retired officials. All these people had connections with the Aligarh movement through the Muslim Educational Conference. The leader of the deputation, the Aga Khan, was a former President of the Educational Conference.[47] In full compliance with the line adopted by Sir Syed, the deputationists claimed that the number of seats to be allotted to the Muslims in the legislatures should be estimated not only on the basis of their numerical strength but also on that of their political impor-

45. Wasti, n. 42, p. 62.
46. M.N. Das, n. 42, p. 167.
47. Matiur Rahman, n. 42, p. 89.

tance and their service to the empire. It was also added that the system of election or nomination to the Legislative Councils so far in practice had failed to give them proper representation and they insisted that they should send their own representatives through separate electorates. It was most unlikely, Minto was told that the name of any Muslim candidate would ever be submitted for the approval of Government by the general electoral bodies. It was also stressed that Muslims were a distinct community with "additional interests of their own which were not shared by other communities and had till then suffered from the fact they had not been adequately represented. Even in the provinces in which the Mohammedans constitute a distinct majority of the population they have too often been treated as though they were appreciably small factors that might without unfairness be neglected."[48] Minto replied that he was sympathetic to these views and that "any electoral representation in India would be doomed to mischieveous failure which aimed at granting a personal enfranchisement regardless of the beliefs and traditions of the communities composing the population of this continent." He further assured the deputationists that Muslim "political rights and interests will be safeguarded in any administration with which I am concerned."[49]

The Congress leaders were quite alarmed at these developments and suspected that the Muslims were being put up as counterpoise to them. This is reflected in the comments by the Congress press. The *Amrita Bazar Patrika* trying to belittle the importance of the deputation commented that it was not an "all-India" deputation and was a 'got up affair fully engineered by interested officials'.[50] The *Bengalee* strongly opposed the Muslim demand for separate representation and considered it "not only indefensible in theory" but feared that it would create "serious political difficulties'.[51]

48. Address presented to Lord Minto, Viceroy and Governor-General of India by A Deputation of the Muslim Community of India on 1 October 1906 at Simla, *Rare Documents*, n. 11, p. 249ff.
49. Wasti, n. 42, p. 72.
50. *Ibid.*, p. 73.
51. *Ibid.*, p. 74.

The organizers of the deputation were quite satisfied as they had succeeded in pacifying the younger section of their community. Mohsin-ul-Mulk expressed his gratitude to the Viceroy for "a clear and sympathetic recognition of the rights of the Mohammedans of India as a distinct community."[52]

The reactions of the Muslim press to the Viceroy's reply were mixed. The *Observer* of Lahore was disappointed as there was no reference to the Muslim demand for more employment in the services and the judiciary.[53] The *Moslem Patriot* (Madras), too found it "disappointing in the extreme" as there was no reference to the idea of a Muslim University.[54] The Viceroy's assurance of safeguarding the interests of the Muslims as a community in administrative reorganization was thought to be "too vague and too indefinite to be assuring in the slightest degree."[55]

The Muslim leaders, who were present at Simla also felt the need for having a political organization of their own with a view to safeguarding the interests of their community. The first concrete step was taken by Nawab Salimullah Khan of Dacca who had failed to join in the deputation. He came out with a scheme for "the Muslim All India Confederacy", the aims of which would be to support the Government and protect the interests of the Muslims. It was also to aim at countering the increasing influence of the Congress and to impress upon the Muslims not to join that body. The Nawab's scheme became the basis of discussion at Dacca on 30 December 1906. The delegates had assembled there from all parts of India to attend the All-India Muhammadan Educational Conference. After the Conference, they all met in a session under the presidentship of Viqar-ul-Mulk and decided to form the All-India Muslim League.[56]

In his inaugural speech Viqar-ul-Mulk outlined the attitude which he wanted the Muslims to adopt towards the British and the Congress. It was emphasized that the Muslims should

52. M.N. Das, n. 42, p. 175.
53. Rahman, n. 42, p. 41.
54. *Ibid.*
55. *Ibid.*
56. Wasti, n. 42, p. 78.

"prove themselves loyal to their Government before they can ask for a recognition of any of their rights." He also pointed out that there was "no quarrel between us and the National Congress. . . nor do we oppose or disagree with every one of their acts and views." The Nawab of Dacca was asked to move the first resolution which defined the aims and objects of the League: (a) to promote among the Muslims of India, feelings of loyalty to the British Government, and to remove any misconception that might arise as to the intention of the Government with regard to any of its measures, (b) to protect and advance the political rights and interests of the Muslims of India, and to respectfully represent their needs and aspirations to the Government and (c) to prevent the rise among the Muslims of any feeling of hostility towards other communities without prejudice to the other aforementioned objects of the League.[57]

The provision of separate electorates under the Indian Councils Act of 1909 was considered a victory for the League. Soon after, however, Muslim opinion began to be influenced by new voices representing certain new trends of thoughts. Among them were Muhammad Ali and Maulana Abul Kalam Azad who had just entered public life. They were rationalist in outlook and also well-versed in Islamic traditions. They spread their views through their journals. Muhammad Ali edited the *Comrade*, an English weekly and Azad an Urdu weekly *Al-Hilal*. Both asserted that there was no conflict between Islam and the Indian nationalism. Their writings had a great impact on the minds of the educated Muslims and helped to bring the League near the Congress. As Jawaharlal Nehru remarks, the League "was drifting though somewhat unwillingly with the tide of nationalism and coming nearer to the Congress."[58] The Muslim attitude also changed because of a number of other developments—both domestic and foreign. The Muslims were disappointed by the negative attitude of the government towards their demands for extension of separate electorates to local bodies and for more employment in various branches of

57. S.S. Pirzada, ed., *Foundation of Pakistan: All Indian Muslim League Documents, 1906-1924* (Karachi, 1969), vol. 1, p. 6.
58. Jawaharlal Nehru, *The Discovery of India* (Calcutta, 1946), p. 416.

public service. The annulment of the partition of Bengal in 1911, particularly proved to be a turning point. A section of the Muslims was convinced that their policy of loyalty to the government would not pay them in the long run. According to this view, unless the League leaders came to an understanding with the Hindus, the future of the community would be bleak. In utter despondency, some members even suggested the winding up of the League so that all Muslims could join the Congress.[59] The international situation also disturbed the Muslims deeply. The events in Turkey, the seat of the Khilafat had created a ferment in the minds of young Muslims. Their sympathies towards Turkey were strengthened when Italy attacked Tripoli in 1911 and subsequently during the Balkan Wars of 1912 and 1913. Muhammad Ali, Azad and Zafar Ali Khan (he had launched *Zamindar* from Lahore) started rallying the support of Muslim masses by writing inflammatory articles in favour of Turkey in their respective weeklies. The traditional policy of loyalty towards the government seemed no longer tenable. At the meeting of the League Council held at Lucknow on 31 December 1912 under the presidentship of the Aga Khan, the aim of the League was laid down as "attainment under the aegis of the British Crown of a system of self-government suitable to India through constitutional means. . . ."[60]

The outbreak of the first World War in August 1914 brought the Muslim League closer to the Congress. During 1915, the movement for Hindu-Muslim reconciliation was accelerated through the efforts of Jinnah, Wazir Hasan and other nationalist Muslims. On the Congress side, Annie Besant also advocated co-ordination of activities between the two organizations so that they could draw up a mutually acceptable scheme of reforms. For this purpose she wanted the Congress not to make an issue of separate electorates. In her presidential address to the United Provinces Provincial Conference in April, she stressed that "it would probably cause too much friction to withdraw separate electorates at present."[61]

59. Rahman, n. 42, pp. 238-39.
60. *Ibid.*, p. 272.
61. Hugh F. Owen, "Negotiating the Lucknow Pact", *Journal of Asian Studies*, vol. XXXI, no. 3, May 1972, p. 573.

Jinnah took the opportunity as President of the Bombay Provincial Conference held at Ahmedabad in October 1916 to warn his fellow Congressmen, stressing the need for granting separate electorates to Muslims:

> Rightly or wrongly the Muslim community is absolutely determined for the present to insist upon separate electorates... I would therefore appeal to my Hindu brethren that in the present state of [the] position they should try to win the confidence and the trust of the Muslims. ... If they are determined to have separate electorates, no resistance should be shown to their demands.[62]

At the two joint meetings of the Congress and League reforms committees at Lucknow in the month of November-December 1916, the Congress accepted the demands for separate electorates and also agreed to co-operate with the Muslim League for demanding weightage for Muslims in all those provinces where the Muslims were in a minority. Under the Congress-League scheme Muslims got over-representation in the provincial legislatures in Bihar, Bombay, Madras and Central Provinces.[63] Being aware of the dominant position of the Muslims in U.P., they were given 30 per cent of the seats there. The price paid for these concessions was that the principle of weightage for the minority community was also applied to Bengal and the Punjab, reducing Muslim representation in the Provincial Legislative Councils from 55 per cent to 50 per cent in the Punjab and to 40 per cent in Bengal.[64]

The Lucknow Pact signified the increasing eagerness of the Congress to win Muslim co-operation in the nationalist movement. The Hindus of U.P. and the Punjab had misgivings regarding the Pact as they felt that their interests had been jeopardized to win Muslim co-operation. On the Muslim side, the

62. *Ibid.*, p. 576.
63. In Bihar (where they were 13 per cent of population Muslims were to have 25 per cent of the seats, in Bombay (20 per cent) 33-1/2 per cent of the seats, in Madras (7 per cent) 15 per cent, and in the Central Provinces (4 per cent) 10 per cent of the seats. *Ibid.*, p. 584.
64. *Ibid.*, p. 586.

Punjab and Bengal were the most vociferous provinces in their condemnation of the Pact. Muhammad Shafi and Nawab Syed Nawab Ali Chowdhury became the chief spokesmen of their respective provinces.[65] Nevertheless it can be said that by entering into an agreement with the League, the Congress gave a formal recognition to communal politics in India as it had consented to recognize the All-India Muslim League as the mouthpiece of the Muslims and also accepted separate electorates.

The end of the first World War found the Muslims in a state of great excitement and unrest. For they were very much concerned with the fate of the Turkish Empire which had fought the war on the side of Germany and thus belonged to the defeated side. As the Sultan of Turkey was also the Caliph and hence the leader of all Muslims regardless of where they lived, it became a matter of religious faith for many Muslims to see that his honour and interests were duly protected. The prospect of the dismemberment of the Turkish Empire and the maintenance of non-Muslim control over the Holy places caused consternation among the Muslims. The Pan-Islamic agitation in India grew very strong indeed. An idea of the views of the Muslims on this question can be had from the following extract from a letter which the Ali Brothers (Muhammad and Shaukat) wrote to the Viceroy at the end of April 1919.

> Muslim loyalty and support had so often been assured to Government in our generation and even Muslim contentment was so often unduly taken for granted that other communities had with some justice made our attitude towards Government almost a matter of reproach. It was strange return for all this loyalty and support that without any effective protest and often with the concurrence of His Majesty's Government blow after blow was aimed at the temporal power of Islam. . . . What the cruel occurrences in Tripoli and the Balkans, at Holy Meshad had led Mussalmans to apprehend was, that the temporal power

65. Owen, n. 61, p. 581.

> of Islam might be so weakened that it might become liable to suffer, without adequate power to prevent, the curtailment of its spiritual influence through the pressure of the temporal power of rival creeds.[66]

Given the large-scale Muslim discontent over the Khilafat question, M.K. Gandhi seized the opportunity of championing the cause of the Muslims in order to win their confidence and enlist their support for the freedom movement. He called Khilafat "the Kamdhenu" as it was for him "an opportunity of uniting Hindus and Mussalmans, as would not arise in a hundred years."[67] On his advice, the Muslims decided at a meeting held at Delhi on 22 December 1919 to withhold all co-operation from the government if the British cabinet did not revise the Turkish Peace Terms. On 2 June 1920, an all-parties conference was held in Allahabad which decided upon the policy of non-cooperation and appointed a committee consisting of Gandhi, Ali brothers, Azad, Kitchlew, Hasrat Mohani and Haji Ahmad Siddiq Khatri to draw up a programme. On 1 August the Khilafat Committee entrusted Gandhi with the leadership of the non-cooperation movement. He merged it with national issues like the Punjab wrongs and the achievement of Swaraj. This was specially done through the special session of the Congress (Calcutta, September 1920) which adopted Gandhi's non-cooperation programme for the redress of the Khilafat and Punjab wrongs and the achievement of Swaraj.[68] At the Khilafat Conference held in Lucknow, 1921, a Maulvi named Abdul Majid of Badaun proposed a resolution to secure Swaraj for India. Gandhi stated that he had joined the Khilafat movement to help the Muslims, for to him their success meant Swaraj. In the course of his speech Muhammad Ali paid a tribute to Gandhi, "I declare today that the Indian Army is the army of Mahatma Gandhi; the

66. P.C. Bamford, *Histories of the Non-Co-operation and Khilafat Movements* (Delhi, 1925), p. 138.
67. Quoted in Mohibbul Hasan, "Mahatma Gandhi and Indian Muslims" in S.C. Biswas, ed., *Gandhi Theory and Practice: Social Impact and Contemporary Relevance* (Simla, 1964), p. 132.
68. Bamford, n. 66, p. 161ff.

Indian Police is the police of Mahatma Gandhi; every man is on the side of Gandhi; nay on the side of religion and country."[69] Similarly in the All-India Khilafat Conference assembled at Meerut on 7 April 1921, a resolution was passed that the Muslims should adhere to non-cooperation until Swaraj was obtained.

Between 1919 and 1922 there was complete unity between the Hindus and the Muslims. The Muslims had pursued their objective with the full concurrence of the Congress, though the main purpose of the latter was enlisting their support in the nationalist movement. But the suspension of the civil disobedience movement in 1922 and the abolition of the Caliphate in 1924 left the Muslims high and dry. Indeed there was a feeling of frustration among both the Hindus and the Muslims, many of whom now turned towards communalism. The Shuddhi and Sangathan movements raised their heads among the Hindus and the Tabligh and Tanzim among the Muslims. The Hindu-Muslim unity was based on a fragile foundation; anti-British sentiment had brought the two communities together but with the collapse of the non-cooperation movement, communal harmony was over. The Moplah rising of August 1921 had already created misunderstanding between the two communities. The Kohat riots of September 1924 grieved Gandhi so much that he went on a twenty-one day fast at Muhammad Ali's house in Delhi. It was over the Kohat riots that differences between Gandhi and Ali brothers were revealed to the public. While the Muslims accused the Hindus of firing the first shot and thus starting the trouble, Gandhi's reaction made them feel that he was partial towards the Hindus. Gandhi was very unhappy because of the damage to temples, breaking of idols and the murder of two Hindus because of their refusal to accept Islam. The statements made by him on the communal disturbances created a chasm between him and the Muslims. On 2 April 1925, he wrote in *Young India* : "The Mussulmans take less interest (in the internal political life and advancement of the country) . . . because they do not yet regard India as their home of which

69. *Ibid.*, p. 164.

they must feel proud."[70] With regard to the communal riots he wrote that the Mussulman as a rule is a bully and the Hindu as a rule is a coward."[71] The same observation was made by him in another article in *Young India* on 19 June 1924 : "the Mussulman being generally in a minority has as a class developed into a bully . . . . The thirteen hundred years of imperialist expansion have made the Mussulmans fighters as a body. The Hindu has an age-old civilization. He is essentially non-violent. He also advised the Hindus to retaliate and not to be "seized with fear."[72] Such remarks were bound to annoy the Muslims. While Muhammad Ali was critical of Malaviya because of his active participation in the Shuddhi and Sangathan movements, Gandhi was lenient towards them. Muhammad Ali believed and Motilal Nehru agreed with him that Malaviya was "out to defeat Gandhism and to become the leader of the Hindus only since he could not be a leader of both the Hindus and Muslims."[73]

The Hindu Mahasabha (founded in 1919) which had been lying dormant for a number of years started making efforts to fortify its position in the country in order to check the demands of the League. The Congress stood discredited in its eyes and was accused by its leaders of bartering away the interests of the Hindus in its desire to appease the Muslims. At the All India Conference of the Hindus held at Banaras in 1923 under the Presidentship of Malaviya, attempts were made to make it an organization exclusively concerned with safeguarding the political, religious, social and economic rights of the Hindu community.[74]

Both the Hindu Mahasabha and the Muslim League now started working for the revision of the Lucknow Pact; the former because it had denied them the advantages of a minority in Bengal and the Punjàb, and the latter because the Punjab Muslims wanted to remedy the injustice done to them

70. *The Collected Works of Gandhi*, vol. 26, p. 442.
71. *Ibid.*
72. *The Collected Works of Gandhi*, vol. 24, p, 270.
73. Muhammad Ali to Gandhi, 21 July 1924, *Muhammad Ali Papers*, Jamia Millia Library.
74. Prabha Dixit. n. 2, p. 155.

by the Pact. When the League met in its annual session in Lahore in 1924, the following resolution was moved by Sheikh Abdul Qadir which received the assent of the majority:

(a) The existing provinces of India should be united under a common Government on a federal basis so that each province should have full and complete provincial autonomy, the functions of the Central Government being confined to such matters only as are of general and common concern.

(b) The basis of representation in the Legislature and in all other elected bodies should be population except that very small minorities may be given representation in excess of their numerical proportion in those cases in which they would remain entirely unrepresented in the absence of such exceptional treatment, subject however to the essential proviso that no majority should be reduced to a minority or even to an equality.[75]

For the next three years, the League was busy defining the position of the Muslims in the forthcoming changes in the constitution of the country. The Congress tried to make attempts at unity by formulating a Hindu-Muslim Pact for settlement of the communal question in Bengal. Another Pact known as the National Pact was drawn up by Lajpat Rai and M.A. Ansari for the whole of India. The Bengal Pact was devised by C.R. Das at the suggestion of the Bengal Provincial Congress Committee. It provided that: (1) representation in the Bengal Legislative Council should be on the population basis with separate electorates subject to such adjustment as might be made necessary by the All-India Hindu-Muslim Pact (the Lucknow Pact) and by the Khilafat and the Congress, (2) representation to local bodies was to be in the proportion of 60 to 40 in every district—60 to the community which was in a majority and 40 to the minority. Thus in a district where the Muslims were in a majority they would get 60 per cent and the Hindus 40 per cent. Similarly where the Hindus were in a

75. Pirzada, n. 57, p. 578.

majority, they would get 60 per cent and the Muslims 40 per cent. The question as to whether there should be separate or mixed electorates was postponed to ascertain the views of both communities. (3) It was decided to give 55 per cent of the Government jobs to the Muslims. (4) And lastly it was decided not to allow any resolution or enactment without the consent of the 75 per cent of the elected members of each community.[76]

Similarly, the Delhi session of Indian National Congress (1923) appointed a committee to enquire into and report on the question of Hindu-Muslim unity. The report was signed by Ansari and Lajpat Rai and proposed the following National Pact: (1) It should be the firm and unalterable object of the communities represented by the signatories to this Pact to secure complete Swaraj for Indians—the Swaraj which would secure and guarantee to Indians, the same status, rights and privileges in India as every free and independent nation enjoyed in its country. (2) The form of Government under Swaraj should be democratic and of the federal type. (3) In view of the existing state of feeling prevailing in the different communities and in view of the insufficient development of political sense and responsibility in them—it was felt necessary for some time to afford adequate protection to the interests of the minority. (4) It was agreed that the various communities should have separate representation in legislatures, both State and Federal. Ansari wanted to extend this principle to municipalities and local boards but Lajpat Rai did not agree to that. As an alternative he suggested that a time limit should be fixed during which communal representation should be enforced, at the expiry of which it would be abolished altogether. He suggested that such representation should be in proportion to the numerical strength of each community in the constituencies.[77]

But the efforts made by the Congress proved futile because these Pacts were disapproved of by the next session of the Congress held in 1924. Even then the hopes of unity were not

76. *Indian Quarterly Register 1923*. pp. 127-28.
77. *Ibid.*, pp. 105-6.

abandoned and all-parties conference was convened in January 1925 by Gandhi in which the representatives of the Congress, the Muslim League, the Hindu Mahasabha, the Justice Party and the Liberal Federation participated. A Sub-committee consisting of 40 members was appointed in order to (a) frame such recommendations as would enable all parties to join the Congress; (b) to frame a scheme for the representation of all communities on the legislative and other elective bodies and to frame a scheme of Swaraj. The Sub-committee was divided into two small committees. While the first of these committees, asked to frame a report on the constitution submitted its report, the other which was asked to devise a scheme of communal representation met only once and adjourned *sine die* without coming to any conclusion because Lajpat Rai and other Hindu representatives were not prepared to attend the committee's meetings.[78] They had become too skeptical and suspicious of the Congress because of the latter's desire to arrive at some understanding with the Muslims. The matter came to a head at the time of the 1926 General Elections to the Legislative Assembly and the Provincial Councils. Before the election there was a split in the Congress (the Swaraj Party had merged itself with the Congress) and Madan Mohan Malaviya and Lajpat Rai had formed the Nationalist Party with the object of opposing the Congress candidates and defeating the Congress programme. Initially Malaviya stood for the Central Assembly against Motilal Nehru, but afterwards he withdrew and a *mahant* contested the election instead. The Congress suffered because malicious propaganda was being spread by the Hindu Mahasabha against Motilal who was denounced as a "beef-eater and destroyer of cows, an opponent of prohibition, of music before the mosque and one man responsible for stoppage of the Ramlila procession in Allahabad."[79] The election results showed that in Bombay and C.P., the Congress fared badly though in Bengal and Madras it had emerged victorious. The U.P. results were characterized

78. *Indian Quarterly Register, 1925*, vol. 1, p. 77.
79. Motilal Nehru to Jawaharlal Nehru, December 1926, *Jawaharlal Nehru Papers*, N.M.M.L.

by Motilal Nehru as "nothing short of a disaster" because the Congress had won only one seat (that contested by Motilal Nehru himself). In the Punjab, it had lost all the seats as Lajpat Rai commanded great influence over the Hindu population.[80] This was the price paid by the Congress for condemning the activities of the Hindu Mahasabha. It was against this background that fresh efforts were made in 1927-28 to bring about a rapprochement between the two communities.

80. *Ibid.*

2

Muslims and the Nehru Report

The appointment of the all-British Simon Commission to review the working of the 1919 reforms gave an opportunity to the Congress and the Muslims to work together for the preparation of the draft Constitution. The ground had already been prepared by the Congress in 1926 at its Gauhati session where it concentrated its attention on the question of Hindu-Muslim unity and asked its Working Committee to "take immediate steps in consultation with Hindu and Mussalman leaders to devise measures for the removal of the present deplorable differences between Hindus and Mussalmans and submit their report to the All India Congress Committee not later than the 31 March 1927."[1]

The next significant step in this direction was taken on 20 March, when prominent Muslim leaders belonging to various groups met in Delhi under the presidentship of Jinnah to discuss the question of Muslim representation in the legislatures. It was unanimously agreed that the Muslims would be prepared to give up separate electorates if the followlng proposals were accepted: (1) Sind to be separated from the Bombay Presidency and constituted into a separate province; (2) reforms to be introduced in North-West Frontier Province and in Baluchistan on the same footing as in any other province

1. *Report of the Indian National Congress, Forty-first Session, Gauhati, 1926*, p. 104.

in India; (3) in the Punjab and Bengal, the proportion of representation to be made in accordance with the population; (4) in the Central Legislature Muslim representation not to be less than one-third. If all these demands were accepted, the Muslims would be prepared to accept joint electorates in all the provinces so constituted and to make to Hindu minorities in Bengal, Punjab and North-West Frontier Provinces the same concessions that the Hindu majorities in other provinces were prepared to make to the Muslims.[2]

According to the Delhi proposals, the Muslims were expected to have majority in the legislatures of five provinces of which no fewer than three—Sind, N.W.F.P. and Baluchistan contained an overwhelming Muslim majority. The end in view was explained by Jinnah in the following words:

> . . . Mussalmans should be made to feel that they are secure and safe-guarded against any act of oppression on the part of the majority and that they need not feel that during the transitional stage towards the fullest development of National Government the majority would be in a position to oppress and tyrannise the minority as majorities are prone to do in other countries.[3]

The Working Committee of the Congress appreciated the preparedness of the Muslim leaders to accept joint electorates and passed a lengthy resolution on the Hindu-Muslim question for presentation at the A.I.C.C. session on 15 May in Bombay. It is significant to note that it accepted all the Muslim proposals. The A.I.C.C. unanimously adopted the same resolution with minor alterations. The principal change suggested was that Sind should not be separated on communal grounds but on general grounds applicable to all provinces. A change in the wording of the resolution removed the objection and it was passed unanimously.[4] The Madras session of the Congress held in December 1927, gave full assurance to

2. Jamil-ud-Din Ahmad, *Historic Documents of the Muslim Freedom Movement* (Lahore, 1970), p. 86.
3. N.N. Mitra, ed., *Indian Quarterly Register*, 1927, vol. 1, p. 37.
4. *Ibid.*, p. 15.

the Muslims that "their legitimate interests should be secured . . . by the reservation of seats in joint electorates on the basis of population in every province and in the central legislature . . . ." It also agreed to other Muslim proposals regarding Sind, N.W.F.P. and Baluchistan.[5]

The Congress leaders were delighted at the prospect of united action with the Muslims. M.A. Ansari, in his presidential address, expressed the gratitude of the Congress for the Muslim leaders in the following words:

> . . . I would be lacking in my duty if I did not place on record the deep appreciation of the Indian National Congress of the spirit of patriotism and statesmanship displayed by the Muslim leaders who rose above prejudice, suspicion and narrow communal outlook and boldly came forward with the proposals which presage a new orientation on Muslim policy in India.[6]

Talking about the resolutions passed at the Madras session, another Congress leader, Govind Ballabh Pant, characterized them "as the best and most suitable arrangement which carried with it the largest amount of support from both the communities." He also said that even though reservation of seats was not "compatible with the complete independence" ' it had been accepted by the Hindus at a meeting of the All-India Committee with the full concurrence of M.R. Jayakar and Madan Mohan Malaviya, both of whom had been the Presidents of the Hindu Mahasabha.[7]

The All-India Muslim League also, at its session in Calcutta on 30 December 1927, accepted the Delhi proposals and decided to co-operate with the rest of the country in boycotting the Statutory Commission and in framing a Constitution for India on lines acceptable to all communities and all parties. This was the result of the lead given by Jinnah, Abdur Rahim, Ali Imam, the Raja of Mahmudabad and others.

5. *Report of the Indian National Congress, Forty-second Session, Madras*, 1927, p. 61.
6. *Ibid.*, Appendix 1, p. 9.
7. *Ibid.*, p. 75.

But at this juncture the solidarity of the League was broken as one section refused to boycott the Simon Commission and also opposed Jinnah and others on account of their readiness to give up separate electorates. A rival session of the League was convened at Lahore on 31 December under Muhammad Shafi. An anti-boycott manifesto[8] was issued whereby Muslims were warned that "a resort to the sterile policy of boycott . . . will bring nothing but shame and sorrow."[9]

On the other hand, the Jinnah section contended that the proceedings of the League at Lahore were conducted in a most arbitrary and unconstitutional manner. A joint statement issued under the signatures of Mohammad Alam, Hissam-ud-din, Chaudhuri Afzal Huq, Mazhar Ali Azhar and Mohammad Sharif pointed out that barely a dozen attended the meeting from provinces other than the Punjab and N.W.F.P.[10]

In accordance with the Madras Congress resolution,[11] authorizing the Working Committee to confer with the other parties to draft a Swaraj constitution for India and to place the same for consideration and approval before a conference, the first meeting of the All Parties Conference was held in Delhi on 12 February 1928. The Muslims had already been offended by the views expressed by the representatives of the Hindu Mahasabha. The latter had categorically rejected the principle of reservation of seats in favour of any majority community in any province. It was also inflexibly opposed to the creation of new Muslim provinces as a price for securing joint electorates. Its attitude made it clear that it considered separate electorates a lesser evil than the creation of new provinces.[12]

8. The manifesto was signed by the Punjab Muslim leaders. They were Zulfiqar Ali Khan, Muhammad Iqbal, Abdul Qayyum, Mian Abdul Haye and Maulvi Mahomed Ali. They pointed out that the Muslims who had signed Jinnah's manifesto belong to provinces in which Muslims were in a helpless minority and asserted that their attitude could not mould the policy of Muslims in such provinces as the Punjab and Bengal, where they were in a majority.
9. *Civil and Military Gazette*, 9 December 1927.
10. *The Tribune* (Lahore), 11 December 1927.
11. Report of the 1927 Congress. n. 5, p. 107.
12. Purshottamadas Thakurdas Papers, Nehru Memorial Museum and Library, New Delhi.

At the All Parties Conference also, the Mahasabha displayed the same intransigence with regard to the Muslim demands. Therefore, the only achievement of the meeting was that a unanimous resolution was passed on N.W.F.P. and Baluchistan placing them on the same footing in respect of their form of government and judicial administration as any other province. With regard to Sind, the Conference made separation subject to two conditions, namely, that the province should be financially self-supporting and secondly, that the majority of its inhabitants must be in favour of separation. It was also pointed out that so long as the scheme of Government in the N.W.F.P. and Baluchistan was not placed on the same footing and Sind was not separated from the Bombay Presidency, separate electorates for Muslims and Sikhs would continue to remain in force.[13]

These resolutions met with adverse criticism from various quarters. The Hindu Mahasabha had practically dissented from them. Sardar Mangal Singh, Secretary, Central Sikh League, stated on behalf of his organization that he could not agree to reservation of seats on population basis nor could he accept a statutory communal majority. Jinnah, Gazanfar Ali Khan and Mohamed Ismail Khan made it clear that they would accept no deviation from the stand taken by the Congress at the time of the Madras session and would accept only those propositions which were in accordance with the principles embodied in the resolution of the League at its Calcutta session. With regard to the conditions laid down for the separation of Sind, which were new, they made it clear that they could not accept them until they had consulted the Council of the All-India Muslim League which was to meet on 26 February.[14]

At the next meeting of the Council of the League, however, Jinnah and Gazanfar Ali emphatically declared that only if the Hindu-Muslim question was settled at the All Parties Conference at its next meeting scheduled to be held on 9 March, would the Committee appointed by the Muslim

13. *Ibid.*
14. *Ibid.*

League proceed to examine other questions and be willing to collaborate with the representatives of other organizations.[15]

On this question the Conference, at its session, beginning on 9 March opined, that it was possible to provide for the safeguards contemplated by the resolutions of the Congress and the League, by devising a system of election on the principle of proportional representation by a single transferable vote or some other similar method. Two sub-committees were appointed: the first one to investigate the whole matter of communal representation and the second to enquire into the financial aspect of the separation of Sind.[16]

The results of the above meetings of the Conference were not encouraging. After long hours of sittings and elaborate discussions, the advance made was insignificant. The initial enthusiasm among the members had also waned.[17] Gandhi who did not participate in the meetings of the Conference but was interested in its achieving Hindu-Muslim unity was grieved at this state of affairs and bemoaned the 'miserable show' being put up by those who were participating in the Conference against the 'insolence' of Lord Birkenhead and his challenge to Indian people to frame a constitution. He disapproved of the Congress resiling from its stand and exhorted the Congress leaders that once they had 'committed' themselves to reservation of seats, they must adhere to it until they were able to evolve another formula which completely satisfied the Muslims.[18] Shuaib Qureshi, the General Secretary of the Congress, supported Gandhi's views and insisted that Congressmen must stand by the resolutions of their Madras session.[19]

But unfortunately Gandhi's views remained unheeded. The Conference could not make much headway. Some Congress Muslims like Shafee Daudi and Shah Muhammad Zubair

15. *Ibid.*
16. *Ibid.*
17. Motilal to Gandhi, 24 February 1928, Motilal Nehru Papers, N.M.M.L.
18. Gandhi to Motilal, 27 February 1928, *The Collected Works of Gandhi*, vol. 30 (New Delhi, February-June 1928), p. 67.
19. Shuaib Qureshi to M.A. Ansari, 5 May 1928, Mukhtar Ahmad Ansari Papers, (Microfilm copy) N.M.M.L.

suggested to Ansari that the provinces should be encouraged to settle their differences on provincial basis.[20] Ansari fully subscribed to their views and commended the example of Bihar where the Hindus and Muslims had been having a sort of Round Table Conference for the purpose of arriving at an understanding between themselves. As a result he instructed various provinces like the Punjab, Bengal, Tamil Nadu, Karnataka and Sind to follow Bihar as an example.[21] The key to the success of the All Parties Conference was in the hands of the Hindu Mahasabha and the Muslim League. The former had made it difficult for the conference to hammer ont an agreed solution by adopting a rigid attitude on the question of reservation of seats in a province for the majority community. On the other hand, in pursuance of the policy formulated by the Council of the Muslim League (Jinnah group) in March, its members had refused to take part in the subsequent deliberations of the Conference. Their main grievance was that the All Parties Conference had modified the Congress resolutions.[22]

Other members had also got weary of the Conference because so far they had failed to secure any substantial results. The work of the Conference was going to be affected by the departure of Jinnah for Europe on 5 May. He had been mainly responsible for the Delhi proposals. The Muslims inside the Congress grew quite pessimistic regarding any definite solution of the outstanding questions being brought about in his absence because they felt Jinnah was the only man who could "deliver the goods on behalf of the Muslim League."[23] The All Parties Conference dispersed after appointing a committee to deal with the communal problem as a whole, particularly in relation to the framing of the constitution.

The committee appointed by the All Parties Conference consisted of members belonging to various organizations. Motilal Nehru was appointed its chairman. Ali Imam and Shuaib Qureshi represented the (Congress) Muslim

20. Ansari to Jawaharlal Nehru, 29 March 1928, All India Congress Committee Papers, N.M.M.L.
21. *Ibid.*, A.I.C.C. Papers.
22. Mohammad Yakub to Ansari, 5 May 1928, Ansari Papers.
23. Ansari to Motilal, 18 May 1928, Motilal Nehru Papers.

viewpoint, M.S. Aney and M.R. Jayakar spoke for the Mahasabha, Sardar Mangal Singh represented the Sikh League and Tej Bahadur Sapru, the Liberal viewpoint. But most of the members did not show any deep interest in the work of the Committee. Out of ten members appointed on the Committee Jayakar resigned and Ali Imam did not attend any meeting. Those who regularly attended the meeting were Shuaib Qureshi, M.S. Aney, Mangal Singh, Tej Bahadur Sapru and Motilal Nehru.[24] Being the chairman of the Committee, Motilal persistently emphasized the supreme necessity of achieving a unanimous formula as he was sure that "an agreed report would be a strong weapon to carry on a campaign in the country against the Government."[25] On the question of separation of Sind and the grant of equal status to N.W.F.P. and Baluchistan, Motilal was prepared to ignore the opposition of the Mahasabha.[26] But the deadlock occurred over the reservation of seats in the Punjab and Bengal. As Shuaib Qureshi was adamant on this question and Aney was not prepared to yield, it led to an impasse and the Nehru Committee (named after Motilal Nehru) dispersed on 22 June without reaching any agreement.[27]

When an informal conference was held on 7 July where Motilal had invited some non-members of both the communities, efforts were once again made to resolve the communal deadlock. The efforts bore fruit and the Muslims were partly satisfied, as their demand for reservation of seats in majority provinces was conceded for ten years. The resolution which was signed and passed by both the members and non-members ran as follows:

> We are unanimously opposed to the reservation of seats in the legislatures either for majorities or minorities . . . . But if this recommendation is not accepted and an agreement can be arrived at only on reservation of seats on the population basis, we recommend that such reservation

24. *Ibid.*
25. Motilal to Gandhi, 22 June 1928, Motilal Nehru Papers.
26. Motilal to Purshottamdas, 23 May 1928, Motilal Nehru Papers.
27. Shuaib to Motilal, 24 June 1928, Motilal Nehru Papers.

> be made for majorities or minorities without any weightage and with a clear provision that it shall automatically cease at the expiry of ten years or earlier by the consent of the parties concerned.[28]

The Muslims suffered extreme humiliation when the first part of the above resolution was modified on the next day and only the reservation of seats for minorities in both central and provincial legislatures was permitted.[29] Shuaib once again argued on behalf of the Muslims that if the question of reservation of seats in provincial legislatures was to be considered then in the Punjab and Bengal seats must be reserved for Muslims in proportion to their population. He based his argument on the fact that in these two provinces, the Muslims were handicapped by poverty and lack of education. On the other hand, the Hindus were well organized, wealthy, educated and in control of commerce and banking of the province. This had resulted in the majority being reduced to a minority in the legislatures of the two provinces.[30]

This view was based on hard facts and was also shared by other Congress Muslims like Shafee Daudi, Tassaduq Ahmad Khan Sherwani, etc. The Muslim community in these two provinces consisted mainly of agriculturists. The principal Muslim castes in the Punjab were Arains, Rajputs and Jats most of whom were cultivators. Among the Hindu population, on the other hand, there were besides Jats and Ahirs who were largely agriculturists, also people belonging to such castes as Banias and Khatris who had taken in large numbers to western education and dominated not only land and commerce but also the various professions. The Muslims were double the number of the Hindus among the ordinary cultivators but among the landlords and urban middle classes, Hindus were nearly twice the number of Muslims. Almost all the big landlords were Hindus.[31] The real opposition of the Punjab Hindus

28. All Parties Conference 1928, Report of the Committee appointed by the Conference to determine the Principles of the Constitution together with a Proceeding of the Lucknow Conference (Allahabad, 1928), p. 50.
29. *Ibid.*
30. Shuaib to Motilal, 2 July 1928, Motilal Nehru Papers.
31. Census of India, 1931 Report, vol. 1, p. 181.

was not due to any high national consideration, but the fear that they might lose their privileged position if the Muslim majority in the provincial legislature was guaranteed.

The Nehru Committee justified its refusal to reserve seats for the Muslim majority by emphasizing that there were 'natural areas' of reservation for Muslims in three-fourths of the Punjab which would ensure their fair representation. Figures were compiled from 1921 census by Jawaharlal Nehru, General Secretary of the Congress. Allowing one member for every hundred thousand of population he had concluded that the Muslims were bound to get over 47.3 per cent of total seats in the Punjab and thus "there was no foundation for the fears entertained by the Muslims."[32] It should not be overlooked that no figures were given for adult population nor was any effort made to collect figures on the economic and educational condition of the Muslims.

At the Lucknow session of the All Parties Conference, held in August, it was announced that Muslim representatives from the Punjab had accepted joint electorates without reservation of seats for majorities. This was largely the result of the efforts made by a group of nationalists in the Punjab belonging to both the communities who had formed provincial committees on the Bihar and Madras model. This Punjab agreement was signed by S.D. Kitchlew, Zafar Ali Khan, Abdur Rahman Ghazi, Mohammad Alam, Afzal Haq, Abdul Qadir, M. Daud Ghaznavi, Lajpat Rai, S. Kharak Singh, Gokul Chand Narang, Sheikh Sirajud-Din Piracha, Satyapal and Mangal Singh.

The Conference approved and adopted the Punjab agreement which read as follows:

> The Punjab Muslims directly with the introduction of the scheme recommended by the Nehru Committee report accept its recommendations on the communal representation including joint electorates without reservation of seats

32. All Parties Conference, 1928, Report of the Committee appointed by the Conference to determine the Principles of the Constitution for India. n. 28, Appendix A.

for any community in the Punjab, provided that franchise is based on adult suffrage.[33]

Akram Khan and J.M. Sengupta accepted on behalf of Bengal Muslims and Hindus respectively the clauses of the report relating to Bengal. The Central Khilafat Committee led by Shaukat Ali expressed its disagreement with the Punjab agreement and stated that it stood for the Delhi proposals in toto. But M. Alam and Abdul Qadir disagreed with him and stated that the Central Khilafat Committee had not authorized him to make the statement.[34]

There is no doubt that the report (commonly known as the Nehru Report) did not have the backing of the entire Muslim community. But the support lent by one section of the Muslims enabled Motilal Nehru to declare to the Conference as well as to the country that some kind of unanimity had been arrived at as a result of the Lucknow Conference. The supplementary report of the Committee stated that the fears of the Muslims were more "imaginary than real" and "it was a matter of great satisfaction that the Punjab and Bengal Provincial Muslim League as well as the Punjab Provincial Khilafat Committee have at their open session fully accepted the agreement." On this ground it was asserted that "the question of reservation of seats for Muslim majorities must therefore be taken as finally settled."[35]

The primary objective of Motilal Nehru was to get the Committee arrive at some kind of unanimity and once this was done he wanted to enlist as much support as possible for the Report. In order to achieve this end, he expressed his desire of dissociating some of the communal parties like the Muslims League and the Hindu Mahasabha if they were dissatisfied with it.[36] Nehru's attitude towards the Hindu Mahasabha and the Muslim League before the Lucknow Conference

33. *Ibid.*, p. 164.
34. All Parties Conference, 1928, Report of the Committee appointed by the Conference to determine the Principle of the Constitution, p. 52.
35. Supplementary Report of the Committee appointed by All Parties Conference, p. 21.
36. Motilal to Gandhi, 26 June 1928, Motilal Nehru Papers.

stands in sharp contrast to the one he displayed after the Conference. Before the Lucknow Conference, when the prospects of the meeting were quite gloomy and he was skeptical about anything substantial coming out of the Conference, he used to be as critical of the behaviour of the Hindu Mahasabha leaders as were the members of the League. Holding the Hindu Mahasabha responsible for the failure of the various meetings of the Conference to achieve any constructive results, he wrote to Ansari:

> . . . the Hindu Mahasabha should really have been kicked out in Delhi, but if that was not done so there, there is no reason why we should not adopt a stronger attitude in Bombay. To repeat an old story it is no use allowing a diseased limb to dangle by your side and obstruct your movement.[37]

He also felt that he should have told the Muslim leaders plainly that the Congress did not identify itself with the resolutions passed by the Hindu Mahasabha and that he would stand by the Madras resolutions.[38]

Once the Lucknow Conference had given its assent to the Punjab ageement despite the persistent demand of the Muslims for reservation of seats, a campaign was started against those Muslims who had stood firmly by the Madras resolution. Endeavours were made to brush aside their opposition by proclaiming that the Report had gained the overwhelming support of the Muslims. Considerable efforts were made by Motilal Nehru to counteract the propaganda of Shaukat Ali, Shafee Daudi and others who were attacking the Congress in the Muslim press by asking the Congress Muslims like Ali Imam, Ansari and Abul Kalam Azad (who had given their whole-hearted support to the Report) to allay the fears of the Muslim community by answering their criticisms and holding public meetings in favour of the Report.[39]

37. Motilal to Ansari, 1 May 1928, Ansari Papers.
38. *Ibid.*
39. Shaukat Ali to Ansari, 26 September 1928, Ansari Papers.

In deference to Motilal Nehru's wishes an organized campaign was launched by these people against the opposition of Shaukat Ali and his party. While speaking at the Lyallpur Conference, Ansari emphasized that the Nehru Report safeguarded the Muslim rights and interests better than the Madras Congress resolutions.[40]

The Hindu Mahasabha was also jubilant. It had succeeded in its strategy of dissuading the Congress from sticking to its Madras resolution. While prominent Muslim leaders like Shaukat Ali, Shafee Daudi, Shuaib Qureshi, Hasrat Mohani, Abdulla Haroon and Abdul Majid Daryabadi were annoyed with the Congress because they felt that their interests had been jeopardized by the Nehru Committee's recommendation, the Hindu Mahasabha felt elated as the privileged position of the Hindus had not been disturbed. The prevailing mood of its leaders can be gauged from the following remarks of Jayakar. Immediately after the Lucknow Conference, he wrote to N.C. Kelkar on 28 August:

> Personally I am inclined to agree with the Nehru Committee's Report not perhaps as an ideal arrangement, yet on the whole being more beneficial to the Hindus than any scheme so far suggested on the Congress side.[41]

In another letter to H.S. Polak on 31 October, he applauded the Congress attitude by saying

> . . . It is for the first time that Congress leaders like Motilal and Dr Ansari and others have descended on *terra firma* and come within the region of practical politics from the aerial clouds which they were chasing for so many years.[42]

The gravity of the situation soon dawned upon the Congress leadership when Jinnah also expressed his indignation over

40. *The Tribune*, 2 September 1928.
41. Jayakar to N.C. Kelkar, 28 August 1928, M.R. Jayakar Papers, File No. 442, National Archives, New Delhi.
42. Jayakar to Polak, 31 October 1928. M.R. Jayakar Papers.

the Nehru Report. Great hopes had been pinned on him and Muhammad Ali who were away since May and had given their wholehearted support to Motilal Nehru in the endeavours for Hindu-Muslim unity. It is pertinent to note here that before Jinnah was to leave for Europe, Ansari had expressed his apprehension to Motilal as to what would happen to the Report if both of them also went against it.[43] His apprehensions proved to be true when Jinnah, after getting the proceedings of the Lucknow Conference, gave a curt reply to Jawaharlal that though he had not gone through the Report fully, since the publication of that Report "much water has run down the Hooghly".[44]

In fact Motilal was so keen on enlisting Jinnah's support that he expressed his readiness to go to Bombay to receive him. Instructions were given to Purshottamdas Thakurdas who was staying in Bombay to "rope in" Jinnah as soon as he returned to impress upon him the effectiveness of the decision arrived at at Lucknow.[45]

Notwithstanding his disapproval of the Report, Jinnah on his arrival, appealed to Muslims not to get alarmed and expressed his appreciation of the efforts made by its authors. He reposed great faith in both the Hindus and the Muslims arriving at some agreement and felt that since the Nehru Report was not the final word, it could be modified in future. He was thus quite hopeful of the communal deadlock being resolved.[46]

At the Lucknow Conference, it had been decided to place the Nehru Committee's proposals before the Convention in order to ascertain the views of various leaders and their respective organizations. The Muslim League, which had abstained from the meetings of the All Parties Conference ever since February, participated in the Convention along with the Khilafat Committee on 28 December in Calcutta. Jinnah on behalf of the Muslim League and Tassaduq Ahmed Khan Sherwani on behalf of the Central Khilafat Committee put

43. Ansari to Motilal, 5 May 1928, Ansari Papers.
44. M.A. Jinnah to Jawaharlal Nehru, 20 October 1928, Jawaharlal Nehru Papers, N.M.M.L.
45. Purshottamdas to Motilal, 29 October 1928, Purshottamdas Thakurdas Papers.
46. *The Tribune*, 8 October 1928.

forward six amendments to the Report. The Convention adopted two of these, namely, (1) a majority of four-fifths of the two houses first sitting separately and then together would be necessary for the amendment or alteration of the constitution by Parliament; and (2) the Punjab pact regarding communal representation should be incorporated in the Nehru Report. The remaining four which were not found acceptable by the Convention were: (1) that one-third of the elected representatives of both Houses of the Central Legislature should be Muslims; (2) that there should be reservation of seats in the Punjab and Bengal in the event of adult suffrage not being established; (3) that residuary powers should vest in the provinces and not in the Central Legislature; and (4) that separation of Sind should not be postponed until the Nehru Constitution was established with adult suffrage.[47] Placing the amendments on behalf of the Muslim League, Jinnah laid more stress on the Muslims getting one-third representation in the Central Legislature. Quoting passages of the Nehru Report where it was argued that the Punjab and Bengal would get many more seats over and above their proportion and the Muslims of the minority provinces would get their representation according to their population, Jinnah stated:

> . . .the method which is adopted is neither quite fair to the provinces where the Mussalmans are in a minority nor does it guarantee that we shall obtain one-third representation in the Central Legislature. Therefore. the two Mussalman's Majority Provinces—Punjab and Bengal—will get more than their population, which means you are giving more to the rich who will, under normal conditions get the largest number of Muslim Representations . . . . We wish to restrict the Punjab and Bengal according to their population and desire that excess should be distributed amongst the minority Muslim Provinces.[48]

47. The Proceedings of the All Parties National Convention (Allahabad, 1928), p. 13.
48. *Ibid.*, p. 79.

It is important to note here that even the Muslim leaders associated with the Congress favoured such amendments like the desirability of residuary powers being vested in the provinces and one-third representation of Muslims in the Central Legislature. Their only difference with the League was that the latter attached great importance to the amendment providing that in case adult suffrage was not established, there should be reservation of seats on population basis for ten years.

Even after four out of his six demands had been strongly opposed, Jinnah made a conciliatory speech. This was the voice of a leader strongly desirous of achieving communal unity:

> It is absolutely essential to our progress that Hindu-Muslim settlement should be reached, and that all communities should live in a friendly and harmonious spirit in this vast country of ours. No country has succeeded in either wresting a democratic constitution from a domination of another nation or establishing representative institution from within without giving guarantees for the securities of the minorities wherever such a problem has arisen. Majorities are apt to be oppressive and tyrannical and minorities always dread and fear that their interests and rights, unless clearly and definitely safe-guarded by statutory provisions, would suffer and be prejudiced but this apprehension is enhanced all the more when we have to deal with communal majority.[49]

For the sake of unity, Tej Bahadur Sapru supported Jinnah with regard to the demand for the reservation of seats in the Central Legislature. Indeed he described that demand as "not inconsistent with the Nehru Report." He told his fellow-delegates: "We must, as practical statesmen, try to solve the problem and not be misled by arithmetical figures."[50] M. R. Jayakar, however, adopted a purely negative attitude. Speaking on behalf of Hindu Mahasabha he alluded to the division

49. *Ibid.*, p. 78.
50 *Ibid.*, p. 84.

in the Muslim group and insisted that Jinnah represented only a small section of Muslims. He gave an ultimatum that if one word was changed in the Nehru Report regarding the Hindu-Muslim question, his party would withdraw its support from it. He warned the members: "If you accede to Mr. Jinnah's demands, the Report will be torn to pieces and will be rejected by important communities who have now accepted it as the final word in the matter."[51] The Sikh League had already declined to accept the Nehru Report while the Liberal Federation had taken up a non-commital attitude with regard to the Hindu-Muslim question.

While replying to the debate, Jinnah once again emphasized the need for Hindu-Muslim unity for the sake of attaining independence and urged upon the delegates the need for a reappraisal of the whole situation. He observed:

> . . . If you do not settle this question today, we shall have to settle it tomorrow, but in the meantime our national interests are bound to suffer. We are all sons of this land. We have to live together. We have to work together and whatever our differences may be let us at any rate not create more bad blood. If we cannot agree, let us at any rate agree to differ but let us part as friends. I once more repeat. Believe me, there is no progress for India until the Musalmans and Hindus are united and let no logic, philosophy or squabble stand in the way of our coming to a compromise and nothing will make me more happy than to see the Hindu Muslim union.[52]

But the Convention failed to secure the Muslim League's concurrence with the Nehru Report and was adjourned *sine die*. In a special interview to the Associated Press representative, Jinnah held the Mahasabha responsible for the failure of the Convention. "The fate of Nehru Report", he said, "was sealed by the speech of Jayakar at the Convention."[53] Even the Congress Muslims regretted the failure of the Conven-

51. *Ibid.*, p. 91.
52. *Ibid.*, pp. 94-95.
53. *The Tribune*, 2 June 1929.

tion and the way the League's suggestions had been treated at the Convention. They also blamed the Mahasabha for its uncompromising attitude. Tassaduq Sherwani deplored the 'stingy' way in which Muslim demands were dealt with at the Calcutta Convention. M. C. Chagla issued a statement to the press where he gave a most grave exposition of his views:

> I wish particularly to point out that the delegates whom the League sent to the Convention represented the most advanced sections of Muslim thought, that a large majority of them had already expressed their approval of the Nehru Report and that several of them have fought their own people and broken with their own organization in order to support the national cause . . . . If these delegates are going to be dubbed as communalists then perhaps there is not a single Muslim nationalist anywhere in the country. . . .I still hope that, before the Convention concludes its labours, it would be able to see its way to accepting the League's demands. Just as the Muslim League has fought and driven out the Shafi section. . . . So also the Convention ought to deal with its Moonjees and Jayakars who threaten to leave the convention every time Muslims make any suggestion to alter or modify any of the provisions of the Report.[54]

The failure of the Convention can only be attributed to the inability of the Congress leaders to stand up firmly against the pressures of the Hindu Mahasabha and override its opinions. From the very beginning Motilal had expressed his desire to adhere to any solution if the contending parties accepted it. He was in favour of the Muslims getting one-third representation in the Central Legislature as he felt it would hardly make any difference to Hindu majority. He had even brought Lajpat Rai round to his point of view. But the sudden death of the latter before the Convention was a great blow to the cause of the Hindu-Muslim unity as his colleagues in the Mahasabha had no knowledge of his understanding with Motilal. The latter had started his negotiations with Lajpat Rai before the

54. *Bombay Chronicle*, 1 January 1929.

Convention and though Lajpat Rai had been influenced by Motilal's arguments, he did not think it expedient to give in at that stage when the Muslims were insisting on other concessions also. It was decided by both of them that Hindu opposition to the Muslim demands might continue and even "stiffen up to the time the Convention was held." The object in view was to reduce the Muslim demands to an irreducible minimum." In accordance with the understanding arrived at between the two, Lajpat Rai, while presiding over the Etawah session of the Mahasabha (27 October 1928) put up a strong opposition to every part of the Muslim demands. Later at the Convention, the Hindu Mahasabha leaders made full use of his Etawah speech.[55]

No attempt was made by Motilal and his colleagues to mollify the dissatisfied Muslims. Probably he did not consider it an act of prudence to "refuse to avail of the opportunity of getting the Report through simply to please that section of Muslims led by Jinnah." He was convinced that Jinnah and Muhammad Ali had been discredited in the eyes of their own party members and had lost their confidence.[56] It is possible that Motilal was influenced by the thinking of men like Jayakar and Lajpat Rai. According to them, Jinnah then did not have much following among the Muslims. Jayakar's views have already been mentioned above. As for Lajpat Rai, in a letter to Motilal Nehru he observed: "Jinnah has really no following. Yaqub is very slippery and Fazl [Fazl-i-Husain] has completely gone out of hand. . . . I think you have more Muslims than Jinnah has with himself. . . .I may frankly tell you that I won't accept any changes."[57]

Jinnah's immediate reaction after the failure of the Convention was that Muslims as a body should reconsider their entire position *vis-a-vis* the Congress. He was confirmed in his belief that the disorganized condition of the Muslims had encouraged the Congress to ignore their demands which they had once accepted. He then started emphasising the supreme need for Muslim solidarity under his leadership for extracting

55. Motilal to Gandhi, 18 August 1929, Motilal Nehru Papers.
56. Motilal to Gandhi, 18 August 1929.
57. Lajpat Rai to Motilal, n.d., 1928, A.I.C.C. Papers.

concessions from the Hindus. Even the Congress Muslims were quite upset with the way the Muslim demands had been treated.[58] The Muslims had been alienated from the Congress to such an extent that when the All Parties Muslim Conference began its first session at Delhi on 31 December 1928,[59] many Muslims were present there who used to figure prominently on the Congress platforms. Shafee Daudi (who was a Khilafatist from Patna) became the Working Secretary and the Ali Brothers were members of the Working Committee. In addition, other prominent leaders associated with this Conference were Muhammad Shafi, the Muslim leader from the Punjab, Fazal Ibrahim Rahimtoola, a member of the Independent Party in the Central Legislative Assembly, Abdur Ghuznavi, one of the principal leaders of Bengal, and Shafaat Karim Ahmed Khan, a member of U. P. Legislative Council. The elected members of the central and provincial legislatures held important places in it and this facilitated its constant contact with the Government. The Aga Khan remained in touch with officialdom as the President of the Conference. Jinnah was the only important Muslim leader who had stood aside. When the Secretary of the Conference invited Jinnah to the meeting in Delhi, Jinnah refused and instead questioned

58. Motilal's correspondence with Purshottamdas Thakurdas reveals that Motilal had differences over the Nehru Report with Ansari also because the latter had misgivings about the treatment meted out to the Muslims. In a letter dated 17 June, Motilal makes a very haughty remark about Ansari's behaviour:
. . .It is going to be a unanimous report. I like your way of putting it that it is disconcerting to find that I have differed from men like Ansari and Shuaib Qureshi instead of saying that it was unfortunate that Dr. Ansari and Shuaib Qureshi should differ from a man like me. How could they dare? Motilal to Purshottamdas Thakurdas, 17 June 1928, Purshottamdas Thakurdas Papers.

59. The objects of the Conference were declared to be "to safe-guard and promote the rights and interests of Indian Musalmans at all stages of constitutional advance towards full responsible government in India and to organize the Indian Mussalmans for the purpose of giving expression to Muslim opinion on questions affecting the Musalmans of India."
K. K. Aziz, ed., *All Parties Muslim Conference, 1928-1935: A Documentary Record* (Karachi, 1972), p. 24.

the representative character of the Conference and its need for the Muslim community.[60]

However, taking advantage of Jinnah's rift with the Congress, several attempts were made by the Shafi group, which had separated itself from Jinnah after the Madras session in 1927, to amalgamate itself with his group. This effort succeeded and soon the two groups were merged into one. A representative meeting of the Council of the Muslim League was attended by both the sections on 3 March 1929. After protracted discussions a draft resolution was prepared by Jinnah to accommodate the various points of views in regard to policy and programme of the Muslim League in respect of the forthcoming constitutional reforms. The Muslim demands became commonly known as Jinnah's Fourteen Points but in substance they represented the same demands which the Muslim leaders had been pressing since 1927. Thus while advocating a federal constitution for India, Jinnah wanted the residuary powers to be vested in the provinces. The legislatures and other elected bodies were to be constituted on the definite principle of adequate and effective representation of minorities in every province without reducing the majorities in any province to a minority or even equality. Muslim representation in the Central Legislature was to be not less than one-third. The Muslims were to be given adequate share in all the services of the state on a communal basis. And lastly it was laid down that when all the other points were accepted by the Congress, the League might agree to joint electorates.[61]

The All Parties Muslim Conference now launched a campaign of vilification against the Congress. A manifesto was issued by its leaders under the heading *Zaruri Ailan* (Important Declaration) whereby the Muslims were asked to disobey the Congress and abstain from participation in its meetings and proceedings. This was reminiscent of those days when the Muslims had been asked by Sir Syed Ahmad to keep aloof from the Congress. A notable success of the Muslim Conference was symbolized by Shafee Daudi who resigned from the Swaraj

60. *Ibid.*, pp. 20-22.
61. *The Indian Annual Register, 1929*, vol. 1, p. 360ff.

Party in the Legislative Assembly as a protest against its anti-Muslim policy. In the words of Shafee Daudi, the main object underlying the manifesto was to counteract the "evil effects" of Motilal's "ill conceived notion about the Hindu-Muslim unity."[62]

The Nationalist Muslims, of course, retaliated by organizing a campaign to counteract the activities of the promoters of the the All Parties Muslim Conference and to carry on a vigorous propaganda in support of the Nehru Report. Efforts were made by Sarojini Naidu to arrange a meeting between Gandhi and Jinnah with a view to arriving at a settlement of those communal differences that had been left unresolved at the Convention. The Mahasabha got alarmed and started making insinuating remarks about Motilal, namely, that he had fallen a victim to the intrigues of Nationalist Muslims under the guidance of Jinnah to get these amendments accepted.[63] Jayakar wrote a letter to Gandhi pressurizing him not to yield to Muslim demands on the ground that the government would deliberately make these concessions part of a constitution which would be entirely different from a scheme which they were struggling to evolve.[64] A meeting of the Hindus was held in Bombay in August when they sent a memorandum to Gandhi asking him not to arrive at any compromise with the Muslims without consulting them. They also added that if anything was settled without consulting the Hindus, it would not be acceptable to them.[65] Even the formation of groups like the Congress Muslim Party and the Nationalist Muslim Party was misinterpreted as a scheme designed to change the decisions of the All Parties Convention and to bring round the Congress towards the acceptance of one-third Muslim representation in the Central Legislature and the unconditional separation of Sind. The whole plan, according to Moonje and Jayakar, was to isolate the Hindu

62. Shafee Daudi to Motilal Nehru, 29 August 1929, Motilal Nehru Papers.
63. Jayakar to Malaviya, 3 August 1929, Jayakar Papers.
64. Jayakar to Gandhi, 25 July 1929, Jayakar Papers.
65. *Ibid.*, 25 July 1929.

the Mahasabha, by getting the Congress and Liberal Federation to agree to the Muslim demands.[66]

It is pertinent to add here that the Hindu Mahasabha had already repudiated the Nehru Report at its Surat session held in April 1929, but now it was claiming to stand uncompromisingly by it and insisting that it should not be altered by one 'jot' or 'tittle'. It had apparently determined to stand firm because of its belief that the Muslims would themselves eventually, come to accept the Report as 'second best'.[67]

A meeting between Gandhi and Jinnah was held in July 1929, but its outcome was not encouraging. After the meeting Gandhi wrote to Motilal in great anguish: "How that can be done [resolving the deadlock] or whether it should be done, you know best. My mind is in a whirl in this matter. The atmosphere is too foggy for me to see clearly."[68] Motilal on his part tried to shelve the issue by asking Gandhi to make the Hindu Mahasabha agree to the Muslim demands. He was sure that if it agreed to the four points on which Jinnah's amendments had been rejected, the whole scheme of the Nehru Report would be adopted by the overwhelming majority of the League and the Khilafat Committee.[69] But this could not be achieved and as a result the differences between the Congress and the Muslims also continued to remain unresolved. It was finally decided to ignore Jinnah and the Ali Brothers completely, as Motilal felt that all the three of them were "totally discredited" and had no following worth the name.[70]

As the succeeding chapters will show, the Congress and the country as a whole had to pay a heavy price for this decision.

66. Jayakar to Malaviya, 31 July 1929, Jayakar Papers.
67. Moonje to Gandhi, 5 August 1929, Jayakar Papers.
68. Gandhi to Motilal, 23 August 1929, Motilal Nehru Papers.
69. *Ibid.*, 23 August 1929.
70. Motilal to Gandhi, 14 August 1929, Motilal Nehru Papers.

3

The Problem of Communal Representation at the Round Table Conference

On 31 October 1929, the Viceroy, Lord Irwin, in a statement announced that His Majesty's Government's intention was eventually to confer Dominion Status upon India. He also added that a Round Table Conference of the representatives of British India, Indian States and British political parties would assemble in London so that adequate expression of Indian views could be obtained before the proposals for the future constitution of the country were laid before the British Parliament.[1]

The general reception accorded to the announcement in India was at first quite encouraging. On 2 November, prominent Indian leaders like Gandhi, Motilal Nehru, Tej Bahadur Sapru and Annie Besant put their signatures to a manifesto which indicated their intention to co-operate in the settlement of Indian political problems. But when an Indian delegation consisting of Mahatma Gandhi, Sapru, Motilal Nehru and Jinnah met Irwin on 23 December to discuss the date and personnel of the Conference, it became quite evident that sharp differences of opinion existed not only between the

1. Lord Irwin's Dominion Status Declaration, 31 October 1929, Halifax Collection, Microfilm copy, N.M.M.L., New Delhi.

Viceroy and Motilal and Gandhi, but among the Indian leaders also. Gandhi doubted the sincerity of British purpose and throughout the conversation insisted that the Viceroy should guarantee that immediate Dominion Status would be granted to India. When reminded of the difficulties, in the form of internal differences, the Congress leaders pressed the right of India to Dominion Status, in spite of those differences. Motilal, in particular, completely denied the existence of any such difficulty. Gandhi's contention was that "he did not the want his people to go to the Conference in their weakness while India was disunited as she was at present and while there was vast difference of opinion among his friends unless they knew that the Viceroy and the British Government were with them."[2] The Congress refusal to recognize the need for communal unity and its unwillingness to participate in the Conference did not deter Jinnah and Sapru from expressing their readiness to go. The differences over the Nehru Report were fresh in their memory and now both of them took the initiative for composing the differences between the Hindus and Muslims. Their opinion was that unless a generous and broad-minded view was taken of the communal question no solution could be possible. They also showed a more realistic attitude as they thought it would be most derogatory if they failed to compose their differences before going to London or if they had to settle them with the help of British officials in England.[3]

For Jinnah, the settlement of the Hindu-Muslim problem was a "national problem" without which there was no hope for any real advance on the part of India towards Dominion Status.[4] Both the All India Muslim League and the All India Muslim Conference welcomed the announcement of the Viceroy. Ever since the Nehru Report, the Muslims had been groaning under a fear that what the Hindus aimed at was to gain political domination over the Muslims. They, therefore,

2. Minutes of conversation amongst Gandhi, Motilal Nehru, Tej Bahadur Sapru, Jinnah and the Viceroy Lord Irwin, 23 December 1929, Motilal Nehru Papers.
3. Sapru to Purshottamdas Thakurdas, 24 November 1929, Tej Bahadur Sapru Papers, Microfilm copy, N.M.M.L.
4. Jinnah to Sapru, 14 December 1929, Sapru Papers.

felt that in any constitution framed for India, definite guarantees must be provided for the Muslims against such a possibility. The Executive Board of the All India Muslim Conference meeting in Lahore in January 1930 advised the Muslims not to close the door to negotiations. It was also made clear that no constitution would be acceptable to the Muslims unless and until adequate safeguards were provided for their rights and interests as laid down in the resolutions of the Delhi Conference held in January 1929.[5]

Similar was the attitude of the Muslim League. Its council meeting in New Delhi on 9 February 1930 appreciated the Viceroy's announcement and described it as "most timely."[6] Muhammad Ali, on behalf of the Khilafat Committee also expressed the same viewpoint. He wrote to Jinnah:

> . . . As for the Mussalmans my advice to them is not to close the door of negotiations with government or any party and to examine every scheme with a view to satisfying that
>
> (1) we are really getting freedom, or Swaraj or full responsible government, whether with or without the British connection, by whatever name people call it and that
> (2) the Mussalmans are getting an adequate and effective share in the governance of India as defined in the points which you and we formulated last year.[7]

In pursuance of his determination to achieve unity, Sapru approached various parties and groups like the All India Muslim Conference, the Nationalist Muslims, National Liberal Federation and the Hindu Mahasabha with the idea of uniting them on a common platform to bring about a settlement of the Hindu-Muslim question. Every party, with the exception of the Hindu Mahasabha, responded favourably and showed

5. K.K. Aziz, ed., *The All India Muslim Conference, A Documentary Record 1928-35* (Karachi, 1972), p. 59.
6. *The Indian Annual Register, vol. I, 1930,* p. 347.
7. Muhammad Ali to Jinnah, 16 January 1930, Ansari Papers.

great enthusiasm for the endeavour.[8] The Hindu Mahasabha refused to co-operate if the communal question was going to be discussed. This time it had been encouraged to maintain this intransigence mainly because of the attitude of Congress leaders who had completely undervalued the importance of solving this problem. Moonje described Sapru's attempts as nothing but "a leap in the darkness and wanted that these should be given up until the Muslims, being disillusioned by the bureaucracy, themselves began to desire rapprochement".[9] It is pertinent to note that Motilal had also characterized Sapru's effort as a "mistake on his part and was sure that he would soon be disillusioned."[10]

At this juncture even the Muslim Congressmen like Ansari, Shuaib Qureshi and Khaliquzzaman expressed their disapproval of the attitude of the Congress towards the communal problem. Ansari had had some disagreement with Motilal at the time of the consideration of the Nehru Report also, but had never come out openly against him. Now the disagreement came to the surface and he openiy expressed his dissent from the policy and programme of the Congress on the Hindu-Muslim question. He found the Congress policy adopted at the Lahore session[11] in 1929 so distasteful that he retired from the Congress executive. He also regretted that the Congress should have utilized the offer made by the Viceroy to its fullest advantage, and blamed it for mishandling the situation. In a letter to Gandhi he wrote:

> . . . I have not the slightest doubt that if we had stuck to it [the the stand of the Madras Congress, 1927 on the Hindu-Muslim problem] we would have gradually overcome the opposition of the Hindu Mahasabha and Hindu-

8. Sapru to Jinnah, 5 January 1930, Sapru Papers.
9. B.R. Moonje to Sapru, 26 January 1930, Sapru Papers.
10. Motilal to Ansari, 17 February 1930, Ansari Papers.
11. There it was decided that "in view of the lapse of the Nehru Report, it is unnecessary to declare the policy of the Congress regarding communal question, the Congress believing that in an independent India, communal questions can only be solved on strictly national lines". *Indian National Congress Resolutions, 1929*, p. 60.

> Muslim unity would have been an accomplished fact by now. But we wanted to be more just and fair . . . we lost at Lucknow and Calcutta what we had gained at Madras . . . . It was the Hindu Mahasabha which completely did the work of destruction.[12]

Indeed, it was a misjudgement of the Congress to have completely neglected the solution of the communal problem at this time. Having failed to achieve unity at the time of the All Parties Convention in 1928, it had given up even a pretence of dealing with it. Motilal Nehru was not prepared to subscribe to the views held by the Muslims and the Liberals as to why the Congress leaders had so far failed to achieve unity and the direction in which further efforts should be made. Motilal contended that the path which the Congress had till then followed had been fundamentally wrong and that Hindu-Muslim unity could not be achieved by preaching it but "would be accomplished without either of them realizing that they were working for it. This could only be done on an economic basis and in the course of the fight for freedom from the usurper."

> As a result of past experience and anxious thought I have now reached the conclusion that the lines upon which we worked were fundamentally wrong. . . . The fact is that we have been appealing to the wrong court all these years. . . . . I have definitely come to hold the opinion that no amount of formulae based upon mutual concessions which those making them have no right to make will bring us any nearer Hindu-Muslim unity than we are at present.[13]

Motilal's views were contradicted by Gandhi. The latter expressed his sympathy with the Muslim viewpoint and stressed that independence could not be achieved without the Muslims and other minorities being satisfied with their position. His views on this question were in complete accord with

12. Ansari to Gandhi,13 February 1930, Ansari Papers.
13. Motilal to Ansari, 17 February 1930, Ansari Papers.

those of Ansari and Sapru. But it is a pity that he did not do anything at this stage to tackle the communal question as he also felt that it had to be approached ". . . not [as] at present by adjustment of the political power but by one or the other acting on the square under all circumstances."[14] His failure in this respect further contributed towards the alienation of the Muslims from the Congress as it confirmed their view that the Congress was not interested in satisfying the Muslims. In desperation Khaliquzzaman wrote to Ansari:

> . . . The reply of Mahatmaji was no doubt felt by everyone of us to be disappointing. In fact it has set everyone thinking. Uptil now we thought that Hindu Muslim unity was the pillar over which the super-structure of the constitution of free Indla was to be laid but from Mahatmaji's letter one can infer that while recognizing the utility of such a unity he does not consider it *sine qua non* for the fight for Independence.[15]

In any case, as a result of the efforts of those desirous of settling the communal problem, an All Parties Conference was convened by Sapru in New Delhi in the month of February 1930. Those present included Annie Besant, Jinnah, Raja of Mahmudabad, Sir Ali Imam, Sultan Ahmed, Muhammad Ali, Sikandar Hyat Khan, Yaqub Hasan, Zulfiqar Ali Khan, Nawab Mohammed Ismail, A. H. Ghaznavi, C. P. Ramaswami Aiyer, Col. Gidney and Col. Crawform. Sapru fully approved of the idea that the Muslims should be given ample safeguards for their representation in the central and provincial legislatures. A manifesto was issued which warned that if the various communities were to go their own ways there would be very little chance of achieving anything worth the name. Therefore it was felt imperative to call a consultative meeting in March to consider those safeguards for the

14. Gandhi to Ansari, February 16, 1930, *The Collected Works of Gandhi*, vol. 42 (New Delhi, October 1929-February 1930), p. 510.
15. Khaliquzzaman to Ansari, 1 March 1930, Ansari Papers.

minorities without which no real constitutional progress could be possible.[16]

The consultative meeting discussed and accepted in principle the demands of the Muslims and other minorities for safeguards that were to be provided for the protection of their religion, education and culture. As regards representation in the legislature, Muhammad Ali came out with a novel suggestion that there should be joint electorates subject to the following conditions:

(a) There should be reservation of seats for Muslims both in provinces where they were in a minority and in those where they were in a majority on population basis.

(b) No right should be given to minorities to contest additional seats. (Here Muhammad Ali differed from his colleagues.)

(c) Everywhere a Hindu candidate must obtain a minimum number of Muslim votes and similarly a Muslim candidate must obtain a minimum number of Hindu votes. The details and the method were not discussed.[17]

The refusal of the Mahasabha to co-operate with Sapru and Jinnah did not deter it from approaching the former in order to enlist its support for the agreement which had been arrived at the March meeting. But the Mahasabha changed its stand now. This was because it apprehended that the Liberals might give in to Muslim demands in their anxiety to win them over. To an invitation from Sapru to attend the conference, scheduled to be held in May 1930, Moonje gave an offensive reply. He told Sapru that there was no possibility of the members of the Mahasabha joining the conference and in the same letter quoted the wire he had sent to Gandhi, imploring him, not to promise concessions to the Muslims which were "incompatible with nationalism". He made it clear that any agreement which might be arrived at with the Muslims would not be binding upon the representa-

16. A Note by Sapru on All Parties Conference, 30 February 1930, Ansari Papers.
17. *Ibid.*

tives of the Hindu Mahasabha.[18] This attitude of the Hindu Mahasabha was enough to show what it was going to do at the Round Table Conference.

The outcome of the meeting held in May was not unexpected, considering the intransigence shown by Moonje. When everything seemed to depend on the ability of Indians to arrive at an agreement the Hindus represented by the Congress and the Mahasabha contrived to shirk the issue. The meeting had to be adjourned indefinitely after passing a resolution that as there was no one who could represent the Hindu viewpoint as a whole, the Conference could not proceed with its work. When the question of a uniform measure of autonomy for all the provinces was under discussion (which Sapru also did not favour as he had lent his whole-hearted support to Motilal in 1928 on Nehru Committee's recommendation for a unitary form of government) Jinnah raised the point whether the Hindus present there would be able to secure their acceptance by the Hindu community as a whole. Since no one came forward, the meeting was wound up with the following remark by Jinnah: "There is nobody with whom I can enter into a pact. I am prepared to take responsibility for the Muslims but where are the representative Hindus who would take such responsibility for their community."[19]

With the Hindu-Muslim problem thus still remaining unsettled, the first session of the Round Table Conference commenced in London on 12 November 1930. Among the Hindus and Muslims the key men were Tej Bahadur Sapru, V. S. Srinivasa Shastri, C. P. Ramaswami Aiyer, Chimanlal Setalvad, Dewan Bahadur Ramaswami Mudaliyar, Moonje, Jayakar, Jinnah, Muhammad Shafi, Muhammad Ali, Zafrullah Khan and the Aga Khan.[20] The Congress being engaged in the civil disobedience movement did not send any representative.

The Muslims were fully aware of the fact that their own organisations were weak; they, therefore, considered it necessary to secure all sorts of assistance from the Government.

18. Moonje to Sapru, 5 May 1930, Sapru Papers.
19. *The Evening News of India*, 7 July 1930, enclosed in Press Clippings File, Jayakar Papers.
20. *Indian Round Table Conference*, Proceedings, 12 November 1930-19 January 1931, p. 331. (Cmd. 3778, 1931.)

The latter was also doing its best to encourage those Muslims who were conducting a campaign against the civil disobedience movement. For the Muslims, the numerical strength of those representing their community did not carry much meaning. What mattered most were the views and the ability of those Muslims. Their main concern, as conveyed to the Viceroy, was that the delegates he chose for the conference should be acceptable to their respective provinces and to India as a whole. Moreover, they questioned Jinnah's right to speak on behalf of the entire community as he was suspected of having one leg in the Hindu camp also. Fazl-i-Husain wrote to Hailey : "...frankly, I do not like the idea of Jinnah doing all the talking and of there being no one strong-minded enough to make a protest in case Jinnah starts upon expressing his views when those views are not acceptable to the Indian Muslims."[21] Therefore Shafaat Ahmed Khan and Zafrullah Khan were deputed to London to counteract Jinnah. Immediately after the launching of the civil disobedience movement, Shafaat Ahmad had tried to dissuade the Muslims from joining the movement, as he felt that it would be 'suicidal' to his community. In an interview with the Viceroy at Lucknow he gave an assurance to him that the Muslims would not join the movement and asserted that without Muslim support it would be a miserable failure. In keeping with the tradition prevalent since the days of Sir Syed, he observed:

> ...Muslims require some assurance, some guarantee that their position will not be endangered by the position and policy they have adopted at this critical juncture. They have loyally supported the government, they have unanimously rejected the offer of the Congress .... If the government or preferably the Viceroy could make a moral gesture and at least reiterate assurance to all minority communities that their interests would be safeguarded it would be of utmost value at this juncture.[22]

21. Fazl-i- Husain to Hailey, 20 May 1930, Hailey Collection, India Office Library, London.
22. Shafaat Ahmad Khan to Captain Blunden, 12 May 1930, Hailey Collection.

As soon as negotiations started at the Round Table Conference a Sub-Committee known as the Minorities Committee was formed to consider the claims of the minorities. Its chief function was to make an endeavour to find a solution of the problem of communal representation. At the outset, the Prime Minister Ramsay MacDonald acting as the Chairman of the above mentioned Committee appealed to the Indian delegates to settle the communal question among themselves.

It must be pointed out that though they were demanding adequate safeguards for their community the Muslims were as vociferous in their demand for self-government as were the other sections of the Indian delegation. Drawing attention to the Viceroy's announcement Jinnah reminded the Prime Minister:

> . . . India now expects the translation and fulfilment of these declarations into action. There never was a more momentous or graver issue in the history of our two nations than the one we are called upon to face today and upon the solution of which hangs the fate of nearly one-fifth of the population of the world.[23]

As far as the Muslim demands were concerned, initially the Muslims favoured separate electorates and in its defence Mohammad Shafi emphasized that joint elactorates instead of helping the cause of nationalism would be detrimental to it. But since the Hindu members like Chimanlal Setalvad, Raja Narendranath, A.P. Patro, who were in full agreement with the other demands of the Muslims, insisted on joint electorates, the latter modified their original position in regard to separate electorates. At the fourth meeting of the Minorities Sub-Committee, Shafi announced that Muslims were prepared to accept joint electorates "in deference to the wishes of the sister communities and to the appeals that have been made to us."[24] Great pressure was exerted upon Jinnah, Aga Khan and Shafi by some other Muslim leaders not to give up separate electorates. Fazl-i-Hussain issued a number of instructions to

23. Indian Round Table Conference, n. 20, p. 22.
24. *Indian Round Table Conference, First Session,* Proceedings of the Minorities Committee, p. 56.

the Muslim delegates urging them not to compromise with the Hindus as he was scared of losing the confidence of the British.[25] Feroz Khan Noon also informed the Aga Khan that the Punjab Muslims would never give up separate electorates.[26] Though Jinnah, Shafi and the Aga Khan decided to take full responsibility for the decision, ultimately they had to give in to the pressures of the Muslim orthodox opinion in India. They were also, however, prepared to give up separate electorates only on certain conditions. These conditions as enumerated by Shafi were that the rights enjoyed by Muslims in the minority provinces should be continued and in the Punjab and Bengal they should have joint electorates on population basis and the reservation of seats should be based on Muhammad Ali's scheme. That scheme had been devised at the time of the All Parties Conference in February but the details were worked out later on. According to it, a candidate was not to be declared elected unless he had secured at least 40 per cent of the votes cast of his own community and at least 5 per cent of the votes cast by other communities wherever he belonged to a minority of 10 per cent or less, and 10 per cent where he belonged to a large minority or majority.[27] These conditions prescribed by the Muslim leaders were not new, but were the repetition of those agreed to by the Congress in 1927, except for the novel idea suggested by Muhammad Ali whereby he wanted to ensure that other communities should also have some say in the election of a Muslim candidate.

Thus the Muslim attitude at the Conference reveals that the crux of the whole problem was not joint electorates or separate electorates but the reservation of seats in the Muslim majority provinces. The argument of the Muslim leaders was that while the Hindus enjoyed power and influence in eight provinces, the Muslims should have the same position in at least four. Shafi described the demand of his community as the "recognition of the just rights of the Mussulmans in these four

25. Fazl-i-Husain to Hailey, 20 May 1930, Hailey Collection.
26. Shafaat Ahmad Khan to Maulana Muhammad Ali, 23 September 1930, Muhammad Ali Papers, Jamia Millia Library.
27. *Indian Round Table Conference*, 12 November 1930-19th January 1931, (Sub-committees Reports, Conference Resolution); and Prime Minister's Statement, (Cmd. 3772, 1931), p. 47.

provinces, of their representation as majority in the majority of provinces. . . .That will be an automatic guarantee to good treatment."[28] Muhammad Ali in his memorandum circulated to the delegates also expressed the same desire more forcefully:

> . . . The Mussalmans desire—and this is the crux of their 14 points and not separate electorates—that there should be federal government so that the central unitary government with a permanent Hindu majority should not override them everywhere ; . . . that in the provinces of the Punjab and Bengal where they have small majorities in population which are unorganized and greatly controlled by Banyas and the Sikhs and the Hindu landlords as in Bengal, these majorities should be reserved . . . the Mussalmans should be allowed to have their majority in all these four provinces as the Hindus have everywhere else.[29]

Muhammad Iqbal's Presidential Address at the twenty-first session of the All-India Muslim League at Allahabad on 29 December 1930 asking for the amalgamation of the Punjab, North-West Frontier Province, Sind and Baluchistan which had given rise to so much misgivings among the Hindu Mahasabha delegates, can also be explained as conveying the same meaning—the desire of the Muslims to have a solid block in the north where they could enjoy their majority rights.[30]

Taking their cue from the Hindu Mahasabha, the Sikhs in the Punjab further complicated the entire situation by putting forward their rival claims. They constituted eleven per cent of the population in the Punjab and they were quite vocal in their demand that their special interests should be protected. This protection, they insisted, should be on lines similar to those

28. *Indian Round Table Conference, Proceedings of the Minorities Committee*, p. 95.
29. "Last Words of Maulana Muhammad Ali", Maulana M. Ali's last letter to the Prime Minister of England, for publication and circulation to the members of the Round Table Conference, 1 January 1930, All India Congress Committee Files, N.M.M.L.
30. S.S. Pirzada, ed., *Foundation of Pakistan : All India Muslim League Documents*, Vol. II, 1924-47 (Karachi, 1970), p. 159.

given to the Muslim minorities in other provinces. They refused to agree to a system of representation designed for the protection of the majority community. They held that their existing share of about 19 per cent seats in the Punjab was "too low in view of their historic, military and economic importance," and demanded that this be raised to 30 per cent.[31] This could be secured only after making deductions from the quota of Muslim seats.

In Bengal the difficulty was created by the over-representation of Europeans, although their numerical strength did not entitle them to more than a seat or two. The need for proportional representation was explained by Fazl-ul-Huq by pointing to the elections held in bodies like municipalities and district boards where there were no separate electorates. He said emphatically that no Muslim could succeed in winning a single seat by means of an election without any reservation. Apart from this a Muslim could be elected only in two ways—either by becoming a member of the Hindu Mahasabha or by agreeing in writing that he would follow his Hindu colleagues on every issue.[32]

Once again the Hindu-Muslim settlement was within the reach of Indian leaders and they would have been able to present a united front to the government, had the Hindu Mahasabha been prepared to accommodate the Muslim wishes. But Moonje had come to attend the Conference fully armed with the determination to maintain his opposition to the Muslim demands until the end.[33] Strict instructions were sent to him by his partymen to be a diehard Hindu. He was asked to concede one-third seats to the Muslims in the central legislature only on the condition that along with provincial autonomy there was a provision for a strong central government with residuary powers.[34]

31. Memorandum submitted by two Sikh delegates Sardar Ujjal Singh and Sardar Sampuran Singh at the first Round Table Conference, n.d., File No. 412, Jayakar Papers.
32. Indian Round Table Conference, Proceedings of the Minorities Committee, p. 117.
33. Moonje to Jayakar, 8 September 1930, Jayakar Papers.
34. "An Appeal to the Hindu delegates of the Round Table Conference", n.d., Jayakar Papers.

Other delegates like C Y. Chintamani, Chimanlal Setalvad and Sardar Ujjal Singh challenged Moonje's right to speak on behalf of the entire Hindu community. Setalvad emphatically countered Moonje's arguments by saying that "the Hindu delegates should not be taken as represented by the views that Dr. Moonje has expressed in the meeting or any other organization in India." He stressed the need for devising adequate safeguards to make the minorities feel safe and satisfied and insisted that there should be reservation of seats either wholly or in some modified form (referring to Muhommad Ali's scheme) so that they would be able to secure their due protection in the legislation.[35] Chintamani also told the Hindu delegates that the "abolition of separate electorates and the substitution therefor of joint electorates is so great a national advantage that the advocates of this change may in justice be called upon to pay a price for that change."[36] Sapru, Setalvad and Sastri had approached Jinnah and the Aga Khan and had offered them a majority of 51 per cent in the Punjab. But the Sikhs refused to fall in line. Even Raja Narendra Nath had privately told Chintamani that although he had no objection to that proposal, he was not prepared to take responsibility for this view, and publicly take a stand opposing the Hindu Mahasabha's approach.[37] Thus the Hindu-Muslim negotiations broke down.

The Government of India's Despatch, published in the same year, alluded to the low economic position of the Muslims and to their voting strength being lower than their numerical strength, and had devised a scheme to meet the Muslim demands. According to it, in the new provincial council in the Punjab the Muslims were to be given a majority of two over the Hindus and Sikhs combined and a proportion of 49 per cent of the House as a whole. But it failed to satisfy either party.[38]

35. Indian Round Table Conference, Proceedings of the Minorities Sub-Committee, p. 108.
36. *Ibid.*, p. 114.
37. Sapru to Raina, 22 December 1930, Sapru Papers.
38. *Government of India's Despatch on Proposals for Constitutional Reforms* (Government of India, Central Publication Branch, Calcutta, 1930), p. 28.

The first Round Table Conference thus ended without a settlement of the communal problem. Winding it up on 19 January 1931 the British Prime Minister observed that he had no intention of imposing his will on the communities through an award as he felt that the conditions were not conducive to that. Instead he exhorted both the Hindus and the Muslims to settle their differences by themselves. He said : "...the British Government has no desire to use your disagreement for any ulterior motives .... We sitting here cannot impose pains and penalties. We sitting here can declare rights and hand over to you the political power to see that those rights are enforced and respected."[39] The Muslims were quite dissatisfied with the Prime Minister's statement and they felt that His Majesty's Government had gone "out of their way" to meet Hindu aspirations and had neglected their demand for safeguards. The Working Committee of the All India Muslim Conference at its meeting on 7 February 1931 recorded its disappointment at the failure of the Conference to find "equitable and just settlement" of the Hindu-Muslim question. Once again it warned that no constitutional structure would appeal to the Muslims which did not safeguard their rights and interests.[40]

The Muslim apprehensions were really unfounded. A perusal of the Prime Minister's secret note on Hindu-Muslim representation reveals that he had decided to concede the Muslim demands. The weightage enjoyed by the Muslims in minority provinces was to continue. There was provision also for Muslim majority in the Punjab and Bengal. Only on the question of separate electorates, he did not commit himself at that stage. Instead he said that Muslims should give a trial to joint electorates with reserved seats or to a small proportion of open electorates in some provinces.[41]

Even Irwin did not want to take the risk of alienating the Muslims and thus strengthening the Congress ranks. An idea of his thinking can be had from the following telegram

39. *Proceedings of the Minorities Sub-Committee*, p. 321.

40. Aziz, n. 5, pp. 68-69.

41. "Note on Hindu-Muslim Representation", copy of Prime Minister's Draft, Secret, Round Table Conference, 1930-31, Hailey Collection.

he sent to the Secretary of State Wedgwood Benn:

> It is of course of first importance that no ground should be given for suspicion, however ill-founded, that Moslems may not in the sequel be fairly treated, or that they may be out-manoeuvred. There have been clear indications of hardening of Muslim opinion in India, and if they believe that Government will not ultimately protect their interests a situation of utmost gravity would be created here. A belief of this kind would at once deprive us of Muslim support. Further they might be driven to make the best terms they could with Congress and join the civil disobedience movement.[42]

The Muslim League did indeed try to seek rapprochement with Gandhi. Mohammad Shafi appealed to him to pay more attention to bridging the gulf between the two communities.[43] Gandhi also was more keen than ever in his desire to reach a communal settlement. The wrecking of the first Round Table Conference because of Hindu-Muslim antagonism had deeply convinced him that it was useless to proceed with the work of framing the Constitution without a prior agreement between the two communities. He assured the Muslims that, in case he could arrive at a settlement with the government, the settlement of the communal question would engage his first attention. As a result of the Gandhi-Irwin truce, the Congress withdrew the civil disobedience movement and agreed to go to the Round Table Conference on the basis of federation as an essential part of the constitution. In a speech at Jamiat-ul-Ulema Conference, Gandhi talked about the need for an early solution of the communal question and his preparedness to agree to the Muslim demands. He said: "... as a Congressman and as a Hindu, I say that I wish to give the Muslims what they want. I do not with to act like a

42. Telegram from Irwin to Wedgwood Benn, 15 January 1931, Halifax Collection.
43. *Bombay Chronicle*, 24 February 1931.

Bania. I wish to leave everything to the honour of the Muslims. I would like you to put down whatever you want on a blank sheet of paper and I shall agree to it."[44]

Now when Gandhi was prepared to agree to all the Muslim demands, the Nationalist Muslims started agitating against separate electorates. A.M. Khwaja wrote a very strong letter to Gandhi imploring him not to accede to the demand for separate electorates and 'betray' the Muslims. He also pointed out that that was only the demand of the Muslims from minority provinces like U.P. and Bihar whose main concern was to safeguard the weightage enjoyed by them.[45]

Efforts were also made by the Nationalist Muslims to influence their co-religionists belonging to the All India Muslim League and All India Muslim Conference not to insist on separate electorates. At the All India National Muslim Conference held in Lucknow on 14 April 1931, negotiations were started with the Muslim League in order to pave the way for settlement conducive "to the best interests of the country and community as well."[46] Emphasizing that there was not much difference (with only one exception) in their viewpoints, Ansari reiterated the view that the anxiety of Muslims to secure certain safeguards and guarantees for their community in the future constitution of India was genuine and assured the anti-Congress Muslims that pro-Congress Muslims would do their best to secure all those demands.[47] Mohammad Shafi reciprocated these sentiments by suggesting the convening of a Muslim Round Table Conference to "formulate unanimous demands of the Muslims" to be submitted to Gandhi. A Conference was held in Simla on 18 April 1931, those attending being Ali Imam and Ansari as the President and Secretary of the Muslim Nationalist Party respectively; Jinnah representing the All India Muslim League; the Aga Khan, Shaukat Ali and Shafee Daudi representing the All India Muslim Conference; Kifayatullah, President of the Jamiat-ul-Ulema; Abdul Rahim,

44. *The Times of India*, 3 March 1931.
45. A.M. Khwaja to Gandhi, 21 March 1931, A.M. Khwaja Papers, N.M.M.L.
46. *The Leader*, 15 April 1931.
47. *Ibid.*

Mohammad Iqbal, Abdul Qayum, A.H. Ghuznavi and Abdulla Haroon representing major Muslim Provinces.[48]

However, the discussions could not make much headway and it was left to the Nawab of Bhopal to make another attempt. It seems that the All India Muslim League had conveyed to the Nationalist Muslim Party that it was prepared to accept joint electorates if a referendum of the Muslims of a province made it clear that such was the wish of the majority among them. In a joint meeting at Bhopal, the following formula was placed for the consideration of the Nationalist Muslim Party by Mohammad Shafi on behalf of his colleagues:

(a) Joint electorates to be introduced at the end of ten years with adult franchise, provided that if the majority of the Muslim members in any legislature, federal or provincial, agree to accept the joint electorates at any time before the expiry of ten years, separate electorates would be abolished.

(b) The first election under the new constitution to be on the basis of separate electorates, with a referendum on the question of joint versus separate electorates at the beginning of the fifth year of the first legislature.

Similarly on behalf of Nationalist Muslim Party, Sherwani placed the following formula for the consideration of those representing the All India Muslim Conference:

(a) Joint electorates to be adopted for the first ten years—on the expiry of which period, a referendum should be held on the question.

(b) In the first legislature 50 per cent of the Muslim members to be elected by joint electorates and 50 per cent by separate electorates. In the second, two-third members to be elected by joint electorate and one-third by separate electorate and thereafter by joint electorate and adult suffrage.[49]

48. *The Indian Annual Register*, 1931, vol. 1, pp. 287-8.

49. "Formulae regarding Muslim representation Proposed and Discussed at an Informal Meeting Held Under the Chairmanship of Nawab of Bhopal", n.d., S.A. Brelvi Papers, N.M.M.L.

The two parties dispersed to ascertain the views of their respective organisations. When they met again on 29 May, the All India Muslim Conference stuck to its guns and put forward its own formula. Its leaders argued that the first elections under the new constitution should be held on the basis of separate electorates and joint electorates shouid be introduced if before the expiry of the life of any legislature, a majority of the elected members demanded that a referendum should be taken on the question of joint versus separate electorates or if ten per cent of the Muslim electorates of any province desired them.

This formula was unacceptable to the Nationalist Muslims as it was inconsistent with the resolutions of the All India Nationalist Muslim Conference held at Lucknow. The prospects of Gandhi arriving at a settlement with the Muslims became remote after the failure of the Muslims themselves to compose their differences.

Gandhi was reluctant to attend the Round Table Conference in the absence of an agreement on the Hindu-Muslim question. He said : ". . . If we cannot set our house in order . . . I cannot speak with one voice." He also felt that he was not in a position to put forth the national demand as he did not have the support of the entire nation. He was realistic enough to admit that the Congress was too weak to seize power from unwilling hands "in the artificial surrounding of the Round Table Conference without the solid backing of Muslims." He was, however, overruled by the Congress Working Committee which did not consider it advisable to postpone attending the Conference because of the failure to obtain a communal settlement. The decision of Gandhi was interpreted as "playing into the hands of the enemy" and exposing the communities to "unnecessary misrepresentation".[50] It was the height of optimism on the part of the Working Committee of the Congress to entertain the hope of getting a Swaraj Constitution at the Round Table Conference without securing the support of the Muslims when Willingdon had

50. "Substance Not Shadow", 18 June 1931, *The Collected Works of Mahatma Gandhi*, vol. 47 (New Delhi, June-September 1931), p. 1.

set his mind on satisfying the Muslims by conceding their demands.

Having accepted the resolution, it was incumbent upon Gandhi to implement it fully. However, even when he agreed to attend the Round Table Conference he repeatedly insisted that his views were more safe and "more truly in consonance with the Lahore resolution on communal question." He also expressed his apprehensions about the proceedings of the Conference and anticipated the failure of his mission. In a statement to the representatives of *Al Ahram*, he expressed his doubts in the following words: "My expectations of the Conference are zero, if I am to base them on a survey of the horizon. . . . The Congress is prepared to pay the cost whatever it may be for gaining freedom."[51]

Thus far from satisfying the Muslims of all the viewpoints and inspiring confidence in them, the policy of the Congress further alienated them as their feelings had been completely disregarded. In a public meeting of Muslims of Calcutta, under the presidentship of Maulana Abdul Majed Badauni, the All India Khilafat Committee, passed a resolution condemning the Congress Working Committee's formula on the communal problem[52] as "more harmful and destructive than even the Nehru Report". Another resolution passed by them was that the Congress resolutions were manifestations of Hindu Raj mentality and would widen the gulf between the

51. Statement to *Al Ahram*, 6 September 1931, *The Collected Works of Mahatma Gandhi*, *ibid.*, p. 397.

52. The Congress Working Committee's formula scheme for a communal settlement laid down that joint electorates should form the basis of representation in the future constitution and that for the Hindus in Sind, the Muslims in Assam and the Sikhs in the Punjab and North West Frontier Province and for Hindus and Muslims in any province where they were less than 25 per cent of the population, seats should be reserved in the Federal and Provincial Legislatures on the bâsis of population with the right to contest additional seats. It also agreed to the residuary powers being vested in the federating units and Sind being constituted into a separate province provided the people of Sind were prepared to bear the financial burden of the separate province.
Indian Round Table Conference, Second Session, 7 September-1 December 1931, Appendix 1, p. 57.

two communities". Shaukat Ali in his fiery outburst gave a warning to the Congress that if it was not willing to recognize the Muslim demands, then they would ask the government to satisfy them and make peace." He also threatened a civil war if the Congress tried to force its views upon them.[53] Before sailing for England to attend the Second Round Table Conference, Jinnah described the attitude of the Hindus as 'foolish' and said that without satisfying the Muslim demands, India could not progress. Explaining his position, he said: "I am an Indian first and a Muslim afterwards and I agree that no Indian can ever serve his country if he neglects the interests of Muslims, because it is by encouraging them that you will be able to serve your country."[54]

When the Second Round Table Conference met in London on 7 September 1931, the difficulties before it were as formidable as they were in December last. The communal deadlock remained unresolved; there was no chance of a communal settlement as the Muslim leaders were not prepared to modify their demands and neither the Congress nor the Hindu Mahasabha was prepared to accept them. In Britain, the Labour Government had been replaced by a coalition Government and though Ramsay MacDonald was still the Prime Minister, a strong conservative element headed by Baldwin had joined the cabinet.

All the parties had arrived in London equipped with a definite programme. The Muslims demands included separate electorates with seats in the Punjab and Bengal on a population basis. The entrance of the Indian states into the federation would mean increased Hindu majority in the federal government. The Muslim representatives were, therefore, keen to counteract the Hindu majority by denying great powers to the Hindu dominated centre. They opposed weightage for the states in the central legislature and stuck to their old demand for one third of the seats in the central legislature. The Aga Khan had told Samuel Hoare even before the Conference had started that the Muslims could not consent to discuss responsibility at the centre in the federal structure

53. *The Times of India*, 5 September 1931.
54. *Bombay Chronicle*, 11 September 1931.

"till they know where they are." He insisted that the centre's power of interference in the provinces in case of emergency should rest with the Governor-General and not with the federal cabinet or federal legislature. He wanted that the administration of law and order should be made a provincial subject and defence a Crown subject, not to be allotted to the Federal Government. He observed : "Unless the Moslem Provinces have some such protection, their position in the majority provinces will become one of absolute dependence on the Federal Government in which they will be always a smaller party."[55]

In the Muslim deputation the real control rested with the conservative Muslim opinion in India like Shafaat Ahmad Khan and Zafrullah Khan who were in close touch with the Muslim representatives who participated in the conference. Also the Muslim Conference leaders had clearly warned Willingdon that if the government contemplated the inclusion of Ali Imam and Ansari, the Muslims would be forced to reconsider their atttiude towards further participation in the Round Table Conference. Their view finally prevailed.

Gandhi had brought with him the Congress scheme for communal settlement, providing for joint electorates as the basis of representation in the future constitution of India and reservation of seats for Hindus and Muslims in provinces where they were less than twenty-five per cent of the population. In the Minorities Committee, the Prime Minister once again acted as the Chairman. Gandhi began by having informal talks with the various Muslim leaders like the Aga Khan and others. In these talks he accepted in his personal capacity a majority of one per cent for Muslims in the Punjab and Bengal. The main points of the agreement which were discussed between Gandhi and the Muslim leaders were:

(a) In the Punjab and Bengal a bare majority of one per cent was to be given to the Muslims in the legislatures; the question whether there would be joint electorates, with the necessary reservation of seats or separate

55. Private Letter from the Aga Khan to Samuel Hoare, 30 August 1931, Private Office Records, L/PO/48.

electorates would be decided by a poll of the Muslim electors before the introduction of a new constitution.

(b) In the provinces where the Muslims were in a minority, the existing weightage of seats was to be maintained, but the question of joint or separate electorates was to be settled in the same way as in Bengal and the Punjab.

(c) In the federal legislature, the Muslim representation in both Houses was to be 26 per cent of the total number of British Indian representatives and of the quota assigned to the states, it was to be at least 7 per cent by convention with a view to Muslim representatives constituting one third of both the Houses.

(d) Residuary powers were to vest in the federating provinces of British India.[56]

Gandhi and the Muslim leaders, however, could not arrive at an agreement because the representatives of the various communities were not able to take decision on their own and were under the strict control of their constituents in India. Even Gandhi told the delegates that he did not have plenipotentiary powers and that any decision reached by him would have to be ratified by the Congress.[57]

The leaders of the different communities had brought different schemes with them and it was very difficult to prepare an agreed plan on their basis. The Congress scheme was rejected by the Hindu Mahasabha. Then both the Hindus and the Sikhs did not agree with the Muslim demands. The common point in all the schemes was that in some provinces the Hindus wanted to ensure their majority with a strong centre while in certain other the Muslims wanted to dominate. No practical suggestion was made in any of these schemes by which the minority in any province, to whichever community it belonged, would be in a position to influence the members of the legislature who would be returned on the votes of the majority community.

56. Shafaat Ahmad to Nawab of Chhatari, 6 October 1931, Nawab of Chhatari Papers, N.M.M.L.

57. Devadas to Jawaharlal Nehru, 2 October 1931, Jawaharlal Nehru Papers.

The Sikhs had suggested an alternative—either weightage of thirty per cent with no single community in majority or redistribution of the Punjab. In a memorandum Sardar Ujjal Singh and Sardar Sampuran Singh ridiculed Iqbal's suggestion made at the All India Muslim League's Conference in December last as making "the dismemberment of India inevitable". They made it clear that the Sikhs were not prepared to accept a constitution which would relegate them to the position of an ineffective minority. For themselves they demanded a territorial rearrangement of the Punjab whereby they wanted Rawalpindi and Multan divisions minus Lyallpur and Montgomery districts, to be separated from the rest of the Punjab. They were overwhelmingly Muslim majority divisions with a population of seven million. Their suggestion was that these districts could be either formed as a separate Muslim majority province or amalgamated with North West Frontier Province.[58]

On 2 October, Samuel Hoare wrote to Willingdon, giving him his impressions about the Conference. He wrote that the delegates were much further off than they were last year. He was convinced of the futility of expecting any resounding results from the Conference as there seemed little chance of a communal settlement emerging from the deliberations of the Minorities Committee. He was most anxious to avoid "an open rupture, particularly a rupture that will align Great Britain on one side and united India on the other."[59]

By the end of November, the Viceroy was also certain that the Secretary of State would have to give the "hookum" on the minorities question and safeguards:

> . . . I have always felt that it was quite difficult for the communities to agree among themselves and His Majesty's Government is bound to have to decide the communal question and say to them, 'you cannot settle this for yourselves, here is a scheme we lay down and this must

58. "Sikhs and the New Constitution of India: Memorandum by Sardar Ujjal Singh and Sardar Sampuran Singh, 12 November 1931", Indian Round Table Conference, Second Session, Appendix IV, p. 64.
59. Samuel Hoare to Willingdon, 2 October 1931, Templewood Collection, India Office Library, London.

hold good until such time as you can knock your heads together and agree'.[60]

Gandhi had already reported the inability of the Indian delegates to find a solution of the Hindu-Muslim question. But as the spokesman of the Congress, he was still keen on broaching the question of India's constitutional status. The cause for the failure of negotiations was laid by him at the door of the government. He accused the latter of deliberately bringing the communal question to the forefront. He also did not agree with the Prime Minister's view that the inability to solve the communal problem was a stumbling block in the way of constitution-making. His contention was that the solution was to be "...the crown of the Swaraj constitution and not its foundation".[61]

The Muslim leaders were reluctant to agree to the proposal made by Gandhi that the proceedings of the Minorities Sub-Committee should be adjourned *sine die* and the work of constitution-making on the Federal Structure Committee should go on. The result of his endeavours to override the wishes of the Muslims was that the latter in association with other minority communities like Depressed Classes, Indian Christians, the Anglo-Indians and the British community evolved a pact embodying an agreement with regard to inter-communal problems. All the five parties to the Minorities Pact pledged themselves to support each other. The Pact also agreed to separate electorates and weightage to all the communities. It also conceded all the Muslim demands including the claim for a majority to be guaranteed by statute in the Punjab and Bengal.[62]

Thus out of two hundred seats in the Bengal legislature, Muslims were to have a hundred and two, thirty-five going to the Depressed Classes, twenty to Europeans and two to Christians. Out of a hundred seats in the Punjab legislature,

60. Willingdon to Samuel Hoare, 13 November 1931, Templewood Collection.
61. Proceedings of the Minorities Sub-Committee, p. 1381ff.
62. "Provision for a settlement of the Communal Problem put forward jointly by Muslims, Depressed Classes, Indian Christians, Anglo-Indians and Europeans", *Indian Round Table Conference, Secona Session*, Appendix III, p. 13.

fifty-one were reserved for Muslims, fourteen for Hindus, ten for Depressed Classes and twenty for Sikhs. Again in the lower chamber of the central legislature, Muslims were to have a hundred out of three hundred seats, forty-five seats were to be reserved for the Depressed Classes, ten for Sikhs and thirty-two for other minorities.

Reports became current in the Conference circles of Muslim *entente* with the British conservatives for the purpose of wrecking the Conference, limiting the reforms at the centre, and Muslims having all their demands contained in the fourteen points met. A report prepared by Sir Edward Benthall, a British Indian representative to the Round Table Conference and a leader of the British commercial community and presented to the Associated Chambers of Commerce revealed the working of the minds of British statesmen and European interests in India. It revealed that the "right wing of the Government had made up its mind to break up the conference and to fight the Congress." It also made clear the fact that Europeans in India only wanted such changes which would make administration more efficient and not democratic government. He wrote on this point: ". . .the two things which really interested Parliament were the safety and prosperity of their own countrymen in India and their trusteeship for the masses."[63] The following statement in the Report is illustrative of Anglo-Muslim *entente*:

> They [Muslims] promised us support and they gave it in full measure. In return they asked us that we should not forget their economic plight in Bengal and that we should without pampering them do what we can to find places for them in European firms, so that they may have a chance to improve their material position and the general standing of their community.[64]

The Prime Minister in his concluding speech at the final plenary session on 1 December reaffirmed his belief in an

63. Report prepared by Sir Edward Benthall enclosed in Purshottamdas Thakurdas Papers.
64. *Ibid.*

all-India federation, but announced that owing to the absence of the settlement of the kev question of how to safeguard the minorities under a responsible central government, the conference would not proceed further with the consideration of the nature of federal executive and its relationship with the legislature. As the Chairman of the Minorities Sub-Committee, he offered to arbitrate on the communal problem if all parties undertook to abide by the decision.[65] In despondency, a group headed by Madan Mohan Malaviya wrote to the Prime Minister that they would agree to it.[66] Even Gandhi gave his assent to this proposal by informing Ramsay MacDonald that his non-signature did not imply that the Congress would resist the Prime Minister's arbitration.[67] Thus the net result of the first and second Round Table Conference was that the communal question remained unresolved and the gulf between the two communities widened. The initiative now passed into the hands of the British Prime Minister, who came forward with his own Award on that question.

65. Second Report of Minorities Sub-Committee, 18 November 1931, p. 546.
66. *Daily Mail*, 21 November, 1931.
67. *Ibid.*, 21 November, 1931.

4

The Communal Award and After

The Communal Award was an inevitable outcome of the repeated failures of the Hindus and the Muslims to resolve the deadlock on the quantum of representation of the various communities in the legislatures. When the communal problem was taken up for discussion after the resumption of the meeting of the Consultative Committee of the Round Table Conference held in Delhi in February 1932, the Muslim leaders brought up the same argument that they would not take part in any discussion on the establishment of responsible government at the centre unless they knew whether the British were going to safeguard their rights and interests. They particularly asked for a definite undertaking that His Majesty's Government would finally take a decision on the communal question.[1] In the Consultative Committee, Zafrullah Khan acting as the spokesman of the Muslims, made a request to Willingdon in the following words:

> . . . as our own efforts have failed, Your Excellency might well press upon the British Government the necessity of giving a decision upon those questions which were before Minorities Committee in order to facilitate and accelerate the work of this Committee and of other committies.[2]

1. Willingdon to Samuel Hoare, 26 February 1932, Templewood Collection.
2. Willingdon to Samuel Hoare, 6 March 1932, Templewood Collection.

Willingdon, who was always distrustful of the Congress, was very keen to help the Muslims representing the Muslim Conference and succumbed to their pressure. The British were in need of Muslim support as the civil disobedience movement had been in full swing since the return of Gandhi from London. He was feeling concerned with the growing restiveness of the Muslims and feared that they might join the civil disobedience movement if no assurances were given to them.[3] Apart from the Congress propaganda, the Muslims were becoming uneasy because of the action taken by the government against the Red Shirt Movement in the North West Frontier Province. Shafee Daudi and Mazhar-ud-din visited that province to watch the conditions there on behalf of the Working Committee of the Muslim League. A Resolution was passed by the Working Committee of the Muslim Conference held at Delhi on 31 January 1932 condemning the activities of Government in the N.W.F.P. and asking the Muslims of India to observe the last Friday of Ramzan as Frontier Day for demonstrating their sympathy with their brothers of that province and showing their abhorrence for the methods adopted by the government to crush the spirit of the Frontier people.[4]

Willingdon considered it imperative that no ground should be given for suspicion that Muslim interests were going to be neglected and they would not be fairly treated in future. He was fully conscious of the fact that a belief of this kind would arouse suspicion in Muslim minds regarding the ultimate intensions of the government. He sent numerous letters to Hoare, pleading the case of the Muslims and conveying their desire for an early announcement to be made by the Prime Minister. From the Muslim side, the Aga Khan was constantly corresponding with Hoare and making an appeal to him to meet the Muslim demands. Thus in March 1932 he sent a memorandum to Hoare for the perusal of the Prime Minister where he formulated a convincing case on behalf of the Muslims. Here he observed:

3. *Ibid.*
4. Home Department, Political File No. 123, 1932. NAI, New Delhi.

> . . . Just as the future existence of England can be assured if she has both her cooperation with her children in the great Dominion as well as her influence and trade in other countries, so our continued existence as a Moslem individuality depends on two facts: the permanence of the real authority of the Imperial Crown throughout India and the minimum safeguards laid down by us at the Delhi Conference of 1929. One without the other will not prevent us from being submerged and absorbed by the Hindu majority . . . . It is our inherent interest to work hand in hand with Great Britain but also to see that the result of their co-operation is not our being handed over by Great Britain to Hindu domination.[5]

Eventually the Government issued a statement on 19 March 1932. It did not go beyond the reiteration of the Prime Minister's pledge at the end of the second session of Round Table Conference. It did not even indicate the time by which His Majesty's Government's decision would be given and only conveyed to the Indian people that the Government had assumed the responsibility for deciding the communal question. The impression given was that the announcement was being made as a consequence of the recommendations of the Consultative Committee and His Majesty's Government was forced to take decision only after an agreement had been found to be beyond the reach of the parties concerned. It stated:

> His Majesty's Government have taken note of the inability of the Consultative Committee of the Round Table Conference to undertake settlement of the communal problem . . . . They have been informed that the absence of a communal agreement is now impeding progress with the programme indicated in the Prime Minister's statement of December. In these circumstances His Majesty's Government think it well to reiterate the pledge which the Prime Minister gave in the same statement that in the event of the failure of the communities to present a

5. Memorandum sent by the Aga Khan to Samuel Hoare, 9 March 1932, Private Office Records, L/PO/49.

> settlement acceptable to all parties as the foundation upon which to build, His Majesty's Government were determined that even this disability should not be permitted to be a bar to progress; and that they are compelled to apply a provisional scheme.[6]

Willingdon had exercised his influence upon the Secretary of State and the Prime Minister in favour of an early announcement. From his correspondence with Hoare, it is not difficult to conclude that he was very anxious that some declaration should be made before the Muslim Conference was held in Lahore on 20 March 1932. It was an apparent move to prevent non co-operation by Muslims which he anticipated would result from the Conference. Willingdon was determined to have his say as far as the Government's policy on the communal problem was concerned. That he put as much pressure as possible on the Government is evident from Hoare's remark to Anderson (Governor of Bengal) that "the Prime Minister and the Cabinet Committee were averse to making any further statement on the communal decision at all. Delhi, however, pressed us very much in connection with the Lahore Conference, and we therefore authorized the statement that you have already read."[7] Indeed Hoare had informed Willingdon that he was not very keen on a fresh announcement regarding the policy of the Government on the communal problem. He had also expressed his doubt whether the British would derive any advantage from a statement which fell short of an announcement of the actual terms of that decision.[8]

Willingdon also saw to it that when the Award was issued, the Muslims should be treated liberally. What the latter desired of the Viceroy was an assurance of the best possible bargain and if that was granted, they promised "not to cavil at the remainder of the decision".[9] This involved a decision

6. Statement issued by the Government of India on 19 March 1932, India Office, Templewood Collection.
7. Hoare to Anderson, 22 March 1932. Templewood Collection.
8. Hoare to Willingdon, 17 March 1932, Templewood Collection.
9. Hailey to Willingdon, 2 April 1932, Hailey Collection.

on the crucial question of Muslim representation in the Punjab and Bengal. Less than a month before the Communal Award was announced, two Muslim leaders from Bengal, A.H. Ghuznavi and Nazimuddin, had a discussion with Anderson and urged that the Muslims should have 51 per cent of seats in the Bengal legislature. Nazimuddin admitted that as a matter of strict equity, the Muslim share could be fixed at less than 50 per cent, but he also added that "... if that view were taken it did not conclude the matter. The British had surely a responsibility for seeing that Bengal was provided with a constitution which offered a reasonable prospect of stable Government and peaceful conditions for the next few years."[10] Nazimuddin also told Anderson that it was a matter of psychology and that "rightly or wrongly the Muslims had set their heart on 51 per cent." He further pointed out that if their demands were not satisfied and they were disheartened, the Muslims might break into groups and "the strong section which has always favoured joint electorates without reservation of seats" would again assert itself and the position would in all possibility be captured by the Congress.[11] Hoare, however, favoured a smaller allotment for the Muslims and preferred the decision to be based on the Government of India's Despatch of 1930. Basing himself on that Despatch, he suggested that the scope and nature of the communal decision should be made on the following lines: (1) His Majesty's Government was not prepared to abolish any existing separate electorates against the wishes of the community concerned. This meant the continuance of separate electorates for the Muslims in all the provinces, for the Sikhs in the Punjab, for the Indian Christians in Madras, for Europeans in Madras, Bombay, Bengal, the United Provinces and Bihar and Orissa and for Anglo-Indians in Madras and Bengal. (2) The Hindus would be entitled to separate electorates in any province in which they were in a minority and desired separate electorates. The Sikhs would be entitled to separate electorates in the North West Frontier Province. (3) In the Punjab, His Majesty's Government might adopt a

10. Anderson to Willingdon, 20 July 1932, Templewood Collection.
11. *Ibid.*

scheme of redistribution on the lines of that indicated in the Government of India's Reform Despatch, the principles of which was to give a statutory majority in the Council to no community. (4) In Bengal, the existing proportion which members representing special interests and communities other than Muslims and Hindus bore to the whole council should be retained. The balance of seats should be divided between Hindus and Muslims in proportion to their population.[12]

Anderson also preferred a distribution of seats which would be more favourable to the Hindus as he felt that the Muslim attitude would not be affected by a few more seats which would still leave them without clear majority though he admitted that this had "unfortunately become an obsession with them." He feared that if the Hindus were unfairly treated they might well say that the plan was "obviously designed to hold them down in the hope that Muslims may eventually gain a sufficient proportion of special constituencies to give them a permanent statutory majority."[13] Hailey (Governor of U.P.) also cautioned Willingdon not to antagonize the Hindus and directed his attention to the fact that the Government had no definite scheme for the constitution at the centre. The Viceroy was advised not to 'purchase' Muslim support by making a decision of "such a range as would be likely to drive Hindus at large into immediate non-co-operation with the constitution."[14]

Willingdon however, did not see any contingency of the Muslims capturing enough special seats to acquire an absolute majority in Bengal because any Commerce and Industry seats lost eventually by European's would pass to the Hindus, thus depriving the Muslims of a statutory majority. He thought that even if the British decision fell a little short of Muslim demands, it would be accepted by them, for he had already communicated to the leading Muslims the substance of the

12. Extract from para II of Note of 9 December 1931 by the Secretary of State (R.T.C. (31) II), Appendix to Memorandum by Hoare for the Cabinet Policy Committee, March 1932, Templewood Collection.
13. Anderson to Willingdon, 29 July 1932, Templewood Collection.
14. Hailey to Willingdon, 7 April 1932, Private Office Records, L/PO/48.

proposed decision and had found many of them, including Fazli-Husain, satisfied with it. This was because it guaranteed to Muslims a 'satisfactory minimum'. His contention was that if the plan chalked out by him was not accepted, it would "alienate from us Muslim support not merely in Bengal but throughout India. The consequences at present political juncture might be disastrous."[15] As he explained his thinking further:

> . . . We are dealing with people emotional, suspicious, apprehensive of their future and apt to be hasty in opinion and violent in action. If the Muslims are now carried away into opposition, we shall be faced with a situation in this country which almost certainly will demand measures more drastic than we have yet taken. We should have the whole forces of the country against us, Hindus and Muslims. The Hindu liberals feel themselves affronted by decision not to continue Round Table Conference. We cannot afford to be wholly without friends. I would therefore very earnestly beg you not to reject the proposals which I have made for the Muslims in Bengal or in the Punjab.[16]

It was in the teeth of opposition of Ramsay MacDonald, Hoare, Anderson and other cabinet members that Willingdon argued for safeguarding the Muslim position. The Prime Minister, in particular, was most distressed at the way the Muslims were sought to be placated. He wrote to Hoare:

> . . .I am sorry to see that the Bengal position is not more harmonious, and also that the consideration has to be used that Moslems should get special privileges in order to be kept quiet. While I fully recognize that any serious rupture between the Moslems and the Bengal Government at this moment should be avoided, this way of doing it keeps

15. Willingdon to Hoare, 9 July 1932, Templewood Collection.
16. Willingdon to Hoare, 10 July 1932, Templewood Collection.

> troubles going and the price is paid not only today but through a long time.[17]

But Willingdon refused to be impressed by such arguments and replied to the criticism of his scheme in the following words: "...I don't anticipate much, for my firm belief is that in this country the hookum is the thing which is accepted by the people, and that after a certain amount of boisterous behaviour in the press and on the platform....they will accept what we have laid down."[18]

The contents of the Communal Award, announced on the 16th August 1932, reveal that Willingdon's views had finally prevailed. The Award conceded most of the Muslim demands. In the Punjab, Muslims were given 89 seats, an obvious majority of two. In Bengal the Muslims were allotted 119 seats, a majority of the Indian seats. Large weightage was given to Europeans so that they could maintain a balance between the two Indian communities. The Muslim demand for the continuation of separate electorates was also conceded.

The announcement of the Communal Award appalled the Hindus. They felt that they were denied the minority rights where these were due to them. For although they were given separate electorates against their will, they failed to secure at least the number of territorial seats which they should have got on population basis. An essential feature of the electoral system in the past was to allot to the minority community seats in excess of its population. This was not done for the Hindus in the Punjab and Bengal as it would have deprived the Muslims of their majority.[19]

The Muslims, on the other hand, were quite pleased with the Award, particularly those from the Punjab who had secured a statutory majority. In Bengal, the reaction was somewhat different. A statement issued by Fazl-ul-Huq and thirty Muslims, including several members of the Legislative Assembly, regarded the Award as a 'distinct advance', though

17. Prime Minister to Hoare, 21 July 1932, Private Office Records, L/PO/49.
18. Willingdon to Hoare, 6 August 1932, Templewood Collection.
19. *Bombay Chronicle*, 20 August 1932.

they demanded statutory majority for the Muslims in the whole Council. While apprising Samuel Hoare about the reception accorded to the Communal Award, Willingdon wrote: "Muslims generally privately well pleased in all provinces though publicly offering some protests as offset to Hindu demands."[20]

Towards the end of September, efforts were made for the revival of negotiations between the Hindus and the Muslims with a view to bringing about an agreement and substituting it for the Award. Malaviya took the lead in urging the Muslims to reconsider their attitude on the communal question. After the Poona Pact,[21] he met Shaukat Ali in order to discuss with him the question of communal unity so as to secure "a permanent honourable agreement between the two communities."[22] The Hindus were more keen to accommodate Muslim interests as the failure at the Round Table Conference had convinced them of the necessity of uniting Indian communities. It was decided by them that in the interests of both the communities as well as of the country as a whole they should once again convene a unity conference to arrive at a definite understanding.

The Nationalist Muslims also gave their full co-operation to these endeavours. Ansari and Sherwani (both of them were in Germany at that time) sent a cable to Shaukat Ali, appealing to him to settle the communal differences while safeguarding Muslim interests "without hampering the country achieving responsible national seft-government". Invitations were sent by Shaukat Ali to Azad, Khaliquzzaman, Syed Mahmud, Nawab Ismail Khan, H.S. Suhrawardy, Feroze Khan Noon, Shafee Daudi, Abdulla Haroon to reach Allahabad by November to take part in the Hindu-Muslim talks.

The Muslim League was prepared to co-operate with the proposed Conference. Its Secretary Mahomed Yakub issued a statement to the Press where he reaffirmed his belief in

20. Telegram No. 1874 from Private Secretary to the Viceroy, to Secretary of State, 26 August 1932, Home Department File No. 41-4/32-Poll and K.W. 1932.
21. By Poona Pact, Gandhi agreed to 30 out of 80 seats in the Bengal Legislative Council being given to the Depressed Classes.
22. *The Leader*, 10 October 1932.

communal unity. He said: "It is my firm belief and conviction that the salvation of our dear Motherland depends entirely upon an honourable settlement between the Hindus and Muslims and therefore I consider that Mr Shaukat Ali's latest pose has a laudable object as its background."[23]

A conference of leading Muslims was held at Lucknow in October where the Nationalist Muslims also fell in line with other Muslims as far as their demand for Muslim majority in Bengal and the Punjab was concerned. The agreement further declared:

> Whereas agreement and unanimity among the Indian Muslims of different shades of opinion is a condition precedent to the realization of the legitimate aspirations of the Muslims of India and an agreement between the various communities of India is essential to the attainment of responsible government and whereas the Conference has reached complete unanimity regarding the Muslim demands as embodied in the All Parties Conference in Delhi on January 1, 1929, other than on the question of the system of separate electorates, this Conference declares that subject to definite acceptance of Muslim demands the method of elections in the Provincial and Central Legislature may be made the subject of negotiations with the other communities preferably on the basis of principles contained in Maulana Muhammad Ali's formula or otherwise on any other satisfactory basis, subject to ratification by a representative conference of the Muslims.[24]

It is not surprising that the Punjab and Bengal Muslims should have expressed strong disapproval of the conference and refrained from attending it. Having secured a majority of 51 per cent in the Punjab and a majority of the Indian seats in Bengal, they were not prepared to surrender their privileges. The position secured by the Communal Award was a political lever in their hands which they exploited to the full in their dealings

23. *The Times of India*, 17 October 1932.
24. Proceedings of the Lucknow Conference, *The Leader*, 19 October 1932.

with the Hindus. Mohammad Iqbal expressed their feelings by saying that by reopening the communal question some leaders were doing disservice to the Muslims as well as to the country. He further stated that they would not be prepared to adhere to any substitute for the Communal Award which "materially and substantially" did not improve the position of the Muslims.[25]

Notwithstanding the opposition of a section of Muslims, the Unity Conference met in Allahabad on 3 November 1932 and appointed a committee with the following as members, with power to co-opt: C. Vijayaraghavachariar, Malaviya, Moonje, Ramanand Chatterji, C. Rajagopalachari, Narendranath, M.L. Chablani, Azad, Shaukat Ali, Raja Saheb Salempur, Maulana Zafar Ali Khan, Maulana Daud Ghuznavi, Sunder Singh Majeethia, Jodh Singh, Ujjal Singh, Gopal Singh and Syed Mahmud. Mahmuddullah Jung and Malaviya were the general secretaries. The Committee was asked to discuss the communal problem and to arrive at agreed recommendations for its settlement.[26]

The various resolutions adopted by the Committee show that Hindus now waived their opposition to the provision for Muslim majority in the legislatures of the Punjab and Bengal. There is no doubt that they had been forced to recognize the validity of the Muslim demands which had been before them for years. It was decided that in Bengal the Muslims would get 51 per cent of the seats and the Hindus and others included in the general electorates would get 44.7 per cent. All reservations of seats and all special constituencies were to cease automatically after ten years. In the Punjab also, the percentage of Muslim seats remained the same; Sikhs were given 20 per cent, while the Hindus got 27 per cent.

The Unity Conference Committee also arrived at an agreement on the question of the separation of Sind with certain conditions. The resoluion stated that "Sind be constituted into a separate province enjoying the same measure

25. *The Leader*, 22 October 1932.
26. Draft Report of the Committee of the Unity Conference, Allahabad, 3-17 November. M.S. Aney Papers, Nehru Memorial Museum and Library.

of autonomy as other major provinces of British India with safeguards for minorities similar to those agreed to in the case of other provinces." In return, the Muslims agreed to surrender their right of separate electorates and the percentage of seats in the Central Legislature.

The method of election now suggested for the next ten years was a modified form of Muhammad Ali's formula. It was stated that out of the candidates who had secured at least 30 per cent of the votes polled of their own community, the candidates who secured the highest number of votes polled on the joint electoral roll would be declared elected. In case there was no candidate who had secured 30 per cent of votes polled of his own community, then out of the two candidates who secured the highest number of votes of their own community, that candidate would be declared elected who secured the highest number of the total votes polled. At the end of ten years this rule of 30 per cent was to cease automatically. In the Central Legislature out of the total elected seats allotted to British India, 32 per cent were reserved for Muslims and 14 per cent for Sikhs. The Committee was adjourned till 3 December, so that meanwhile its members could have the agreement ratified by their respective organisations.[27]

Malaviya felt so much enthused with the results of the conference that he even sent a telegram to London, informing the British Government about the success of the Conference. The British officials in India refused to be swayed by the Conference; they thought it was impossible that "it would arrive at any decision on which further action can be based." There is no doubt that the Hindu leaders were making very serious efforts to secure the support of their Muslim counterparts. But it proved to be of no avail because the Muslims who participated in the Conference were practically all of the nationalist group. Hailey, who was in Allahabad at that time remarked : " . . . The Muslims who really count are those who were not at the Conference itself . . . . I have seen letters from Muslims in the Punjab and elsewhere

27. Text of the agreement arrived at by the Committee of the Unity Conference. 18 November 1932, M.S. Aney Papers.

which take the line that the Muslims appearing at the Conference were not authorized to make any agreement which modified the original demand of the 13 remaining points of Jinnah." He also asserted that those Muslims had informed him that "nothing will induce them to give up separate electorates even if the Hindus now accept the whole of Jinnah's 14 points."[28]

An All Parties Muslim Conference was held in Allahabad to consider the proposals hammered at the Unity Conference on 11 December. The delegates numbered about 200, among them being eleven members of the Muslim Conference and seven of the Muslim League. The Khilafat Conference, the Nationalist Muslim Party, the Shia Political Conference, the Ahrar Party, the Jamiat-ul-Ulema of Kanpur and Delhi were also represented. Khaliquzzaman, the Chairman of the Reception Committee, condemned the activities of those Muslims who had dissociated themselves from the Conference and said that they were "prepared to barter away the interests of the community for the sake of unadulterated separate electorates." In his opinion these were wholly detrimental to the interests of the Muslims in provinces where they were in a minority and 'not very desirable in provinces where they were in a majority'. Zulfiqar Ali Khan in his presidential address stated that the Unity Conference had demonstrated to the world that "Indians, Hindus and Muslims were capable of solving their differences in a decent manner." He also denounced the activities of those "Muslim cliques working in India, who for their own selfish ends were sacrificing the interests of the country and the community."[29]

In spite of these laudable sentiments, the fate of this Unity Conference was not different from the previous conferences of this nature. The majority of the Muslim leaders were not prepared to whittle down their demands. The acceptance of the Allahabad decisions by ths Muslims would have meant the abandonment by them of the much coveted right of

28. Hailey to Haig, 19 November 1932. Hailey Collection.
29. Proceedings of the Allahabad Unity Conference, *The Leader*, 26 December 1932.

separate electorates without any compensating concession. Another factor responsible for the Muslim opposition was the fact that they had their eyes fixed on the session of the third Round Table Conference which was opened by the Prime Minister on 17th November 1932. Besides, the only two demands of the Muslims which were not tackled by the Communal Award (representation in the Centre and separation of Sind) were also conceded by the Government while the Unity Conference was still in session. On 24 December, Hoare announced that the Muslim community would have a representation of 33-1/3 per cent of the British Indian seats in the federal chambers. On the question of separation of Sind, he reiterated that "His Majesty's Government have accepted [it] in principle subject to the discovery of satisfactory means of financing the new Province."[30] This amounted to the acceptance of all of Jinnah's Fourteen Points by the Government. Whatever hope still remained of the success of the efforts initiated at the Allahabad Unity Conference was finally extinguished now. The new situation was clearly reflected at the Round Table Conference. The Muslim delegates presented to it a memorandum expressing their dissatisfaction with the Muslim position in the Centre. The government had conceded a representation of 33-1/3 per cent of the British Indian seats, therefore it was emphasized in the memorandum that they should have one-third of the seats in an all-India centre. They demanded 33 seats out of every hundred both in the Lower and the Upper Houses. They also insisted that of their share of 33 seats out of one hundred in either House, 25 should be guarnteed to them out of the British Indian quota, and the remaining eight should form the Indian states' quota. They were also opposed to the grant of any weightage to the states because this would be a further handicap to the Muslim minority. In addition, they expressed their strong dislike for joint electorates and insisted that for the lower chamber the Muslim representatives should be chosen by direct election through separate Muslim constituencies. For the upper chamber also, they wanted that their

30. Abstract of the Secretary of State's Statement to the Conference on 6 December 1932, *Indian Round Table Conference, Third Session, November-December 1932*, pp. 57-8.

representatives from British India should be elected through separate constituencies, i.e., by the Muslim members of the various provincial legislatures and by them alone. Besides, they attached great importance to the vesting of residuary powers in the provinces both in regard to legislation and taxation.[31]

The Hindu delegates at the Conference, on the other hand, were feeling very sore over the Communal Award and tried to convince the Government of its being detrimental to Hindu interests. In a memorandum submitted on behalf of the Sikhs and the Hindus, they pleaded for a revision of the Award in order to make it more fair and just from their point of view. They also regretted that the differences between the Hindus and the Muslims were being exploited by the Government for denying the claims of Indians on matters concerned with political issues relating to the transfer of power and responsibility from the British Parliament to the Indian people.[32]

Another memorandum was submitted by a Hindu representative from the Punjab where the Hindus had been denied representation even according to their population minus the weightage. Nanak Chand, the author of the memorandum, did not criticise the Government but reminded it of the constant alignment of the Punjab Hindus with the Government and characterised the Communal Award as the result of "anti-Hindu prejudice which has been created in the minds of the authorities by the Congress activities, the non-cooperation movement, civil disobedience and other movements of like nature." He also gave reasons for the opposition of his community against the grant of statutory majority to the Muslims by saying that "the absolute majority of a community based upon separate electorates—unchangeable, unalterable—is opposed to all canons of fair play and justice." He further added that the Hindus of the Punjab were worried that "a religious, fanatical majority of Muslim rule should not be based upon separate electorates, situated as the Punjab is

31. "Muslim Position in the Centre", Memorandum submitted by the Muslim delegation, 27 December 1932. Proceedings of the third session of the Round Table Conference, pp. 193-4.

32. Memorandum by N.C. Kelkar, Pandit Nanak Chand and Sardar Tara Singh, *Ibid.*, pp. 179-81.

close to the frontiers and close to Afghanistan and other Muhammadan countries."[33]

After the final session of the third Round Table Conference, a White Paper, embodying the proposals of the British Government for constitutional reforms was issued. Later a Joint Select Committee consisting of members of both Houses of Parliament was convened to discuss the whole question. The scheme put forward by the Committee was in two parts—one proposing a federation of Indian states and British Indian Provinces, the other conferring autonomy on the provinces.[34]

Differences between the Hindu and the Muslim points of view were again reflected in the evidence presented before the Joint Select Committee. The general substance of the memorandum submitted by the Hindus implied a fundamental objection to separate electorates and dissatisfaction with the Communal Award. Nanak Chand was the spokesman of the Hindus and he argued that if the Muslims were entitled to receive excessive representation in the legislative and local bodies of the U.P., why should the same concession be denied to the Hindu minority in respect of the legislative and local bodies in the Punjab, Bengal, the North West Frontier Province and Sind? Also, with regard to services in the Punjab, he stressed that minorities should receive the same treatment as the Muslim minority in U.P. did. B.C. Chatterjee, on behalf of Bengal Hindus also urged the introduction of joint electorates which he characterized as the "solution of the whole difficulty."[35]

The views of the All-India Muslim Conference and the All-India Muslim League on the White Paper proposals were placed before the Committee in a memorandum which pointed out that "the scheme outlined in the White Paper will not be a complete success until the Muslim community is assured of

33. "The Communal Award: Statement of Reasons against its acceptance by the Hindu of the Punjab", submitted by Pandit Nanak Chand, *ibid.*, pp. 166-68.

34. *Joint Committee on Indian Constitutional Reform, Evidence*, vol. 2 (1932-33), p. 1383.

35. *Ibid.*, vol. 20 (1932-33), p. 1391.

those rights which the White Paper has ignored."[36] Particular stress was laid on the point that there should be no delay in the introduction of provincial autonomy. It was also pointed out that there were great difficulties in working out an All-India Federation where the Indian states were bound to influence British Indian policy while British India would be debarred from interfering in the internal affairs of the states. It was urged, therefore, that as many subjects as possible should be transferred to the provinces and very few retained for the Centre & that Muslims should be guaranteed one third of the total number of seats in the whole House and therefore slightly increased proportion of seats in the British Indian share over the one-third promised to them by the Communal Award.[37] It is to be noted here that while the Muslim leaders expressed their disappointment with the scheme of reforms outlined in the White Paper as they felt that they had not been properly treated, the Hindu representatives in all those provinces where the Muslims were in a majority, did not hesitate to admit that they preferred the autocratic rule of British Government to that of an autonomous Indian legislature.

The timely criticism of the Hindu Mahasabha, which was most vociferous in its condemnation of the Communal Award, by Nehru did a lot to soothe the Muslims. It was the first open attack made against the Mahasabha since 1928 when the two communities had started drifting away from each other. While denouncing the Mahasabha as communal, anti-national and reactionary, he also made the Congress stand on Communal Award very clear:

> ... It is also true that the Communal-Award is an utter negation of nationalism and is meant to separate India into communal compartments and give strength to disruptive tendencies and thus strengthen the hold of British imperialism. But it must be borne in mind that nationalism cannot be accepted only when it profits the majority community. The test comes in the provinces where there

36. *Ibid.*, p. 1475.
37. *Ibid.*, p, 1476.

> is Muslim majority and in that test the Hindu Mahasabha has failed. Nor is it enough to blame Muslim communalists .... The point is that a special responsibility does attach to the Hindus in India because they are the majority community and because economically and educationally they are more advanced.[38]

The Congress had also condemned the Award as "anti-national, undemocratic and intrinsically bad". Despite such criticism, now, out of a desire to accommodate Muslim interests, it adopted an attitude of neutrality towards the Award. It seemed to have realized the fact that the lack of a united front had operated as an effective barrier hindering India's advance in every direction. In a letter to Madan Mohan Malaviya, Gandhi wrote : "... I have given it as my opinion that there is no escape from the Communal Award if we are to secure Musalmans' co-operation and if we are to secure any advantage for the nation. The other alternative is retention of the status quo."[39] In a statement to the Press on 21 May 1934, Ansari explained the Congress policy:

> ...The Congress knows that while a large number of Hindus and Sikhs have taken strong exception to the Communal Award, a considerable section of Mussalmans, Harijans and Christians have accepted it for so long as an agreed substitute is found. The Congress will always strive to help to find a national solution of the question, but in my opinion such a solution of the question cannot be found except by a Constituent Assembly convened to frame a national Constitution. Until then, the question of acceptance or rejection of the mode or proportion of representation as continued in the Award does not arise.[40]

The Working Committee at Bombay on 17 June 1934 also reiterated that it could neither reject nor accept the Award

38. *The Tribune*, 30 November 1933.
39. Gandhi to Madan Mohan Malaviya, 1 April 1934, Syed Mahmud Papers, N.M.M.L.
40. *The Indian Annual Register, 1934*, vol. 1, p. 296.

given the sharp division of opinion among the different communities in India.[41]

This attitude led to a split in the Congress ranks. When the Award was discussed by the Working Committee on 21 July 1934 both Aney and Malaviya resigned from the Congress because the Working Committee had decided that no nationalist who would be elected on the Congress ticket as a member of the legislature could vote against the Communal Award if a resolution on this subject was brought forward. He was also bound to abstain from making any representation against the Award to the British Government and there was to be no propaganda by Congressmen against the Award.[42] Such an attitude on the part of the Congress seemed to jeopardize the position of the Hindu minority in the Punjab. Aney and Malaviya, now formed a new party called the Nationalist Party to organize a campaign throughout the country against the Communal Award as well as the White Paper and to set up in the Punjab and Bengal candidates for election to the Assembly scheduled to be held in the same year. The Nationalist Party held that there should be no tampering with the Lucknow Pact except with the consent of the parties concerned. The Hindu Mahasabha announced its whole-hearted support to the Nationalist Party.[43]

In the Assembly Elections held in October 1934, though the Congress lost 2 seats in the Punjab and 3 seats in Bengal to the Nationalist Party, it captured all the general seats in Madras, Orissa, U.P. and C.P. On a suggestion made by some members of the Nationalist Party in Bengal to the Congress for a reconsideration of its attitude on the communal problem, in view of the verdict of the Hindu electorates in the Punjab and Bengal, the Working Committee of the Congress reiterated its opinion:

> The policy of the Congress in the matter of the Communal Award is already recorded in a resolution passed at the Bombay session of the Indian National Congress. The

41. *Ibid.*, p. 300.
42. "Congress and Communal Award", Correspondence between Nehru and Jagat Narain Lal, 30 October 1936, A.I.C.C. Papers.
43. Moonje to Ganpat Rai, 9 August 1934, Hindu Mahasabha Papers.

> fact that in some constituencies, some Congressmen have chosen to differ from the Congress policy on this matter . . .does not and cannot affect the Congress policy until the same is reconsidered and revised by the Congress, particularly when the said policy has been overwhelmingly endorsed in the country at large. Until then all Congressmen and Congress organizations are expected to abstain from working against the policy of the Congress as solemnly decided.[44]

The attitude of the Congress undoubtedly contributed to a considerable lessening of tension between the Hindus and the Muslims in the political field, at any rate for the time being. The crux of the whole issue, which had led to disagreement between the two communities was that the Muslims had asked for assurances that the safeguards to which they attached importance should be embodied in the future constitution of India. The Government had acceded to all their demands and the Congress had also not denied them unequivocally. After his arrival from Europe in 1934, Jinnah voiced his unequivocal condemnation of the entire constitutional scheme. On the question of the Communal Award also, the League did not rule out the possibility of modifying it. The Council of the League which met at New Delhi on 1 April 1934 passed the following resolution:

> Resolved that they accept the Communal Award as far as it goes until a substitute is agreed upon by the various communities and on that basis express their readiness for co-operation with other communities and parties to secure such future constitution for India, as would be acceptable to the country.[45]

Giving his impression of the above-mentioned session of the Council of the Muslim League in an interview to the Associated Press, Jinnah said that the Muslims would not lag behind any other community in serving the best interests of India. He also expressed his deep interest in opposing the White

44. *The Indian Annual Register, 1934*, vol. II, p. 219.
45. *The Indian Annual Register*, n. 40, p. 318.

Paper proposals being foisted upon India. He, however, felt that opposition could be effective only if there was unity between the Hindus and the Muslims. He said:

> . . .nothing will give me greater happiness than bring about complete co-operation and friendship between Hindus and Moslems and in this desire my impression is that I have the solid support of Mussalmans. . . .On my return to India, I have seen abundant evidence that public opinion both Hindu and Moslem, thinks alike in terms of the political evolution of the country.[46]

At a meeting of the Working Committee of the All-India Muslim Conference held at Aligarh on 23 December 1934, the Nawab of Chhatari who was the President, also remarked that the constitutional advance proposed by the Joint Parliamentary Committee was disappointing as it fell short of the aspirations of Indians. As for the Communal Award, he pointed out that it formed the basis of co-operation among the communities in the absence of any settlement among them.[47]

Opening the All-Bengal Muslim Young Men's Conference held in Calcutta in October 1934, Fazl-ul-Huq, who presided, urged the Muslims to end communal strife and jealousy which might "shatter all hopes of the future of India." He said:

> We are on the threshold of momentous constitutional changes. . . .Great as our hopes of political advancement are, we cannot shut our eyes to the fact, that flitting across our vision of the future, there are sinister phantoms of communal jealousy and strife. . . . If we have not made ourselves fit for the changes that are coming we will be pushed to the wall despite all the provisions contained in the White Paper or the momentary Communal Award. The besetting sin of Muslim Politics has all along been the unfaltering faith in the sense of justice of the British officials.[48]

46. *Ibid.*, p. 319.
47. *The Indian Annual Register*, n. 44, pp. 310-11.
48. *Ibid.*, p. 311.

With the dawn of the year 1935, negotiations were started between the Hindus and the Muslims for the substitution of the Communal Award by agreement. They got an early start particularly because Jinnah had expressed his readiness to accept an honourable compromise. On 1 January 1935, after receiving a letter from Jinnah, Iqbal wrote to Ansari, "...I think the time has come for Hindus and Muslims to work together. ...If this opportunity is lost, present tensions will only stiffen more and more making co-operation impossible."[49] Rajendra Prasad, the President of the Congress, wrote to Jinnah on 23 January that the only way for progress was "to jointly formulate some proposals which you and I could put before our respective organizations as jointly emanating from us." For him, the sorest point in the Award was separate electorates and he wrote to Jinnah that no progress was possible if this was retained. He put forward a formula which was based on the Working Committee's resolution adopted at Bombay in 1931, which included joint electorates, reservation of seats on population basis with freedom to minorities to contest more seats, the franchise being so arranged as to reflect the proportion of various communities in the electorate.[50]

Jinnah also was very keen that they should arrive at a settlement and ask the government to accede to it because such "a settlement would remove the cloud of suspicion and we would work together with confidence". He was prepared to accept joint electorates and expressed his readiness to proceed on that basis. He pointed out that in the formula under discussion, there would be difficulties in Bengal where a large proportion of the seats had been reserved for Europeans. Rajendra Prasad pointed out that it was argued by the Hindus that both in the Punjab and Bengal, although the Hindus were in a minority, weightage was given to Europeans not only at the cost of the majority party but also at the cost of the Hindus which was most unfair to them. Talking about the chances of an agreement on the communal question, Jinnah said that if the Congress did not

49. Iqbal to Ansari, 1 January 1935, Ansari Papers.
50. Notes of conversation held between M. A. Jinnah and Rajendra Prasad on 28 January 1935. Rajendra Prasad Papers, National Archives of India, New Delhi.

insist on its demand for complete independence and sat down with others to define the demand in terms of transfer of power regarding Defence, Foreign Relations and Finance, there were good chances of a formula being evolved which would be acceptable to the Liberals and the Muslims. Rajendra Prasad's conclusion was that "if the Congress insisted on demanding 14 annas, and Mr. Jinnah felt that we should not demand more than 12 annas, he would not press his views to a breaking point and fall in line with us."[51] He proceeded to suggest a formula for Bengal and said that if as a result of joint efforts some seats were secured from Europeans they might be divided between the Hindus and the Muslims on population basis.

In their next meeting on 30 January, Jinnah, while talking about the resolution which might be tabled in the Central Assembly about the Report of the Joint Parliamentary Committee, assured Rajendra Prasad that if the Congress tabled a resolution rejecting it, the Muslims would not vote for it as they held that the rejection of the Report included rejection of the Award also. In his opinion the foundations of the provincial constitution with an extended franchise, transfer of all departments to responsible Ministers and a wholly elected House were all sound. The objectionable features were the Governor's special powers and powers relating to the police. As regards the Centre, the scheme was fundamentally wrong and no changes would make it acceptable.

Jinnah also suggested to Prasad that in place of separate electorates, something should be given to the Muslims as compensation. He added that (1) they should have the electoral register so framed as to reflect the proportion of their population, if necessary by a different franchise, (2) that the constituencies should not be overlapping, and (3) that in the Punjab when the constituencies were demarcated, he would give the Sikhs, being the smallest community the first chance to select those they liked and then the Hindus would be given a similar chance and lastly what would be left would be given to the Muslims. So far as Bengal was concerned, he was prepared to accept the proportion of seats allotted in the Award

51. *Ibia.*

but wanted that joint efforts should be made to secure some seats from the Europeans. He admitted that the caste Hindus in Bengal had suffered a double blow—one in the Award which gave them less than their population and the other by the Poona Pact. He wanted the seats obtained from the Europeans to be distributed among upper class Hindus and Muslims.[52]

As a result of the conversation the following formula was drafted as a basis for further discussion and it was decided to ascertain the reactions of Hindus, Muslims and Sikhs:

1. Franchise should be so framed and adjusted as to reflect the proportion of population of the various communities in the electoral rolls for the provinces and the Centre and for that purpose differential franchise should be adopted wherever necessary.
2. There should be no overlapping of electorates of different constituencies.
3. In the Punjab the Sikhs should choose the number of constituencies for the seats allotted to them in the Award and thereafter the Hindus would have the choice to fix on such constituencies as they might desire for the number allotted to them and the remaining constituencies would be allotted to the Muslims according to the number of seats fixed in the Award, excluding the seats allotted to Europeans, Anglo-Indians, Indian Christians and special constituencies.
4. In Bengal it was agreed between the Hindus and the Muslims that if any seats were obtained from the Europeans, the same would be divided between them in proportion to their population in that province. Joint efforts would be made by the Hindus and the Muslims to persuade the Europeans to release as many seats as they possibly can from the quota allotted to them by the Award. Subject to this, the seats allotted to the Muslims under the Award were to remain reserved for them excluding the seats given to Europeans, Anglo-Indians, Indian-Christians and special constituencies.

52. *Ibid.*

5. Similar seats allotted to the Muslims for the Central Legislature by the Award were to remain reserved for them.
6. On this basis it was agreed that joint electorates would replace separate electorates in all the provinces and in the Centre.[53]

In substance, it meant that seats were given to the Muslims as in the Award but elections were to be held on the basis of joint electorates formed on the basis of a franchise which would reflect the population of various communities. Prasad preferred a reduction of seats for the Muslims in the Centre as they had got more than 33-1/3 per cent of the seats in British India. He also wanted a time limit to be fixed on the reservation of seats. But on both these points Jinnah argued that it would be hard for him to get Muslim acceptance if they reopened the question of seats along with that of electorate. Prasad was quite convinced with Jinnah's arguments as is clear from his remark : "...If we consider the allotment of seats, we notice that a majority of seats is not reserved for them [Muslims] even in Bengal and the Punjab. They may get a bare majority only if they capture some of the special constituency seats." He gave more weight to securing joint electorates and felt that on the whole the formula "furnished a fair basis of agreement." He was prepared to "pay some price" in order to secure joint electorates.[54]

Maulana Azad had also requested Prasad to take full advantage of the situation as he had found Jinnah in a conciliatory mood and considered him a person who could deliver the goods on behalf of the Muslims. He also desired that if joint electorate could be obtained by the Congress acceding to Muslim demands for reservation of seats, the Congress should not hesitate to go for it. He was conscious of the fact that the Award had turned the scales in favour of the Muslims, but since the Congress had always attached great significance to

53. Notes on conversation between Jinnah and Rajendra Prasad held on 13-14 February 1935. A.I.C.C. Papers.
54. Rajendra Prasad to Sardar Patel, 14 February 1935, Rajendra Prasad Papers, microfilm copy, Nehru Memorial Museum and Library.

joint electorates, it should not fail to secure them.[55] Jinnah had also given an assurance to Prasad that if the communal problem was solved, the Muslims would be prepared to join in any national demand or struggle. Personally, Prasad had no objection to the points put forward by him.[56]

Prasad now started talks with Bengal and the Punjab Hindus to ascertain their views on the draft formula. He had already received telegrams from Bengal Hindus exhorting him not to commit himself to any scheme without consulting them.[57] Malaviya had also adopted a very stiff attitude and made it plain to Prasad that if the seats given to the Muslims in the Centre which were more than 33-1/3 per cent were not reduced, he would not accept any settlement. He also desired that while the Muslims in Bengal should get 51 per cent, the Hindus should get 44.5 per cent, and not in proportion to their population, as that would amount to perpetuating their unfavourable position.[58] When Prasad argued that the Muslims had the Award in their favour and that the Hindus should "make the best of a bad position", Malaviya replied that only if he pressed the Hindu viewpoint they would accept a reasonable settlement.[59] When Prasad asked Jinnah to reconsider his attitude on 20 February, he expressed his inability to do so as he had already faced difficulties in persuading his colleagues to give up separate electorates. He pointed out to Prasad that the Congress should recognize that "what may have been possible some years ago was not possible to-day and those who made such suggestions ignored the basic fact of the Award being in favour of Mussalmans."[60]

Confronted with the opposition of the Hindu Mahasabha leaders, Jinnah started insisting that Prasad should try to get the signatures of Malaviya and other leaders. This demand

55. Maulana Azad to Rajendra Prasad (Urdu), 18 February 1935, Rajendra Prasad Papers, N.A.I., New Delhi.
56. Rajendra Prasad to Tushar Kanti Ghosh, 29 March 1935, Rajendra Prasad Papers.
57. Telegram from Indra Narayan Sen to Rajendra Prasad, 15 February 1935, Rajendra Prasad Papers.
58. Daily Notes taken by Rajendra Prasad, 20 February 1935, Rajendra Prasad Papers.
59. *Ibid.*
60. *Ibid.*

was not unreasonable, because so far the Unity Conferences and talks between the Hindu and Muslim leaders had proved abortive because of the stubborn refusal of the Hindu Mahasabha to yield to Muslim demands. Meanwhile an Anti-Communal Award Conference had met at Delhi on 23 February 1935 and was carrying on an intensive campaign against the Award. It also sent a memorial to Zetland signed by the Hindu leaders of Bengal, including the members of the Bengal Legislative Council to make an amendment to the following effect:

(a) that the method of choosing the members of the legislature in Bengal should be by Joint Electorates in which the Hindu minority of Bengal believed as a matter of principle and not by forcing upon them separate communal electorates which was a negation of responsible government;

(b) that the composition of the Legislature should be so altered as to restore to the Hindu minority their due share of representation on the basis not merely of their population strength but also of their established culture, economic, political and administrative importance, on the basis of which they had been granted their existing representation and on no account should this be curtailed;

(c) they protested strongly against the unfair and unprecedented provision to protect a majority community by conferring upon it a position of permanent and statutory predominance in the Legislature and making that position unalterable by any appeal to the electorate. In conclusion they submitted that pending decision on their claims to a larger amount of weightage in representation, the *status quo* should be maintained in the matter of communal representation in the Legislature in the absence of any fresh communal agreement.[61]

In view of such divergence of opinion, Prasad and Jinnah could not achieve anything. On 1 March, they issued a joint statement announcing their inability. It read as follows:

> We had made an earnest effort to find a solution of the communal problem which would satisfy all the parties concerned. We regret that in spite of our best efforts we

61. The memorial of the Hindus of Bengal including the Hindu members of the Bengal Legislative Council, Hindu Mahasabha Papers.

> have not been able to find such a formula. We realize that communal harmony and concord are essential for the progress of our country and we can only hope that forces will arise which will make a future attempt more fruitful.[62]

At its twenty-fourth session held in Bombay on 11 April 1936, the All-India Muslim League formally defined its attitude towards the Constitution, and falling in line with the Congress, it decided to utilize its provincial part. In his presidential address Syed Wazir Hassan accused the Government of forcing a constitution upon India and described it as "anti democratic". This session of the League is significant because, in marked contrast with the previous sessions, there did not figure any remarks hostile to the Congress or any advocacy of communal interests. Instead, more emphasis was laid on achieving unity. Currimbhoy Ebrahim, Chairman of the Reception Committee observed: "Unity is the bedrock of nationhood, as it is also the essence of all religions. And no Constitution, however advantageous from our point of view, can work well or survive in the absence of inter-communal goodwill and harmony."[63]

In moving the resolution regarding the constitution, Jinnah said that there was only 2 per cent responsibility and 98 per cent safeguards and special responsibility of the Governor-General. He severely criticized those reactionary conservative Muslims whose sole aim was to secure office and places for themselves and who had received every encouragement and support from the Government. They were accused of being the main hindrance in the way of independence. The main principles of the election manifesto issued by the League's Parliamentory Board on the basis of which Muslim representatives in various legislatures were supposed to work were defined as follows: (1) The provincial constitution and the proposed central constitution should be replaced by full self-government on democratic lines, (2) and that in the meantime representatives of the Muslim League in the various legislatures should utilize

62. Joint Statement by Rajendra Prasad and Jinnah, 1 March 1935, Rajendra Prasad Papers.
63. S.S. Pirzada, ed., *Foundations of Pakistan : All India Muslim League Documents*, vol. II (Karachi, 1969), p. 238.

the legislatures in order to extract the maximum benefit out of the constitution for the uplift of the people in the various provinces. The Muslim League Party must be formed as a corollary so long as separate electorates existed but there would be free co-operation with any group or groups whose aims and ideals were approximately the same as those of the League Party.

The Manifesto also laid down the following programme for the ensuing election: to protect religious rights of the Muslims in which connection, for all matters of religious character, due weight should be given to the opinion of the Jamiat-ul-Ulema-i-Hind and Majrahids to make every effort to secure the repeal of all repressive laws; to reject all measures which were detrimental to the interests of India, which encroached upon the fundamental liberties of the people and led to economic exploitation of the country; to reduce the heavy cost of the administrative machinery, central and provincial, and allocated substantial funds for nation-building departments; to nationalize the Indian army and reduce military expenditure; to encourage development of industries; to work for social education and the economic uplift of the rural population; to sponsor measures for the relief of agricultural indebtedness; to make elementary education free and compulsory; to protect and promote the Urdu language and script; and to devise measures for the amelioration of the general condition of the Muslims.[64]

This programme was not fundamentally different from that of the Congress, except that some emphasis was laid on Muslim interests. This augured well for the future, but as we shall see in the next chapter, there took place a trememdous change in the nature of Muslim politics in India between 1937 and 1940.

64. *The Indian Annual Register*, vol. 1, 1936, p. 301.

5

Provincial Autonomy

As a result of the Provincial Assembly elections under the Act of 1935, held in 1937, the Congress commanded a majority in the Legislative Assemblies of six—out of eleven provinces and emerged as the largest party in two other provinces.[1] Its position in the country thus became quite strong and formidable. In contrast, the performance of the Muslim League was not at all impressive; it had won only 109 out of 482 seats contested. Besides, it also failed to win a majority of seats in any

1. *Provinces*	*Total number of seats in Legislative Assembly*	*Seats won by the Congress in the election*
Assam	108	35
Bengal	250	54
Bihar	152	95
Bombay	175	88
C. P.	112	71
Madras	215	159
N.W.F.P.	50	19
Orissa	60	36
Punjab	175	18
Sind	60	8
U.P.	228	133

Return showing the Results of Elections in India, 1937 (Cmd. 5589).

of the four Muslim-majority provinces.[2] The results created despair among the League's leaders as all their calculations had proved wrong. They had contested the elections in the hope that as a result of the Communal Award, they would be able to have full sway over the majority provinces, but now this hope was dashed to the ground.

The only redeeming feature for the Muslim League was that the performance of Congress in the Muslim majority areas was also not impressive. The results of the election showed that except in the North-West Frontier Province, it was not popular with the Muslim masses. Jawaharlal Nehru, President of the Congress at that time, admitted that the latter had failed in its efforts to secure Muslim seats. After the elections, he remarked: "Only in regard to the Muslim seats did we lack success. . . . We failed because we had long neglected working among Muslim masses and we could not reach them in time."[3] But on the whole the Congress leaders were thrilled at the results. The failure of the Muslim League to win enough seats was interpreted as the vindication of the Congress policy towards the communal problem.

The Congress now started an intensive effort to establish contact with the Muslim masses. Nehru issued a circular to all Provincial Congress Committees to pay special attention to the enrolment of Muslim members. Each Provincial Congress Committee was asked to appoint a special committee to increase

2.

Provinces	*Total No. of seats allotted to Muslims in the Legislative Assembly.*	*Seats won by the Muslim League in the election of 1937*
Assam	34	9
Bengal	117	39
Bihar	39	—
Bombay	29	20
C.P.	14	—
Madras	28	10
N.W.F.P.	36	—
Orissa	4	—
Punjab	84	2
Sind	33	3
U.P.	64	27

Ibid.

3. *The Times of India*, 3 March 1937.

Congress contact with the masses—rural and urban. The office of the All India Congress Committee started a special department and orders were issued to district and local authorities to issue notices in Urdu in all areas where there was a sizeable Urdu reading population.[4] The Congress also adopted a very rigid attitude towards the Muslim League. Nehru openly expressed doubt about the capability of the League to function on a political plane since it was, according to him, only a religious body and stressed that "the time has gone when religious groups as such can take part in the political and economic struggle. That may have been so in medieval times: it is inconceivable today."[5] He also refused to consider the Muslim League as the representative organization of the Muslims. In a letter to Khaliquzzaman, he wrote:

> . . .Why should I accept it as the representative of the Muslims of India when I know it represents the handful of Muslims at the top who deliberately seek refuge in the name of religion to avoid discussing mass problems?. I have a certain measure of intelligence and I have studied political, economic and allied problems. Am I to insult my intelligence by talking baby-talk of an age gone by? . . .Do you not see that this communal policy which the Muslim League here has fathered is a policy more injurious to the Muslims of India than anything that a majority could do would be?[6]

The attitude of the Congress, particularly that of Nehru was not unjustifiable. It was not inconsistent with the results of the elections and also the disorganized and weak condition of the Muslim League. The Ahrars, the Muslims inside the Congress and the Jamiat-ul-Ulema were co-operating with the Congress. The youth of Aligarh University were exasperated wih the League.[7] In the Punjab, the Unionist Party and the

4. Circular dated 31 March 1937, issued by Jawaharlal Nehru, the Congress President, to the Provincial Congress Committees, Rajendra Prasad Papers.
5. *The Times of India*, 23 April 1937.
6. Nehru to Khaliquzzaman, 1 July 1937, Nehru Papers.
7. *The Times of India*, 27 April 1937.

Ahrars were quite strong. In Sind and North-West Frontier Province, the League was quite insignificant. In Bihar, the majority of the Muslim seats had been captured by Independents and in Bengal Fazl-ul-Huq's Krishak Praja Party was supreme. Only in U. P. and Bombay the League had some standing.

The Congress victory coupled with the Congress decision to contact the Muslim masses over his head seriously alarmed Jinnah. The immediate reaction to its electoral defeat on the part of the League was the realization of its own disunity and lack of organization. Jinnah set his mind on remedying these two shortcomings. He started making efforts to consolidate the League. The realization dawned upon him that it did not represent the entire Muslim community and was "a preserved conclave of titled and conservative people." In an appeal to Muslims, he said:

> For the upliftment and advancement of Mussalmans and working for their welfare much work remains to be done in the political, economic and social spheres of life by establishing different centres in India for supplying up-to-date information and knowledge and establishing relief centres to aid and assist Muslims in different parts of India.[8]

Need was also felt for an independent press for which donations were made by a few Muslims of U. P. for the advancement of Muslim cause and interests. A plan for mass-contact among the Muslims was also chalked out. At the meeting of the U. P. Muslim League Parliamentary Board held at the residence of the Raja of Mahmudabad, it was decided that all the twenty-seven members of the Muslim League elected to the U. P. Legislative Assembly would raise Rs. 100 each from their respective constituencies, and that each member of the Working Committee of the Board was to pay Rs. 500 for the purpose of carrying propaganda among the Muslim masses.[9]

Jinnah's influence was also at a low ebb. After his first meeting with the Indian leaders, Linlithgow had gathered the

8. *The Times of India*, 5 June 1937.
9. *Ibid.*, 27 July 1937.

impression that Jinnah did not command the full allegiance of his followers. Jinnah himself had complained to him that the government did not pay sufficient attention to the Muslims and also mentioned the risk of Muslims being driven into the 'arms' of the Congress because of the weak position of the League.[10] After the acceptance of office by the Congress Ministers, a growing number of Muslims, thinking that Congress Ministries would be in a position to help them, shifted their allegiance from the Muslim League to the Congress. Given the weak and disorganized condition of the League, the defections inside its own rank further undermined its position in the eyes of the Congress. This was the background of the Congress-League coalition talks.

The coalition issue in U. P. has been the subject of much controversy and it has been repeatedly alleged that the decision of the Congress to back out from its promise to form coalition ministries was a fateful decision which led to the demand for partition.[11] While there is no doubt that the failure to have a coalition ministry in U. P. had a major impact on the evolution of Muslim attitude towards the Congress, evidence from unpublished sources does not indicate the existence of any prior agreement about the formation of coalition ministries. However, it is a fact that at the time of elections, the relations between the League and the Congress were quite cordial and there was a general hope that they might work together after the elections also. The League election board had some old Congressmen on it and the most powerful worker on behalf of the League was Maulana Husain Ahmad who had always been sympathetic towards the Congress. The election campaign was more a tussle against the Agriculturist Party of big zamindars headed by the Nawab of Chhatari than a confrontation between the League and the Congress. During his tours even Nehru had sometimes supported the League candi-

10. Linlithgow to Zetland, 26 August 1937. Linlithgow Papers, India Office Library, London.

11. See Penderel Moon, *Divide and Quit* (London, 1961) ; H. V. Hodson, *The Great Divide : Britain, India, Pakistan* (London, 1969); and A. K. Azad, *India Wins Freedom* (Bombay, 1959).

dates. The Jamiat-ul-Ulema leaders had also supported them.[12]

After the elections, however, the anti-Congress group in the League became dominant: the President of U. P. League Parliamentary Board joined the Interim Ministry. Many members of the Parliamentary Board had resigned in disgust; chief among them were Maulana Husain Ahmad and Hafiz Ibrahim. Towards the end of June Khaliquzzaman, the U. P. Muslim League leader, approached the Congress with the idea of forming coalition ministries. Before that in March their Parliamentary Board had offered co-operation to the U. P. Congress Party on the basis of its Wardha programme and had also expressed its readiness to abide by the discipline of the Congress. The idea conveyed by Khaliquzzaman to Nehru was that he was working for a close co-operation with the Congress. When Nehru objected to his close association with the League leaders who, he felt, had joined hands with British imperialism, Khaliquzzaman replied that he had associated himself with League with the intention of rooting out the influence of the reactionary group. He also informed Nehru that he was "torn between two loyalties." At the same time he complained against the Congress policy of contact with the masses which he felt had further contributed towards stiffening the opposition of reactionaries.[13]

Towards the end of June, overtures were made by him and Nawab Ismail Khan to the Congress with the idea of securing ministries for themselves. Already in April Harry Haig, the Governor of U.P. who had some inkling of these developments had informed Linlithgow about Khaliquzzaman's flirtation with the Congress. He had also mentioned about Govind Ballabh Pant telling him that the Congress had offered two seats in the cabinet to the Muslims. Khaliquzzaman who was Chairman of the U. P. Parliamentary Board, had also invited Pant to perform the hoisting of the Congress flag over the Municipal Office in Lucknow.[14] In a subsequent meeting with Maulana Azad held in Lucknow, Khaliquzzaman went to the extent of expressing his readiness to give him a 'blank cheque'

12. Nehru to Rajendra Prasad, 21 July 1937. Nehru Papers.
13. *Ibid.*, 21 July 1937.
14. Haig to Linlithgow, 23 April 1937, Linlithgow Papers.

provided he was prepared to include himself and Nawab Ismail Khan in the ministry. The Congress leaders particularly Azad got attracted by the idea of the whole Muslim group in the U.P. League ceasing to exist as a separate political group and being practically absorbed by the Congress. The Congress could not resist the temptation of liquidating the League, as is clear from Nehru's letter to Rajendra Prasad:

> . . . the alternative was worth having if it could be secured. This was the winding up of the Muslim League group in the U.P. and its absorption in the Congress. This would have a great effect not only in the U.P. but all over India and outside. This would mean a free field for our work without communal troubles. This would knock over the British Government which relied so much on these troubles.[15]

Maulana Azad contends that the effort to have a Congress-League coalition failed because of Nehru's insistence that the League should not be given more than one seat in the Ministry. This seems to be an oversimplification because the negotiations did not break down over the number of Muslim Leaguers to be taken. Maulana Azad seems to have relied on his memory when he asserts that the refusal of Nehru torpedoed the negotiations. The fact is that the latter was prepared to include both Khaliquzzaman and Nawab Ismail Khan provided they agreed to the conditions put before them.[16]

No doubt, Nehru feared reaction among the Congress Muslims in particular who were going to be excluded from office in preference to those who might appear as just opportunists. Eventually it was decided to offer 'stringent conditions' to the Muslim League group and to include two of their leaders in the Ministry only if they accepted those conditions. The conditions laid down were that the March resolution of the Working Committee on Congress policy in the legislatures was

15. Nehru to Rajendra Prasad, 21 July 1937, Nehru Papers.
16. *Ibid.*

to be accepted fully.[17] The Muslim League group including the U.P. Parliamentary Board was to be wound up. All the Muslim League members of Legislative Assembly were to become full members of the Congress Party and to abide by the discipline of the party. In the by-elections the League could not put up a separate candidate. Khaliquzzaman had agreed to all the conditions except two: the winding up of the League's Parliamentary Board and desisting from setting up separate candidates at the by-elections.[18] In his autobiography, Khaliquzzaman has tried to exonerate himself from the lure of a minister's post and has instead put the blame on Maulana Husain Ahmad by saying that the latter was 'preparing' ground for a coalition with the Congress and for securing ministership in the Cabinet.[19] But he has exposed himself by also enclosing a letter from Maulana Ahmad Said, the Secretary of the Jamiat-ul-Ulema. An excerpt from this letter speaks for itself:

> . . .do let me know how far it is true that if seats for yourself and Nawab Ismail Khan could be found in the cabinet, a settlement might have been possible with the Congress, and the Congress was ready to give one seat but you were not prepared to leave Nawab Ismail Khan behind and there was no room for him. Therefore, an agreement could not be reached. Is it also true that Rafi Ahmad Qidwai to whom you had offered full help and did not put up a candidate against him proved disloyal to you?[20]

It is to be noted here that Khaliquzzaman had started negotiations with the Congress without any direction from the Muslim League. He had, of course, hoped that his party

17. The Working Committee at its meeting held in Wardha on 1st of March 1937 had stipulated that any member of a provincial assembly, not elected on behalf of the Congress but willing to take the Congress pledge and abide by Congress principles and discipline, might be taken into the Congress Party in that legislature. *The Indian Annual Register, 1937*, vol. 1, p. 176.
18. Nehru to Rajendra Prasad, 21 July 1937.
19. C. Khaliquzzaman, *Pathway to Pakistan* (Lahore, 1961), p. 157.
20. Ahmad Said to Khaliquzzaman, *ibid.* p. 158.

would accept his lead. However, when Jinnah came to know of Khaliquzzaman's overtures to the Congress, he did not spare any efforts to frustrate them. Jinnah succeeded in exerting his influence and did not let Khaliquzzaman enter into any bargain with the Congress. At the meeting of the Muslim League Parliamentary Board at Lucknow in May, he reiterated that the League would not tolerate any policy of merging with the Congress.[21]

Something similar to U.P. had happened in Bombay also. The information as given by K.M. Munshi reveals that Jinnah had offered to co-operate with the Congress provided the two persons nominated by him were included in the cabinet. It was suggested to Jinnah that his nominees would have to accept the Congress discipline so long as they were ministers and also accept the principle of joint responsibility. Jinnah insisted that his nominees would not be amenable to the discipline of the Congress and they would not even accept the doctrine of joint responsibility.[22] Jinnah was determined not to yield to Congress dictates and saw in the Congress attempt to annihilate the League a portent of the treatment the Muslims would receive at the hands of the Hindus in the future. It was clear to him that the Congress was not prepared to associate the Muslim League in the administration of the country unless it merged itself with it.

Jinnah issued a rejoinder to Khaliquzzaman not to pursue his efforts to conciliate the Congress. He wrote: "... it would be useless for any individual or individuals to effectively carry the Muslims behind them if any settlement is arrived at with a particular group." He described the coalition talk in U.P. as the Congress attempt to create disruption in the League's ranks.[23] He indeed felt that the Congress was not keen on a settlement and was only making attempts to split the League. The Bundelkhand by-election held in July 1937 had served as a morale booster for the League as it had defeated the Congress candidate.

21. *The Leader*, 17 May 1937.
22. Oral History transcript of K.M. Munshi's interview, Nehru Memorial Museum and Library.
23. *The Times of India*, 26 June 1937.

The Muslim League had won this election by carrying on a communal propaganda. An atmosphere of hatred against the Congress was created by raising the slogan 'Islam in danger'.[24] In fact it had been a 'trial of strength' between the Congress and the League. Nehru had taken a personal interest in this election as he felt that ". . . a victory . . . in this [election] would indeed be a triumph for the Congress and our cause" and also a "point of honour".[24a] At the annual session of the League held in Lucknow, the Congress was severely criticized. The Chairman of the Reception Committee, the Raja of Mahmudabad, expressed his regret at the Congress attitude and said:

> A delicate political situation has been created in our own country. The majority community refuses to recognize even the existence of the Muslim community as such and it refuses to work in co-operation with our leaders for national advancement.[25]

In his presidential address, Jinnah spoke very bitterly against the Congress because of its "demand for unconditional surrender and attempts to liquidate the League" and exhorted the Muslims to organize themselves and be united:

> . . . They [Muslims] must realize that the time has come when they should concentrate and devote their energies to self organization and the full development of their power to the exclusion of every other consideration. . . . We must develop power and strength till the Mussalmans are fully organized and have acquired that power and strength which must come from the solidarity and the unity of the people.

24. An appeal to the electorate of Bundelkhand" in Urdu by Shaukat Ali, All India Congress Committee File, 1938.
    In another by-election in the Punjab held in May 1938, a Muslim League candidate, Sheikh Muhammad Sadiq with the support of Unionist party defeated Saifuddin Kitchlew who stood as the Congress candidate and also Chaudhuri Afzal Haq, the Ahrar candidate.

24a. Nehru to A.G. Kher, 30 June 1937, A.I.C.C. Papers.

25. *The Indian Annual Register 1937*, Vol. II, p. 402.

> No settlement with the majority is possible as no Hindu leader speaking with any authority shows any concern or genuine desire for it. An honourable settlement can only be achieved between equals; and unless the two parties learn to respect and fear each other, there is no solid ground for any settlement. Offers of peace by the weaker party always mean a confession of weakness and an invitation to aggression. Appeals to patriotism, justice and fairplay and for goodwill fall flat.[26]

What Jinnah had in mind was that sufficient pressure brought upon the Congress by a solid Muslim front might result in the Congress adopting a more reasonable attitude towards them.

Jinnah also changed his stand on the question of federation. Earlier it was condemned as not being democratic—now his plea was that it was detrimental to the interest of Muslims. He urged the British government to refrain from its enforcement as he considered the scheme to be detrimental to the interests of the people of India generally and to those of the Muslims particularly. Instead of pleading for Hindu-Muslim unity as he often used to do at the League sessions, he now started insisting that League should be treated as its equal by the Congress. Jinnah's main concern was that it should be accepted as the sole Muslim organization.[27]

Other Muslim leaders were no less worried about the political future of their community. Iqbal had also exhorted Jinnah to expedite the work of organization "more vigorously than ever" and stated that they "should not rest till Muslim governments are established in the five provinces and reforms are granted to Baluchistan."[28] It was for the first time at the Lucknow session that the League became a mass organization and opened its membership to all Muslims who had attained

26. S.S. Pirzada, *Foundations of Pakistan : All India Muslim League Documents*, 1924-47, vol. 2, pp. 268-269.
27. Jamil-ud-din, ed., *Speeches and Writings of Mr. Jinnah* (Lahore, 1943), vol. 1, p. 29.
28. Iqbal to Jinnah, 30 October 1937, Appendix II, p. 31. Mohammad Noman, ed., *Our Struggle, 1857-1947 : A Pictorial Record* (Karachi, n.d.).

the age of eighteen. It changed its creed and decided to demand full independence. It also chalked out a programme for revitalizing the organization. The greatest achievement for the League at this session was that its lead came to be acknowledged by the Muslim majority provinces also. Sikander Hayat Khan, Premier of the Punjab, entered into a pact with Jinnah whereby he pledged to follow his lead in all-India matters. Similarly Fazlul Huq of Bengal also acknowledged Jinnah's leadership. This gave a new position of strength to the League.

While trying to unite all the Muslims under his leadership, Jinnah had not yet given up all hope for a settlement with the Congress. He requested Gandhi to formulate some proposals for Hindu-Muslim unity. But Gandhi did not seem to be very keen on arriving at an understanding with him. He gave an unconvincing reply to Jinnah and wrote: ". . .What proposals can I make except to ask you on bended knees to be what I had thought you were."[29] He told Jinnah that since he had accepted Azad as his guide, Jinnah could open conversation with him. Jinnah, of course, did not have any constructive proposal to make. He again and again emphasized that the matters which were agitating the Muslims were the Fourteen Points, and demanded that the Congress should withdraw all opposition to the Communal Award. His other demands were: the share of the Muslims in state services should be fixed by statutory enactment; Muslim personal laws and culture should be guaranteed by statute; Muslims should have religious and cultural freedom; Muslim majorities in the provinces should not be affected by any territorial adjustments; the Bande Mataram song should be given up; Urdu should be the national language of India; Muslim representation in the local bodies should be governed by the principles underlying the Communal Award, separate electorates and population strength; setting up of coalition ministries and the recognition of the Muslim League as the one authoritative and representative organization of Muslims.[30]

29. Gandhi to Jinnah, 3 February 1938. Nehru-Jinnah *Correspondence including Gandhi-Jinnah and Nehru-Nawab Ismail Correspondence* (Allahabad, 1938), p. 83.

30. Extract from *New Times*, Lahore, dated 1 March 1938. Nehru Papers.

As far as withdrawal of the Congress opposition to the Communal Award was concerned, Nehru told Jinnah that the "Communal Award, unsatisfactory as it is holds the field for the present and till such time as it may be altered by mutual agreement of the parties concerned." In his correspondence with Subhas Bose, the Congress President, Jinnah insisted that "any agreement arrived at should be based on a clear understanding of the position of the Congress and the League." All the time Jinnah was deliberately insisting on the most extravagant demand of the Muslim League being accepted as the only representative organization of Muslims since he must have gauged that the Congress could not afford to accede to it.[31] Khaliquzzaman has also mentioned that Jinnah had not yet made up his mind on any definite ideas and the basic question which was confronting the Muslims at that time was what their demand was to be now. In a tone of self-adulation, he writes:

> ...The question was: What should be our demand now? We had already secured our weightage and separate electorates under the Communal Award and after 1936 no demand by the Hindu community as such was made for its abrogation....
>
> It was a piece of good luck for us that Congress fought shy of accepting the Muslim demand for the recognition of League as an authoritative representative organization of Muslims on such a flimsy pretext while yet at the same time wooing and running after the League. If Congress had accepted the position at the time when the demand was made by the League, I wonder what positive demands we could then have made.[32]

On the other hand, the Congress leaders, particularly Nehru, adopted a complacent attitude. His reply to Jinnah was quite vague. He refused to consider the demands outlined by Jinnah and told him that before taking them into consideration "the political and economic background of the free India we are working for has to be kept in mind for ultimately that is the

31. Nehru to Jinnah, 6 April 1938.
32. Khaliquzzaman, n. 19, p. 192.

controlling factor." He made no reference to the communal issue, but referred instead to the general international situation and to the condition of the masses:

> . . . Another matter has assumed an urgent and vital significance and this is the exceedingly critical international situation and the probability of war. . . . This must therefore be considered the governing factor of the situation and almost everything else becomes of secondary importance for all our efforts and petty arguments will be of little avail, if the very foundation is upset.
>
> . . . I have carefully looked through the various matters to which you have drawn attention in your letter and its enclosure and I find that there is nothing in them which refers to or touches the economic demands of the masses or affects the all important question of poverty and unemployment.[33]

Nehru was not prepared to consider the League's demand for statutory guarantees because it involved changes in the constitution, while his main concern was to do away with the then existing constitution. What he was prepared to do was to commit that in a future constitution of India, certain guarantees would be added. About coalition ministries he said that a ministry must have a definite political and economic programme and policy.[34]

Jinnah was repelled by the "militant spirit" and "arrogance" showed by Nehru.[35] It was obvious to him that the Congress had decided not to recognize the Muslim League as a force to be reckoned with. Apart from Jinnah, other Muslims like Syed Mahmud[36] and Maulana Azad were also growing

33. Nehru to Jinnah, April 6, 1938, Nehru Papers.
34. *Ibid.*
35. Jinnah to Nehru, April 12, 1938, Nehru Papers.
36. Syed Mahmud had been a close associate of Nehru in political matters. But after the installation of Congress ministries, they started drifting away from each other because Syed Mahmud had some misgivings regarding the working of the ministries. What was most unpalatable to Nehru was a remark made by Syed Mahmud in a letter where he had said, "What is little understood and never learnt in India is facing facts." He had also desired

critical of the Congress attitude towards the Muslims.[37] Syed Mahmud, who had been a very close friend of Nehru, was drifting away from him so far as their approach to communal question was concerned. The immediate cause for resentment on the part of Syed Mahmud was the Nagpur session of Bharatiya Sahitya Parishad held on 24 April 1936, where the Congress conceded that Hindi or Hindustani would be the national language. This had upset Syed Mahmud so much that he decided to retire from political life. In desperation he wrote that if this Hindu-Urdu controversy was not solved, there would not be any chance of united action between the two communities. He was particularly disturbed by Gandhi's speech where he had used the word "Hindi yani Hindustani" to be the national language of India.[38] The explanation given by Nehru was that a large number of people from South India had attended the session and they apprehended that attempts were being made on behalf of Hindustani to overshadow them. Gandhi's attempt was to "win over those reluctant and suspicious writers from the South and the West to the ideal of

that the minorities should be given such powers by the constitution that they could throw out the Government of the day. Nehru's replies to Syed Mahmud's letters show that he was not prepared to change his views. He openly said, "There is nothing strange for me to differ from others. In some ways I differ from every one of my colleagues . . . . It has dawned upon me that both on the political question and the communal question, our approaches are entirely different and in fact somewhat hostile to each other . . . I hold strong views and I am not likely to give them up." Nehru to Syed Mahmud, 12 October 1940, Nehru Papers.

37. In a letter written on 15 August 1938 to Rajendra Prasad, Azad made a critical evaluation of the Congress policy on the communal question. Making a retrospective analysis of the communal question since 1928, he concluded that the Congress had delayed the solution of the Hindu-Muslim question. That was the main reason why it had taken such a complicated turn at that moment. His contention was that if "we had settled the matter at that time [In 1928 Jinnah was asking for reservation of seats in the Punjab and Bengal in case adult franchise was not established], the whole misunderstanding between the Congress and Muslims would have disappeared for ever." Azad to Rajendra Prasad, 15 August 1938, Urdu, Rajendra Prasad Papers.
38. Syed Mahmud to Rajendra Prasad, 24 April 1936, Urdu, Rajendra Prasad Papers.

Hindustani as a common language for India."[39] Nehru also explained that Hindi meant the use of both the scripts. While the explanation offered by Nehru can partially explain the use of the word 'Hindi' by Gandhi, yet a letter written by the latter in August 1937 leads one to doubt the correctness of the justification given by Nehru. Gandhi had written to Nehru:

> ...You should not hesitate to express the hope that as Hindus and Muslims are one day bound to be one at heart, they will also, who speak Hindustani adopt one script, i.e., Devanagari, because of its being more scientific and being akin to the great provincial scripts of the languages descended from Sanskrit.
>
> ...I take it that my endorsement of your suggestion does not mean that I must ask the Hindi Sammelan to give up the use of the word 'Hindi'.[40]

While Azad regretted that the question of the script should not have been taken up for discussion, Zakir Hussain pleaded to Rajendra Prasad to "grant the advocates of Urdu what they wanted for in the interests of a united Indian people you can never give them too much."[41] But the Congress leaders failed to realize the seriousness of the growing ill-will among the Muslims on the language and other questions. Nehru had told Syed Mahmud that he was unable to get excited about the communal problem as it seemed to him an unreal affair. For him "the vital factor in the world is the fierce tussle that is going on between progress and reaction." His own way of looking at things was completely different from others. "The vital factor is the problem of poverty and unemployment" and everything else was 'subsidiary' to it. He was also sure that this was the "right way" and regretted that this attitude was "strangely lacking in most other people especially

39. Nehru to Syed Mahmud, 24 September 1936, Rajendra Prasad Papers.
40. Gandhi to Nehru, 3 August 1937, Nehru Papers.
41. Zakir Husain to Rajendra Prasad, 24 August 1937, Rajendra Prasad Papers.

in those who talk and write so much about Hindi and Urdu."[42]

Because of this attitude Muslim uneasiness and distrust of the Congress continued to grow. The Muslim League, in its bitterness, tried its best to fan the flames of discontent by publicising the alleged insolent behaviour of the Congress Ministries. Most of the complaints related to forcing Muslim school children to sing Bande Mataram, the Hindu-Urdu controversy, unpleasant incidents outside mosques and efforts made by the Congress to prevent Muslim representatives from being elected to local bodies.[43] A committee was appointed by the Council of the All India Muslim League to make an enquiry into Muslim grievances in the various Congress governed provinces. The report presented by the Committee known as the Pirpur Report confirmed these charges against the Congress ministries. The Pirpur Report pointed out:

> . . .Whatever may be the underlying principle of Congress nationalism and whatever may be the justification for the foregoing incidents—the fact remains that the average Hindu is inclined to associate Swaraj with Ramraj and Congress Government with Hindu government. The Muslims feel that notwithstanding the non-communal professions of the Congress and the desire of a few Congress leaders to follow a truly national policy, a vast majority of the Congress members are Hindus who look forward, after many centuries of British and Muslim rule to the establishment of a purely Hindu raj.[44]

A sub-committee was also appointed by the Working Committee of the Bihar Provincial Muslim League to make an enquiry into the grievances and hardships of Muslims at the hands of the Congress government, including cases of injustice towards them during the Hindu-Muslim confrontation on the occasions of the Bakr-Id, Muharram or Hindu festivals. The

42. Nehru to Syed Mahmud, 24 September 1936, Syed Mahmud Papers.
43. *Report of the Enquiry Committee appointed by the Council of the All India Muslim League to enquire into Muslim Grievances in Congress Provinces*, 15 November 1938 (Pirpur Report) (Delhi, 1938), p. 7.
44. *Ibid.*, p. 14.

report which has been published is known as the Shareef Report. This report alleged that the Muslims in Bihar were living in a state of constant fear of attack upon their life and property in different parts of the province.[45]

The common complaint of Muslims in all the Congress-ruled provinces was that they were now much worse off than when they were under the previous government. Pointing out the communal tendencies of the Congress regime in Central Provinces and Berar, the Pirpur Report mentioned that the Central Provinces Congress Committee had issued instructions that while a Hindu could enlist himself as a member of the Hindu Mahasabha and the Congress at one and the same time, no Muslim could become a member both of the Muslim League and the Congress.[46] This has been corroborated by Maulana Azad also. In a letter written to Rajendra Prasad he referred to the discriminatory action of the Congress and contended that it was not only a complaint of the other groups but also of the Congress Muslims. If the latter could not have any connection with the Muslim League why was it tolerated that a member of the Hindu Mahasabha was simultaneously a member of Congress also? He requested him to remove the complaints of Muslims which had perturbed Muslim nationalists also and implored him to take some immediate decisive action to remedy the situation. Fazlul Haq had made a statement that the Muslims were being oppressed in Bihar, particularly in Bhagalpur. Azad also requested Rajendra Prasad that the Bhagalpur affairs should not be allowed to get worse and asked him to take some action personally as appeals had been sent by the Congress Muslims also.[47] Syed Mahmud fiercely criticised the working of the Congress ministries and asserted that "such belief was not the effect of propaganda alone." In a very frank letter to Nehru he wrote : ". . .let me tell you in general terms again that the Congress has failed to properly and efficiently govern particularly in this province

45. *Report of the Enquiry Committee appointed by the Working Committee of the Bihar Provincial Muslim League to enquire into some grievances of Muslims in Bihar* (Patna, 1938), p. 9.
46. Pirpur Report, n. 43, p. 49.
47. Azad to Rajendra Prasad (Urdu), 8 December 1937, Rajendra Prasad Papers.

[Bihar] where it has definitely misgoverned." He also criticized the Congress Ministers as being full of provincialism, caste prejudices and revivalism.[48]

A similar account of the Congress misgovernment in U.P. was given by Sapru to Inglis (special correspondent of *The Times*) on 7 March 1940. According to him it was evident that an alternative government was impossible and therefore it led to "much demoralisation of public life and great deal of arrogance on the part of Congress ministries" which was the main cause for the dissatisfaction with their conduct and policy among non-Congress elements. He also wrote that Congressmen openly interfered with the magistrates and judges and he cited some cases of such interference, which came up before the Allahabad High Court. He did not accuse the Congress of having committed atrocities on the minorities but expressed the view that "there is no doubt that the rank and file of the Congressmen in the district alienated the Muslim sentiment . . . and gave rise to the impression that the Congress government could do anything."[49]

Sultan Ahmed also used very harsh words against the Congress ministers and his letter shows the disgust of Muslims with the Congress. He wrote in a letter:

> . . . So far I had blamed the Mussalmans, for their hot-headness, impracticable suggestions and unreasonable demands but after having seen the working of the Congress ministries in at least two or three provinces I am veering round to the view that the apprehension of the Muslims is justified. The meanness to which some of the Congress people stoop when power has been given to them has been an eye-opener to me. Their tall talk of nationalism is a perfect humbug and I find that in the chair of authority they are quite guilty of bias, bigotry, inequalities and meanness which are absolutely astounding.[50]

The growing discontent among the Muslims was fully exploited

48. Syed Mahmud to Nehru, 9 December 1939, Syed Mahmud Papers.
49. Sapru to Inglis, 7 March 1940, Sapru Papers.
50. Sultan Ahmed to his friend (name of the person not known), 26 October 1938, Rajendra Prasad Papers.

by the League leaders to extend their influence.

At the annual session of the League held on 26-29 December 1938, Jinnah vehemently criticized the Congress. He felt that the Congress High Command wanted the Muslims to be "a mere understudy of the Congress, mere footpages of the Congress leaders, to be used, governed and brought to heels when they had served the purpose of the Congress." He made it obvious that he did not want any settlement with the Congress. As a matter of pride he declared: "I want to make it plain to all concerned that we Muslims want no gift. The Muslims want no concessions."[51] It was clear from his outburst that now he had no qualms about gaining the support of the British as he stated that the Muslim League would be "the ally of even the devil if need be in the interests of Muslims." The address was marked by the absence of any reference to the need for Hindu-Muslim unity. His line of action had changed. His belief was that "in politics one has to play one's game as on a chess-board."[52] While the Muslim League did its utmost to magnify the highhandedness of the majority community, the Congress tried to minimise them or pretended to disbelieve them and did nothing to assuage the Muslim fears. The response of Rajendra Prasad, for instance, to the Muslim League's propaganda was one of complete indifference. He wrote : ". . .So far as I am concerned the Congress ministry has done nothing to the prejudice of Mussalmans."[53] The gravity of the situation dawned upon the Congress leaders quite late. Nehru had put an end to mass contact committee and a minorities committee consisting of leading Congress Muslims and Hindus was formed. In 1939 Nehru wrote to Rajendra Prasad:

> . . .There is no doubt that we have been unable to check the growth of communalism and anti-Congress feeling among the Muslim masses . . . One of the most

51. Annual Session of the All India Muslim League, 1938, *op cit.*, n. 26, p. 304.
52. *Ibid.*, p. 309.
53. Rajendra Prasad to Sultan Ahmad, 2 February 1938, Rajendra Prasad Papers.

remarkable signs of the times is the ferment amongst the Muslims in India both the intelligentsia and the masses.[54]

Rajendra Prasad had also written to Nehru in the same vein: ". . .For the last two or three years I have been feeling very much the want of some provisions which could ensure adequate representation of the Muslims in the Congress Committee.[55]

This awakening among the Congress leaders had come quite late. The cumulative effect of the aggravation of Muslim fears and uneasiness was the growth of opposition in the Muslim League to the idea of an all-India Federation. By the end of the year 1938, the Muslim League leaders were united in their determination not to let the Muslims be dominated by the Hindus in a future central government. They began to feel that the Congress demand for complete independence was detrimental to Muslim interests as it would place the Hindus permanently in power at the Centre. The League leaders now began to look for some alternative scheme.

Sikandar Hayat Khan formulated a scheme which was meant to secure the Muslims against Hindu domination. In an interview with the Governor of Punjab Henry Craik he explained the reasons for the Muslim objections to the idea of federation. He apprehended that the tendency would be for the "party in power at the Centre to intervene in all provincial matters." Although recruitment to the armed forces might be a reserved subject, he felt that the Congress ministry would exert its influence in regard to that question. He visualized a situation where the position of the Muslims would be affected as the Congress would "work steadily against the reservation of the existing large share of recruitment for the martial classes of the Punjab."[56]

Sikander's next worry was that the Congress ministry would insist on the establishment of a convention through which the Governor-General would be bound to accept the advice of a ministry even in regard to reserved subjects. The

54. Nehru to Rajendra Prasad, 18 October 1939, Nehru Papers.
55. Rajendra Prasad to Nehru, 11 July 1939, Nehru Papers.
56. Sikander Hayat Khan to Henry Craik, 27 June 1938, Linlithgow Papers, India Office Library, London.

safeguard prescribed by him was the "establishment of a Central Executive so constituted as to reflect the opinion of those elements who are not prepared to surrender completely to the Congress or purely Hindu policy". He concluded by saying that His Majesty's Government would be committing a mistake by pressing for the introduction of federation in the near future. He asked the government to give an assurance to the Muslims that the government would not do anything which would be detrimental to Muslim interests.

He had evolved an alternative scheme of a federation of zones in place of a federation of provinces and the states which will be discussed in the next chapter. It will suffice to point out here that his chief concern was to secure a Centre in which both the Legislature and the Executive would represent the different federating units, i.e., each federal unit would have an equal share of representation both in the Legislature and in the ministry. For this purpose he had divided the whole of India into seven units or zones.

It should be noted that the alternative scheme to federation was actually referred to by Sir Sikandar at the Lucknow session of the League held in October 1937. He had submitted his scheme to the Viceroy before the session but the latter dissuaded him from placing it before the public. Similarly certain Muslims in the Punjab were giving serious consideration to the movement started at the time of Lucknow session for a federation of the North-West comprising of the Punjab, Sind, N.W.F.P. and the Punjab States.[57]

In the month of March 1939, Khaliquzzaman and Abdur Rahman Siddiqi met Zetland in London where they also discussed with him the position of the Muslim community in India in the event of a scheme of federation coming into existence. At the outset they told him of the Muslim decision not to acquiesce in its introduction. Zetland tried to probe their mind to find out if they had any alternative suggestion to put forward. What they proposed to him was the establishment of three or four federations of provinces and

57. Note of an interview between Linlithgow and G.D. Birla at New Delhi on 1 February 1938. Enclosure 1 to Letter dated 7 February 1938, Linlithgow Papers.

states which would be co-ordinated by a small central body. The whole object of their scheme was also to give the Muslims as great a measure of control at the Centre as the Hindus. When they enumerated the details, Zetland felt that they were also aiming at a federation of Muslim provinces and states in the North-West India, a federation of Bengal and Assam, and a federation of Bihar and Orissa in the east. This was the reason why he had informed Linlithgow about his apprehension that Muslims might create hurdles in the way of federation (which proved to be correct). He wrote : "...What they told me confirms to some extent the views which I expressed to you not very long ago to the effect that we should probably have greater difficulty in bringing the Muslims into the federation than the Congress." He also realized "the difficulties of bringing the federation into existence", which according to him were "gaining in magnitude."[58]

Jinnah was no less dissatisfied with the federation idea. It was evident that he would turn to the Viceroy to seek redress of his grievances. Already in a meeting with Brabourne he and Sikander Hayat Khan had expressed their apprehension that the government and the Congress were working for an early federation and had given the assurance that the Muslims would stand by the government through "thick and thin" if their demand was conceded. Jinnah had ended up with the suggestion that they "keep the centre as it is now", that they should "make friends with the Muslims" by "protecting" them in the Congress provinces, and if they did that the Muslims would protect them at the Centre.[59]

The Viceroy was not less anxious to support Jinnah as he saw in the Muslim League opposition an effective barrier against the Congress. That he also held Jinnah in high esteem is evident from his remark that "it would be the greatest mistake in any way to discount the importance of expression of opinion [that the government should redress Muslim grievances] particularly from a man of the standing of Jinnah and we must give full weight to them."[60]

58. Zetland to Linlithgow, 20 March 1939, Linlithgow Papers.
59. Brabourne to Linlithgow, 19 August 1938, Brabourne Collection, India Office Library, London.
60. Linlithgow to Zetland, 28 March 1939, Linlithgow Papers.

Linlithgow did his best to mollify the Muslims as he harboured the misconceived notion that by supporting the Muslims he would mitigate their hostility to the scheme. He was convinced that an all-India Federation was the only practicable line of constitutional advance and a corollary to provincial autonomy. This was the time when he was looking forward to the early implementation of the federal scheme. He had written to Zetland:

> ...We cannot for a moment contemplate substantial modification—much less the jettisoning of the federal plan on account of Muslim fear. Indeed the fact is that no conceivable amendment of the scheme would meet Muslim objections which are directed against qualities which belong inevitably to any conceivable scheme of federation. The moment we weaken in our resolution to push federation through we shall find ourselves without a policy and without a future. Our prestige is deeply involved. If we fail we shall incur the contempt of all parties and (whatever the surface signs) we shall disappoint the greatest majority of politically minded Indians.[61]

He did not consider the Muslim League to be formidable enough to prevent the attainment of federation or to make it unworkable. When he offered his hand of friendship to Jinnah, he did not foresee that this would be at the cost of his federation scheme. In his own way he felt that by enlisting the support of Jinnah, he would make him act according to his own dictates and guide him in the direction he desired. His contention was that only the achievement of federation would help to alleviate the tensions. He wrote:

> I shall be very greatly mistaken if we do not find that the two communities will work much more closely together with the degree of resposibility at the Centre which Federation involves and with the Centre based to so large an extent directly or indirectly on popular

61. *Ibid.*, 28 March 1939.

> election; and thus when the Hindu-Muslim problem would be transferred to the Central Government, the chance of leaders bearing greater influence on their community in independent province is a real one.[62]

Linlithgow had also met Gandhi when the latter had put forward various concessions which the Congress might be prepared to make on the Hindu-Muslim question. The Viceroy had conveyed those proposals to Sultan Ahmed, Feroz Khan Noon, Nawab of Chhatari and Nazimuddin to let them know what concessions Gandhi was prepared to make in return for an arrangement with the League. They were as follows:

(1) Population proportion or else weightage in minority provinces for appointments in all branches of the services. A corresponding arrangement to be made in respect of provinces in which the Hindus were in a minority.

(2) A committee to be set up consisting of equal numbers of Hindu and Muslims philologists to prepare a dictionary of Hindustani and to meet the difficulties which had arisen over the Hindi-Urdu question. If the Muslims attached importance to the retention of Urdu, he would be ready to agree to the amount spent in the case of Muslims on education in Hindu majority provinces to be handed over to a Muslim body entirely outside the Ministry of Education, on the understanding that a similar arrangement would be introduced in respect of Hindus in provinces in which they were in a minority.[63]

But nothing concrete came out of Gandhi's proposals. The Muslim League was now more keen on securing Linlithgow's support than on gaining concessions from the Congress. Jinnah had approached the Viceroy on the assumption that the government was not yet contemplating to withdraw from India. On 28 February 1939 when he had talks with Linlithgow he laid more emphasis on the fact that in any federal scheme, the government should ensure an adequate equipoise between the Hindu and Muslim votes. In order to secure that, he told

62. *Ibid.*, 25 March 1939.
63. Note of an interview between Gandhi and Linlithgow, Enclosure 2 to the letter dated 23 January 1939, Linlithgow Papers.

Linlithgow that he had in mind the 'manipulation' of territorial votes and the adjustment of territorial divisions. He felt that his scheme was better than Sikander's. It is significant here to note the conversation Linlithgow had with Jinnah on this point in the words of the former:

> . . .I thought I would take him a little further and ask him whether in his judgement the equipoise to which he referred could be maintained in the event of our leaving the country. He admitted coyly that it might possibly prove very difficult in that event; and I asked him whether he wanted us to stay. He again admitted with some reluctance that it looked very much as though that was the position that was going to emerge.[64]

Linlithgow was not willing to discuss that contingency with Jinnah and asked him whether he was seriously contemplating that he should go back to Parliament "after ten years of endeavouring with the help of Indians" and after two years' experience of provincial autonomy "to suggest that in the Provinces the scheme devised and admitted of being worked. . . was all mere nonsense and that something completely different on the lines which Jinnah now indicated would have to be devised." That was what Jinnah wanted him to do because he felt that "so long as there was any shadow of authority in exercise by His Majesty's Government the government should be landed with every possible responsibility by Hindus and Muslims alike."[65]

Jinnah also conveyed to Linlithgow that the country was not 'competent' to run a democracy and that he and others who had been advocates of this system of government had misjudged "the capacity of India to run such a system." They also had been carried away by their "patriotic and nationalist" feelings and he felt in the light of the practical experience that it would work to the detriment of Muslim interests. Jinnah also added that the Muslims did not get a fair treatment in the Congress majority provinces.[66]

64. Linlithgow to Zetland, 28 February 1939, Linlithgow Papers.
65. *Ibid.*, 28 February 1939.
66. Linlithgow to Zetland, 28 March 1939, Linlithgow Papers.

Linlithgow was quite sympathetic towards the Muslim grievances but he did not give much importance to any of the schemes that had been put forward by the Muslims nor was he "unduly perturbed" because he did not feel that "any of the schemes that have so far been ventilated have the least chance of surviving critical examination." He did not consider them worth consideration and felt that it was just a "formless apprehension" which was so evident among the Muslims throughout India. At the same time he was convinced that Jinnah was not the only person who was voicing opposition to the federal scheme. He had granted interviews to other Muslims like Muhammad Yamin Khan, Mohammad Yakub, Ziauddin Ahmad, all of whom had put forward the same grievance that the arrogant Hindu majority was bent upon undermining their position."[67]

But Linlithgow along with Zetland was also not prepared to brush aside the fears entertained by the Muslims against the Congress government. Zetland had informed Linlithgow after having been apprised of the widening gulf between the Hindus and the Muslims that due weight should be given to the Muslims as they lacked an "adequate mouth-piece". He wrote, ". . .the deep-seated dislike and fear of Hindu domination on the part of 90 million Muslims is a thing which we cannot possibly brush aside."[68] Speaking at the Empire Day Banquet in London, he made a reference to Hindu-Muslim differences and though he held that both the communities had to make efforts for reconciling communal differences, he exhorted the Congress to accede to the Muslim demands and placate them. He said :

> ...I have no hesitation in saying that on this issue the present generation of Indians has it within its power to make or to mar future of their country. Only if minorities in the country be they princes or Moslems feel assured that they collaborate as equal partners in a common enterprise without a haunting fear of finding their civic rights constantly overborne or disregarded

67. Linlithgow to Zetland, 12 April 1939, Linlithgow Papers.
68. Zetland to Linlithgow, 19 May 1939, Linlithgow Papers.

> can we hope for sure and steady progress towards the goal. Whether or not this condition is to be fulfilled must depend in the main on the attitude of Hindus towards minorities. Much is at stake. Is it too much to ask that leaders of Congress as politically organized representing broadly speaking Hindu India should take this aspect of the matter seriously into account?[69]

Much was indeed at stake. For the failure of the Congress leadership to work out a settlement with the Muslim League in the new context (provincial autonomy and federation) had led the latter to search for an alternative scheme under which the Muslims might be able to shape their destiny without any fear of interference from the Hindu majority. This was to result very soon in the emergence of the demand for India's partition.

69. Zetland to Linlithgow, 24 May 1939, Linlithgow Collection.

6

The Emergence of the Demand for Partition

The Second World War began on September 3 and India was immediately dragged into it by the Viceroy, Lord Linlithgow without any consultation with Indian leaders. This very much irked the Congress and it was prepared to offer only conditional support to the war effort. Its Working Committee seized the opportunity to ask the Government for a clear declaration of the British war aims and made it plain that it would not countenance the country being made a party to the war unless India was treated as an independent nation whose policy would be guided in accordance with the wishes of the people.[1]

This tipped the scales in favour of the Muslim League. Linlithgow sought the help of Jinnah towards securing the wholehearted support of the Muslims and showed an increasing tendency to treat the League on terms of equality with the Congress. In an interview held on 4 September he reminded Jinnah of the usefulness of British rule for safeguarding the interests of Muslims, and asked whether Jinnah had not told him "again and again that he regarded the influence of the British in India as essential to the survival of his own community."[2] Linlithgow also told Jinnah that the British had

1. *Congress and War Crisis* (Allahabad, n.d.), p. 118.
2. Linlithgow to Zetland, 4 September 1939. Linlithgow Collection.

decided "in view of the onset of war, to suspend the work in connection with the Federation."[3] The reasons given for this decision were that the complicated process of arranging for a large number of Instruments of Accession of Indian states and the negotiations to be carried on for this purpose could not be undertaken while the war continued. When Linlithgow referred to Sikandar Hayat Khan's expression of loyalty and cooperation[4] with the British in the war, Jinnah could not resist assuring him that he also "shared those sentiments of loyalty and that same readiness to give his full support." He, however, took care to point out that "he was a public man and had to think of his followers."[5]

Being a shrewd politician Jinnah was convinced that the Government was desperately in need of the Muslim support to maintain the *status quo* and resist the Congress demands. He wanted that the Congress should be meted out the same treatment by Linlithgow as had been done by Willingdon. Linlithgow's correspondence with Zetland, giving the account of his interview with Jinnah is quite revealing. Linlithgow informed Zetland:

> He [Jinnah] hoped I would do what I could to strengthen his hand. That was why he wanted something positive to take to his followers. They were saying to him: "Why should we fight to perpetuate conditions in India that must shortly bring about complete domination by the Hindus." What could he say to that? Hence his anxiety that His Majesty's Government should soon, if not immediately, announce that the constitution was to be completely overhauled and reshaped. . . . His friends in the Congress provinces were suffering cruelly. Let His Majesty's Government at least protect them in the enjoyment of their lives, their property and their own culture and mode of living.

3. *Ibid.*
4. On 3 September Sikandar Hayat Khan sent him a message assuring that the Punjab and Bengal were behind the government in the prosecution of the war. Linlithgow to Zetland, 5 September 1939, Linlithgow Papers.
5. Linlithgow to Zetland, 4 September 1939, Linlithgow Papers.

> I said, "Do you want me to turn Congress ministries out?" To this Mr Jinnah at once replied, "Yes! Turn them out at once. Nothing else will bring them to their senses. Their object, though you may not believe it, and though I did not believe it till 2 years ago was nothing less than to destroy both you British and us Muslims. They will never stand by you." On this I made no comment.[6]

Linlithgow also tried to probe Jinnah's mind about the statement made by him that he did not believe in democratic government in India and raised the question that "if democratic government was unsuitable to this country, how was she to obtain her goal of self-government. Was such a policy not to condemn India to a perpetual condition of communal strife?"[7] It is significant to note that this elicited from Jinnah the reply that "an escape from the impasse. . .lay in the adoption of Partition."[8]

At the Working Committee meeting on 18 September, the Muslim League passed a resolution on the outbreak of war. It appreciated the invitation extended to Jinnah by Linlithgow to apprise him of the international situation. In order to impress Linlithgow it emphasized that the Viceroy's declaration regarding the suspension of Federation was in the interests of India and particularly those of the Muslims. It demanded that the federal scheme instead of being suspended should be abandoned completely without further delay. It also urged upon the government that the entire problem of India's future constitution should be considered *de novo*.[9] Enumerating the reasons for the change in the League's stand the Committee pointed out:

> . . .It had hoped to occupy an honourable place in the national life, government and administration of the country and work for a free India with free and independent Islam in which they could play an equal part with the

6. Note of an interview between Jinnah and Linlithgow, 5 October 1939, Linlithgow Papers.
7. *Ibid.*
8. *Ibid.*
9. *Indian Annual Register, 1939*, vol. 2, p. 351.

> major community with a complete sense of security. . .but the developments that have taken place and especially since the inauguration of the provincial constitution based on the so called democratic parliamentary system of government and the recent experiences of over two years have established beyond doubt that it has resulted wholly in a permanent communal majority and the domination of the Hindus over the Muslim minorities whose life and liberty, property and honour are in danger and even their religious rights and culture are being assailed and annihilated every day under the Congress government in various provinces.[10]

Linlithgow's answer to the demand of the Congress for "more marked constitutional changes" and the Muslim League's demand for "special protection" was the reiteration of the intention of the British government that "Dominion Status was the natural issue of India's progress."[11] He announced that at the end of the War, His Majesty's Government would enter into consultation with representatives of the "several communities, parties and interests in India with a view to secure their aid and co-operation in the framing of such modifications in the details of the plan embodied in the Act of 1935."[12] Alluding to the communal differences between the Congress and the Muslim League, he made it clear that they could not be brushed aside. He said : ". . . these differences of view, deeply and sincerely held . . . by those who have abandoned them to me, should be borne in mind when we consider our present problems, for they have a very direct and obvious relevance to them.''[13]

Feeling encouraged Jinnah now demanded that "no new pronouncement or new constitutional departure should be made without the approval of the League." Though this would place him in the commanding position of being the arbiter of

10. *Ibid.*
11. Speeches and Statements of Linlithgow, 18 October 1939, Linlithgow Papers.
12. *Ibid.*, 18 October 1939.
13. Linlithgow to Zetland, 5 November 1939, Linlithgow Papers.

future policy,[14] Linlithgow was prepared to give him this power. While conveying Jinnah's demand to Zetland, he wrote: "We ought to recognize that in dealing with Muslim leaders we were dealing people who were reasonable men and also that they were out, as anyone else, for India's advance."[15]

Nehru now realized the dangers of the developing situation and approached Jinnah with a view to persuading the League to forge a united front with the Congress in its opposition to the war aims of the government. He confessed to Jinnah that he had neglected the solution of the communal problem. In a rather apologetic tone, he observed:

> . . . I entirely agree with you that it is a tragedy that Hindu-Muslim problem has not so far been settled in a friendly way. I feel terribly distresssed about it and ashamed of myself in so far as I have not been able to contribute anything substantial towards its solution. I must admit to you that in this matter I have lost confidence in myself though I am not usually given that way. But the last two or three years have had a powerful effect on me.[16]

A draft statement was also prepared by the Congress which it was hoped, might be issued under the signatures of Rajendra Prasad, Nehru and Jinnah. It was said there that the Congress and League leaders had met together on several occasions and "although there was much in common" between them on the political issue (political crisis in India caused by the European war) and their general objective, they did not see eye to eye in regard to "some matters affecting the approach to the communal question and the immediate steps to be taken."[17] It was also specified that they had discussed only the political issue and the communal problem was left for future discussion.

14. "Note of a conversation between Linlithgow and Jinnah," Linlithgow to Zetland, 12 January 1940, Linlithgow Papers.
15. *Ibid.*, 12 January 1940.
16. Nehru to Jinnah, 18 October, 1939, Nehru Papers.
17. Draft to be issued under the joint signatures of Rajendra Prasad, Jinnah and Nehru, 4 November 1939, Nehru Papers.

But Jinnah refused to agree and the statement could not be issued.

In the same month Prasad had also approached Jinnah in order to break the communal impasse.[18] He stressed that the charges of atrocities levelled against the Congress ministries were unfounded and were based on "misapprehensions" and "one-sided reports". He broached the subject of appointing Maurice Gwyer, Chief Justice of the Federal Court, to inquire into the matter. But now Jinnah had pinned his entire faith on the Viceroy.[19] His reply to Prasad's proposal was that the matter was under His Excellency's consideration and he was "the proper authority to take such action and adopt such measures as would meet our requirements and would restore complete sense of security and satisfaction among the Mussalmans."[20] In a meeting held with Gandhi at Delhi in October he flatly stated that (1) so long as the Congress was not prepared to treat the Muslim League as the authoritative and representative organization of the Mussalmans of India it was not possible to carry on talks regarding the Hindu-Muslim settlement, and (2) that the League would not endorse the Congress demand for the declaration of British war aims till the two organizations had reached an agreement with regard to the minority problems.[21]

In the meanwhile, the Congress Working Committee at its meeting on 22-23 October 1939, considered Linlithgow's declaration about British war aims as a reiteration of the old imperialist policy. It took particular objection to the stress on the differences among Indian parties, describing it as a 'screen' to hide the true intentions of Great Britain. The Working Committee categorically declined to admit any necessity for

18. Rajendra Prasad, President of the Congress, showed a genuine desire for settlement with Jinnah and in October he had stressed its urgency to Nehru. His contention was that the communal question was the dominant question because "not only the decision of the British government but any future line of action that we may decide upon depends to a large extent upon its satisfactory solution". Prasad to Nehru, 14 October 1939, Rajendra Prasad Papers, National Archives of India, New Delhi.
19. The *Indian Annual Register, 1939*, vol. II, p. 234.
20. *Ibid*
21. Jinnah to Nehru, 13 December 1939, Nehru Papers.

prior agreement with the Muslim League as a condition precedent to the fulfilment of its demands. Its contention was that the Constituent Assembly would adequately secure protection for the Muslims. To express its disapproval of the Viceroy's statement the Committee called upon the Congress ministries to tender their resignations.[22]

This led to the resignation of Congress ministries from office and left the field open for Jinnah to raise his demands and extract concessions from the government. He made an appeal to the Muslims to observe 22 December 1939 as the "Day of Deliverance". He also expressed a deep sense of relief and rejoiced that the Congress ministries had ceased to function. In an appeal to the Muslims, he ridiculed the High Command of the Congress and accused it of being mainly responsible for the "wrongs that had been done to Muslims." He accused the Congress of flouting Muslim opinion both in the discharge of their administrative duties and in the legislature and of destroying Muslim culture and interfering with their religious and social life. He also emphasized that if the appeals had been heard at the proper time no such action would have been necessary.[23] While this action of Jinnah made the Congress 'bang' the door of negotiations with him as it was considered futile to have any further meeting with him, Linlithgow sent him an assurance that "His Majesty's Government are not under any misapprehension as to the importance of the contentment of the Muslim community to the stability and success of any constitutional development in India." He was also asked not to entertain any fears regarding the weight which his community was going to exercise in future.[24]

The strategy adopted by Linlithgow was to lay continuous stress on divergence of views between the two communities in his public speeches and in his dealings with the Congress. At the same time he went on assuring Jinnah that he had decided to safeguard the position of the minorities. In January 1940 he wrote to Zetland about his decision to "effectively safeguard the minority position and his determination to avoid

22. *Congress and the War Crisis*, n. 1, pp. 137-38.
23. Jamilud-din, ed., *Speeches and Writings of Jinnah* (Lahore, 1942), p. 95.
24. Linlithgow to Zetland, 4 January 1940, Linlithgow Collection.

allowing ourselves to be stampeded into measures for which this country was not ripe."[25] Linlithgow was determined not to hand over the government machinery to the Congress nor to assist the latter in keeping 'their opponents' in India under effective control. He was so contemptuous of the Congress that he felt it was not capable of running the machinery of the government. His contention was that one of the main difficulties in considering constitutional progress in India was the "finding of shoulders broad enough to carry the burden which we should relinquish."[26]

Unlike Linlithgow, Zetland was not averse to giving some consideration to the Congress.[27] He prepared a memorandum where, while opposing the possibility of imposing on any large section of India's population a self-governing constitution against its wishes, he also added that the British could not allow any minority to interrupt the course of reforms. He desired that Linlithgow should tell the two communities that the British had their own 'desiderata' which must be secured. The outlines of the 'desiderata' as framed by Zetland were as follows:

(A) Arrangements for the defence of India as part of the Empire;
(B) Security for the service of the sterling debt held in this country;
(C) Sufficient control of the services to secure their reasonable rights including their rights to careers for which

25. *Ibid.*
26. Linlithgow to Zetland, 30 January 1940, Zetland Collection.
27. Of course to Zetland too the Congress was an anathema. But the repeated exhortation of the opposition that the policy of inaction as pursued by Linlithgow would do considerable harm as it was widening the gulf between the two communities and might lead to a civil war in India prompted him to take some decisive action. Salisbury had complained to Zetland about Linlithgow's policy: ". . . What is good of his reiteration about Dominion Status? Of course we all know that Dominion Status is the settled ultimate goal of the policy of His Majesty's present Government." He stressed that it was neither "accurate nor dignified to say again and again that communal difficulties were the biggest hurdle in the way of constitutional development."
Zetland to Linlithgow, 4 February 1940, Zetland Collection.

they were recruited, though recruitment by the Secretary of State was to end at a fixed date;

(D) The maintenance for some time at least of the commercial safeguards in the existing constitution;

(E) Such a position in India as would enable the British to discharge their obligation to the states in so far as the states were not incorporated in the new Dominion of India.

Zetland felt that if all this was made clear, the British could avoid the accusation that they were insincere in their professions and establish that they were anxious to help India to achieve Dominion Status at the earliest possible and that they were not using the minorities "as pawns in a Machiavellian game of Divide and Rule". He had also asked the Cabinet that it should assume responsibility for telling the Congress and the minorities that "provided our desiderata were met to our satisfaction we would accept a constitution framed by Indians themselves."[28]

But Linlithgow had firmly committed himself to a policy of inaction. He wrote to Zetland that the British must refrain from taking any concrete action. Thus he was doing what Jinnah wanted him to do—to avoid committing himself to any scheme. He told Zetland that ". . .We should make a very great mistake were we in the present circumstances to start running after the Congress." His strategy was to keep "reiterating the generous offer we have made dressing it, if necessary in somewhat different garments," a process to which he had been completely devoting himself during the last three months and not "extending or amplifying" it. What he favoured was a continued insistence on the necessity of the Hindus and the Muslims getting together themselves.[29]

As has already been mentioned, Jinnah had not completely ruled out the prospects of working with the Congress, though this had to be on his own terms. In an interview with Linlithgow in January 1940, he enumerated his terms for an understanding with the Congress: coalition ministries in the

28. *Ibid.*
29. Linlithgow to Zetland, 13 February 1940, Linlithgow Collection.

provinces; no measures to be forced through any legislature if two-thirds of the Muslim members of the Assembly objected to it; Congress flag not to be flown on public institutions; Bande Mataram to be abandoned as a national anthem; and the Congress to abandon its wrecking tactics against the Muslim League.[30] Any prospect of the Muslim League joining hands with the Congress in its demand for complete independence was, obviously inimical to British imperial interests. Linlithgow certainly did not like it. As early as October 1937, he had remarked: "from our point of view, desirable as agreement between all parties may be made in principle, I am not sure that such a consummation is entirely to be welcomed."[31] By 1940 the need for continuing disagreement between the main political parties in India, from the British point of view, had only increased, and not been reduced. It is, therefore, not surprising that the Viceroy set himself the task of prompting the League leaders to devise a constructive scheme of their own and to present the Muslim League as a formidable opponent of the Congress.

Linlithgow's chief concern now was to bring home to these leaders that their ambivalent attitude towards the constitutional issue would prove to be disastrous to them. It should be noted here that Jinnah had already mentioned about having recourse to partition in case the Muslims were asked to evolve an alternative to the federal scheme. Now he also stopped characterizing the Muslims as a minority. Instead, he started emphasizing that Hinduism and Islam "represent two distinct and separate civilizations and moreover are as distinct from one another in origin, tradition and manner of life as are nations in Europe."[32] He, however, did not yet insist on partition and observed:

> A constitution must be evolved that recognizes that there are in India two nations who both must share the

30. Note of a talk between Linlithgow and Jinnah, 13 January 1940, Enclosure 2 to letter dated 16 January 1940, Linlithgow Papers.
31. Linlithgow to Zetland, 17 October 1937, Linlithgow Papers.
32. Article on the Constitutional Maladies of India sent at special request of the "Time and Tide" London, on 19 January 1940, Jamilud-din, n. 23. p. 112.

> governance of their common motherland. In evolving such a Constitution, the Muslims are ready to co-operate with the British Government, the Congress or any other party so that the present enmities may cease and India may take its place amongst the great countries of the world.[33]

Thus it is clear that he had not ruled out his association with the Congress if the latter decided to agree to his demands. Apparently Linlithgow did not relish this. In a meeting with Sikandar Hyat Khan on 3 February he complained that Muslim position as maintained by Jinnah was unhelpful and "static to a dangerous degree."[34] When he met Fazlul Huq to ascertain his views on the Muslim position, the latter started convincing Linlithgow of his entire support to the government by declaring that "He was a Muslim first, always and his duty to his community was one which he could not at any stage forget." He also complained to Linlithgow that the Muslim case had not been fully understood either in India or Britain. He also pleaded with Linlithgow for an assurance that the latter would not try to enlist the support of the Congress which was constantly making trouble for the government. But to the great despair of Linlithgow he also referred to the contingency of working with the Congress if it finally decided to accept the principle of coalition in provinces with joint policies to carry out a common programme. Referring to the Muslim position he said: "the Muslims were in the constant difficulty of being on the defensive. They could not recommend any recession from the present position in regard to constitutional advance or publicly reject the principle of Home Rule or Dominion Status."[35]

Linlithgow's letter to Zetland about the account of the above meeting is self-explanatory. Taking credit for what he had done for Muslims he wrote:

33. *Ibid.*, p. 119.
34. Enclosure 2 to letter dated 30 January 1940. Note of a conversation between Linlithgow and Sikandar Hayat Khan at Delhi on 25 January 1940, Linlithgow Papers.
35. Note of a conversation between Linlithgow and Sikandar Hayat Khan and Fazlul Huq, 14 February 1940, Linlithgow Papers.

> I said . . . whether I had thrown away the Muslim, or the minority case in any respect, and if so how? They both replied at once "No" Sir Sikandar later amending his reply to "Not yet"! I said that I had listened with interest to Mr Huq's exposition of the position as he saw it. . . . I would take only one point which he had raised. He had made the complaint that the Muslim case had not been properly presented. Why was that? Who was to blame? . . . I went on to say that if he and his friends could secure that the Muslim case was better understood nobody would be better pleased than I would.[36]

Linlithgow also informed Fazlul Huq and Sikandar Hayat Khan that so long the Muslims adopted a negative attitude and unconstructive policy, it would be very difficult to make it understood in Great Britain, the United States and even in this country. He gave an illustration that during a conversation between one Kline, the representative of the Associated Press of America, and his Private Secretary, the former had mentioned that in fifty minutes, Gandhi had given him enough press material while after his two hours discussion with Jinnah he had been left with the impression that the League had no constructive programme.

As for Fazlul Huq's suggestion that coalition on some common agreed programme might be the solution of their estrangement with the Congress, the Viceroy impressed upon him the seriousness with which the Muslims would view any concession to the Congress if it was unaccompanied by some satisfaction of their demand. He also reminded him that the Congress would not be allowed to return to office in the provinces and at the same time secure advance at the Centre, until it had satisfied the minorities. If the Congress was not prepared to satisfy the minorities before returning to office in the provinces, then it was in his view "essential that no concession should be made to them at the Centre."[37]

Khaliquzzaman has written that on 6 February Jinnah had

36. *Ibid.*
37. *Ibid*:

informed Linlithgow about the partition scheme but the Viceroy's note of the interview between the two immediately after the above mentioned meeting bears no evidence of it. It is true that Linlithgow enumerated to him the advantage of an alternative scheme for the benefit of Muslims and repeated the argument he had put forward before Fazlul Huq and Sikandar Hayat Khan. Jinnah had asked him what the Muslim League should do in those circumstances? Linlithgow encouraged him to have a positive scheme of his own and emphasized the disadvantages of maintaining only a negative attitude. Jinnah's reply to him was that given the failure of his effort to arrive at an agreement satisfactory to all parties he should "make it clear to the Congress without undue delay that there was nothing doing and this nonsense had to stop, in the same way as Lord Willingdon had done some years ago."[38] It shows that Jinnah wanted Linlithgow to take some stern measures against the Congress which would enable it to be more reasonable and accommodating towards the Muslim League.

About the future constitution Jinnah had told Linlithgow that he was not in a position to present in detail "the considered opinion of his colleagues and himself on this very important subject and that he would be very shortly ready to do so."[39] Probably Jinnah was unwilling to divulge the details of his scheme; quite often his colleagues also used to complain that he never took them into confidence regarding any of his schemes.

Thus Linlithgow remained dissatisfied with the stand taken by Jinnah and even told him that this would not ease the situation as it would become very difficult for him to educate public opinion in Great Britain and more particularly the "600 odd representatives of constituencies by the submission of a formal memorandum to his Majesty's Government."[40] It can be discerned from Linlithgow's interview with Jinnah that he was doing his best to encourage Jinnah to have an alternate scheme of his own; he, of course, knew that since the previous

38. Note of an interview between Linlithgow and Jinnah, Enclosure 3 to Letter dated 6 February 1940 from Linlithgow to Zetland, Linlithgow Collection.
39. *Ibid.*
40. *Ibid.*

year various schemes were being examined to formulate an alternative to the federal scheme. Jinnah's interview with Linlithgow leads to the conclusion that he was perhaps not yet in a position to bring out his scheme in full details. Even then Linlithgow continued to insist that the negative policy being pursued by the Muslims would do them great harm. The following remarks of Linlithgow addressed to Jinnah are indeed extremely important for a proper understanding of the prelude to the emergence of the demand for Partition:

> If he and his friends wanted to secure that the Muslim case should not go by default in the United Kingdom it was really essential that they should formulate their plan in the near future. At the risk of wearying him I was bound to repeat what I had often said before that I was convinced that it was quite useless to appeal for support in Great Britain for a party whose policy was one of sheer negation.[41]

Jinnah had replied that he and his friends would "make public at any rate the outlines of their position in time to enable him to explain the Muslim position in Great Britain and in India." This he was able to do by the end of February. On 25 February at a meeting of the Council of the All-India Muslim League, he asked the Muslims to organise themselves and to convey the message of the League to every Muslim. He also said:

> . . . People ask me what is our goal. . . . The whole question is very simple. Great Britain wants to rule India. Mr Gandhi and the Congress want to rule India and the Mussalmans. We say that we will not let either the British or Mr Gandhi rule the Musalmans. We want to be free.[42]

On 22 March, Jinnah came out with the proposal of separating the Muslim majority provinces from India. His

41. *Ibid*
42. Jamiluddin, n. 23, p. 132.

presidential address was in the nature of a rejoinder to the Congress and its proposal (affirmed at its Ramgarh session held in March) that the Constituent Assembly elected on the basis of adult franchise would satisfy the minorities' legitimate inteɹests. His analysis of the Hindu-Muslim problem was that it was not of an "inter-communal character bur manifestly of an international one" and the best course would be "to allow the major nations separate homelands by dividing India into autonomous states." To make the demand for separation more convincing and justifiable it was emphasized by Jinnah that Hinduism and Islam were "different and distinct social orders because they belonged to two different religious philosophies, social customs and literatures. They neither intermarry nor interdine together and indeed they belong to two different civilizations." Arguing that "Muslim India could not accept any constitution which must necessarily result in a Hindu majority government" Jinnah made it clear that since Muslims werc a nation, they must have their "homelands, their territory and their state." He further added: "We wish our people to develop to the fullest our spiritual, cultural, economic, social and political life in a way that we think best and in consonance with our own ideals."[43] The Muslim League session adopted a resolution which declared:

> . . . no constitutional plan would be workable in this country or acceptable to the Muslims unless it is designed on the following basic principles, viz., that geographically contiguous units are demarcated into regions which should be so constituted with such territorial readjustments as may be necessary that the areas in which the Muslims are numerically in a majority, as in the North-Western and Eastern Zones of India, should be grouped to constitute independent states in which the constituent units shall be autonomous and sovereign.
>
> That adequate, effective and mandatory safeguards should be specifically provided in the constitution for minorities in these units and in the regions for the

43. S.S. Pirzada, *Foundations of Pakistan : All India Muslim League Documents* (Karachi, 1971), Vol II 1924-1947 pp. 337-38.

> protection of their religious, cultural, economic, political, administrative and other rights and interests in consultation with them; and in other parts of India where the Mussalmans are in a minority, adequate, effective and mandatory safeguards shall be specifically provided in the constitution, for them and other minorities for the protection of their religious, cultural, economic, political, administrative and other rights and interests in consultation with them.[44]

A perusal of the several schemes framed during the last decade with a view to safeguarding Muslim interests would show that the demand for partition was neither sudden nor new. Nor was it the handiwork of Jinnah alone. We may begin with Muhammad Iqbal's presidential address delivered at the annual Muslim League's session at Allahabad in 1930, because very often Iqbal has been held responsible for devising a scheme for the separation of India. What he had advocated there was the creation of "Muslim India within India" (he did not include Bengal) by the creation of an autonomous state based on the unity of language, race, history, religion and identity of economic interest. This was not only his desire but also the desire of other Muslims like Jinnah, Muhammad Ali, Shaukat Ali and Muhammad Shafi at that time. Iqbal was not a politician but was first and foremost a student of Islam. Defining his solution of the communal problem, he had stated in his presidential address that:

> . . . if the principle that the Indian Muslim is entitled to full and free development on the lines of his own culture and tradition in his own Indian homelands is recognized as the basis of a permanent communal settlement he will be ready to stake his all for the freedom of India.[45]

He had also emphasized that "the life of Islam as a cultural force in this country very largely depends on its centralisation

44. *Ibid.*, p. 341.
45. Shamloo, comp., *Speeches and Statements of Iqbal* (Lahore, 1948), p. 11.

in a specified territory." Pointing out the advantages of this scheme, he had explained that "... possessing full opportunity of development within the body politic of India, the North-West Indian Muslims will prove the best defenders of India against a foreign invasion."[46]

That Iqbal did not ask for partition of India has been acknowledged by Chowdhry Rahmat Ali who pioneered the Partition scheme and had coined the word 'Pakistan' in 1933. He has written that Iqbal was supporting the Muslim League's demand for an Indian federation comprising of the Muslim majority provinces. According to Rahmat Ali : "... By the word 'state' he meant not a separate or sovereign state but a big province within and as a part of the proposed Indian federation."[47] As for himself, Rahmat Ali had believed from his very childhood[48] that: "Muslims are a Millat distinct from the caste Hindoo Jati, that our destiny lies in integration with other Muslims and not with caste Hindus; that among other territories the north-western provinces of present day 'India' belong to us." He had always deprecated the activities

46. *Ibid.*, p. 13.
47. C. Rahmat Ali, *Pakistan . The Fatherland of the Pak Nation*, 3rd edn. (Cambridge, 1940), pp. 219-20.
48. Rahmat Ali has written that this belief—that Muslims should be treated as a distinct nation and not as a minority belonging to Indian nation was imparted to him in his childhood by his father Haji Choudhary Shah. "I grew with it and it grew with me." It became the dominating passion of his life. He gave his first political expression to it in 1915 when in his inaugural address at the *Bazm-i-Shibli*, he said :

    North of India is Muslim and we will keep it Muslim. Not only that, we will make it a Muslim state. But this we can do only if and when we and our North cease to be Indian. For that is a pre-requisite to it, so the sooner we shed 'Indianism' the better for us all and for Islam.

    The immediate occasion for this statement was the negotiation which was going on between Hindu and Muslim leaders for an understanding on the basis of the national unity of India and whch resulted in the Lucknow Pact of 1916. After the Pact, he severed his connection with a revolutionary society of Hindu and Muslim young intellectuals, most of whom had supported the Lucknow Pact.
    Ibid., p. 214.

of other Muslim leaders as leading to "Indianization of our nation and our lands."[49]

Rahmat Ali was particularly vehement in his condemnation of the federal idea which according to him involved the "renunciation of Pak nationhood" and the Muslims' acceptance of Indian nationhood. It was his contention that this made "our absorption by the caste Hindus a certainty and its acceptance by us an act of self-immolation." By 1933 when the scheme of an all-India federation became a reality he became more vociferous in his condemnation of this development, because "it portended an immediate peril to the life and liberty of our nation." His reaction to it should be noted in his own words:

> . . . I warned the Muslim delegates. I knew that their action had obliterated the twelve centuries of our history, destroyed the very foundations of our heritage and crippled all hopes of the fulfilment of our mission. I begged them to realize their responsibility before Allah and his Rasool and to withdraw their demand for the Indian Federal Constitution and ask for a separate federation of our north-western homelands.[50]

Having failed in his efforts, the feeling gripped him that "Allah had assigned that fateful task to me"; and he directed all his energies towards the achievement of a Muslim homeland. Thus inspired by this objective he concluded that "it was now or never; that any further silence would be fatal." In pursuit of that decision he drafted the statement, 'Now or Never', which embodied the first part of his plan. This statement was a proclamation of "the freedom of the Muslims from the British-Bania domination, the release of our nation from the bonds of minorityism." Here he condemned the activities of Muslim delegates to the Round Table Conference and denounced their attempts to include Muslim 'homelands' in the all-India federation. He also demanded the 'recognition of our distinct nationhood in Pakistan and

49. *Ibid.*, p. 213.
50. *Ibid.*, pp. 222-3.

urged the creation of a Federation of India."[51]

The word 'Pakistan' as coined by him was composed of letters taken from the names of various states which, according to him constituted the Muslim homelands—Punjab, Afghania (North-West Frontier Province), Kashmir, Iran, Sindh (including Kachch and Kathiawar), Tukharistan, Afghanistan and Baluchistan. Its meaning was defined as "land of the Paks —the spiritually pure and clean."[52] In 1935 when final shape was being given to the Government of India Act, he issued a circular letter from Cambridge where he emphasized that the "Government of India Bill, based on the Indian Federal Scheme has created an acute crisis in the national life of Pakistan and has raised a supreme issue—an issue of life or death for its national future." He also hoped that fullest support would be given to the "inexorable demand of Pakistan—a demand based on justice and equality—for the recognition of its sacred right to a separate national existence as distinct from Hindoostan." His primary concern was to draw the attention of the British people and Parliament and also that of 'Hindoostan' to the vital distinctions—social, cultural, religious—which separated 'Pakistan' from Hindoostan. The following excerpt from his letter pointed out the vital distinctions between the two communities:

> . . . The very basis and content of our national life is founded on fundamentals essentially different from those on which Hindooism lives and prospers. Our age long social system and our ancient national tradition have given us a civilization with a philosophy—a culture, language, a literature and an art basically and fundamentally different from that of Hindoostan. This is not all. We do not interdine; we do not intermarry. Our national customs and calendars, even our diet and dress are different.[53]

He also emphasized that "geographically also the lands comprising Pakistan form a separate and distinct Unit."

51. *Ibid.*, p. 227.
52. *Ibid.*, p. 224.
53. C. Rahmat Ali to [name of the person not given], 8 July 1935, enclosed in M.R. Jayakar Papers, File No. 752/1941-45.

Therefore, according to him, nature had decreed that Jumna should flow as 'boundary river' between Pakistan and Hindoostan. He also emphasized that the "Indo-Pakistan problem is not an inter-communal issue but is an international problem"[54] and would be solved on that basis alone.

The scheme as outlined by Sikandar Hyat Khan in 1937 was in the form of an alternative to the federal scheme of the government and the idea of Constituent Assembly as desired by the Congress. Some of the salient features of the scheme were:

(1) Instead of bringing British Indian Provinces and Indian states into the Federation as two distinct components, it provided for their entering it together on a regional basis which would be conducive to the solidarity of the country and the stability of the central government.

(2) It would encourage collaboration between contiguous units, including British Indian Provinces and Indian States, whose geographical proximity, common language and affinity of economic and other interests formed natural ties to bind them together. For instance,

(a) In administrative matters, particularly those pertaining to law and order, this scheme would encourage the various units in a zone to make reciprocal arrangements and when necessary to devise a common line of action.

(b) In the economic field it would enable the units to share in common arrangement for the establishment of institutes for industrial and agricultural research, for experimental and demonstrative forms and other similar matters.

(3) By thus encouraging collaboration between British Indian Provinces and Indian States it would tend to reduce causes and occasions for friction which would otherwise be constantly present if British Indian and Indian States units were kept in two watertight compartments.

(4) By confining the jurisdiction of the Federal Executive

54. *Ibid.*

and Legislature to a few specified subjects of common concern, it would enable both the British Indian units and the Indian States to enter the Federation on a uniform basis. At the same time it would allay the doubts and misgivings of the units by eliminating the possibility of undue interference by the Centre in their internal affairs.

(5) It would ensure the willing and loyal co-operation of the units with the Federal Centre and thus avoid the growth of any fissiparous tendency among the units.

(6) It would effectively safeguard the integrity and autonomy of British Indian and Indian States units; and

(7) It would give to the Minorities a greater sense of security.

For the establishment of an All India Federation on a regional basis, the country was to be demarcated into seven 'zones' as under:

Zone 1 : Assam and Bengal (*minus* one or two Western Districts in order to reduce the size of the 'Zone' with a view to approximate it to other zones) Bengal States and Sikkim.

Zone 2 : Bihar and Orissa (*plus* the areas transferred from Bengal to Orissa). This would benefit Orissa which was handicapped to some extent on account of its limited resources and area.

Zone 3 : United Provinces and U.P. States.

Zone 4 : Madras, Travancore, Madras States and Coorg.

Zone 5 : Bombay, Hyderabad, Western Indian States, Bombay States, Mysore and C.P. States.

Zone 6 : Rajputana States (*minus* Bikaner and Jaisalmer), Gwalior, Central Indian States, Bihar and Orissa States, C.P. and Berar.

Zone 7 : Punjab, Sind, NWF Province, Kashmir, Punjab States, Baluchistan, Bikaner and Jaisalmer.

Sir Sikandar also laid down that there would be a regional legislature for each zone consisting of both British Indian and Indian States units. One-third of the total number of members of the various regional legislatures were to constitute the Central Federal Assembly.[55]

Another scheme was put forward by Syed Abdul Latif of Hyderabad in 1939 before the committee appointed by the working committee of the League an 25 March 1939. He contended that India was not a composite nation and Hindus and Muslims belonged to two distinct social orders and prescribed the division of India into four cultural zones for the Muslims and eleven zones for the Hindus: The Indian States were to be distributed between the different zones in accordance with their natural affinities. Each zone would form a homogeneous State with a highly centralized form of government. The following zones were demarcated to be assigned to the Muslims:

1. *North-West Block*—There was a great Muslim block in the North-West consisting of Sind, Baluchistan, the Punjab, North-West Frontier Province and Kashmir, the Indian States of Khairpur and Bahawalpur. This area might be converted into a single autonomous state formed on the basis of federal relationship between the six units thereby allowing over 25 million of Muslims a free home of their own.

2. *North-East Block*—Right on the other side of India, the North-East, there was also a solid block of Muslims in Eastern Bengal and Assam of over 30 millions, who might be assigned a free political existence.

3. *Delhi-Lucknow Block*—In between the two blocks mentioned above the Muslims were unevenly distributed. Those of this area living close to each of the two blocks should be attracted for naturalization to the one nearer to them. The rest, the great bulk, belonging to the United Province and Bihar numbering about 12 million might be concentrated in a block extending in a line from the eastern border of Patiala to Lucknow and rounding up Rampur on the way. The block was carved out to allow the Hindu nationality to keep within its zone all its great religious centres like Banares, Hardwar, Allahabad and Mathura. To shift it on to any other part of the North would defeat that purpose.

4. *The Deccan Block*—The case of the Muslims below the Vindhyas and Satpuras called for a special consideration. They were scattered all over the South in colonies of varying

55. Henry Craik to Linlithgow, 5 June 1938, Linlithgow Papers.

size and exceeded 12 million in number. From them a zone was to be carved. The Dominion of Hyderabad might provide such a zone with a strip of territory in the South running through the districts of Kurnool, Cuddapah, Chittoor, North-Arcot and Chingleput down to the city of Madras. Such a strip with an opening to the sea would be found absolutely necessary to settle the large Muslim mercantile and marine community living for ages on the Coromandel and Malabar coasts.

According to this scheme, exchange of population was also desired "to assure Hindus and Muslims freedom to live their own cultural lives in homelands of their own and to promote the cause of India's unity."[56]

The scheme known as "Confederacy of India" by "A Punjabi" published in 1939 was also worked out in great detail. The underlying assumption behind that scheme was that Hindus and Muslims were two separate nations with different religions, cultures and conflicting political and economic interests. Like other 'schemes', he also advocated the reshaping of the map of India. His scheme was as follows:

1. The Indus Region's Federation with the Punjab, NWFP, Kashmir, Baluchistan, Bahawalpur, Amb, Dir, Swat, Chitral, Khairpur, Kalat, Las Bela, Kapurthala and Malerkotla as its federal units.

2. The Hindu India Federation with the United Provinces, Central Provinces, Bihar, with some portions of Bengal, Orissa, Assam, Madras, Bombay and the Indian States other than the Rajasthan and the Deccan States included in the States' Federations as their federal units.

3. Rajasthan Federation with the various States of Rajputana and Central India as its federal units.

4. The Deccan States' Federation comprising the Hyderabad, Mysore and Bastar States.

5. The Bengal Federation: The prominent Muslim tracts of the Eastern Bengal and Goalpara and Sylhet districts of Assam as its provincial unit, and Tripura and other states lying within the provincial unit or cut off by its territories

56. For Syed Abdul Latif's scheme, see *The Indian Annual Register, 1939*, vol. I, pp. 366-70.

from the Hindu India as its State units.

Each federation joining the confederation of India was to have a governor-general, with the governor of its provincial units under him, who was to be responsible to the central confederal authority, in relation to the confederal subjects and matters relating to the rights and obligations of the Crown in respect of the Indian States within the federation. The confederal authority would be vested in the Viceroy assisted by a confederal assembly consisting of members drawn from the various Indian Federations.

The author did not favour exchange of population. His contention was that in case the Hindus disagreed with his idea of a confederacy then the Muslims should insist on separation. He said:

> . . . We should be separationists-cum-confederationists and if the Hindus disagree with the idea of a confederacy of Hindu India and Muslim India, then we should be simply separationists, demanding secession of our regions from Hindu India without any link between them. We should desire separation simply because we want to evolve a happier and more contented India, whether it be by separation of the Hindu cultural zones and Muslim cultural zones to be linked together in a confederacy, quite independent of and separate from each other except for the confederal bond or complete separation in order to constitute our regions into federated states independently and separately from Hindu India.[57]

Explaining the reasons for advocating such a scheme, he observed:

> "The failure of Hindu-Muslim relations . . . point to the one conclusion that the Muslims will either have to remain content with the present state of affairs or discover some new political ideal wherein all clash between their various loyalties could cease. Through the scheme the territorial loyalties of the Muslims and their allegiance to their faith would find a "happy compromise".

57. "A Punjabi", *Confederacy of India* (Lahore, 1939), p. 17.

It would also ensure them their economic and cultural interests backed by "an absolute political power." It was further stressed that it was the "legitimate heritage" of the Muslims to enjoy full state powers in all those parts of India where they were in an overwhelming majority and the establishment of their own states would mean "revival of Islamic culture and orthodox Islam, the betterment of the Muslim masses, the securing of trade and industrial interests and the restoration of 'self-respect'."[58]

Lastly, the Aligarh scheme proposed by Syed Zafrul Hasan and Mohammad Afzul Hussain Qadri in 1939 aimed at the division of the country into Hindu India and Muslim India. The principles on which it was based were as follows:

(1) The Muslims of India were a nation by themselves. They had a distinct national unity wholly different from the Hindus and other non-Muslims. Indeed they were more different from the Hindus than the Sudetan Germans were from the Czechs.

(2) The Muslims of India had a separate national future and had to make their own contributions to the betterment of the world.

(3) The future of the Muslims of India lay in complete freedom from the domination of the Hindus, the British, or for the matter of that, any other people.

(4) The Muslim majority provinces could not be permitted to be enslaved into a single All India Federation with an overwhelming Hindu majority at the Centre.

(5) The Muslims in the minority provinces should not be allowed to be deprived of their separate religious, cultural and political identity and should be given full and effective support by the Muslim majority provinces.

The scheme envisaged the division of India into several wholly independent and sovereign states:

1. Pakistan comprising the Punjab, NWFP, Sind, Baluchistan and the States of Kashmir and Jammu, Mandi, Chamba, Saket, Sumin, Kapurthala, Malerkotla, Chitral, Dir, Kalat, Loharu, Bilaspur, Simla Hill States, Bahawalpur, etc.

58. *Ibid.*, p. 147.

Population — 3,92,74,244
Muslims — 2,36,97,538; 60.3 per cent

2. Bengal (excluding Howrah and Midnapore districts), Purnea district (Bihar), Sylhet division (Assam)

Population — 5,25,19,232
Muslims — 3,01,18,184; 57.0 per cent

3. Hindustan comprising the rest of India and Indian States (excluding Hyderabad, Pakistan, Bengal and the States included therein).

Population — 21,60,00,000
Muslims — 2,09,60,000; 9.7 per cent

4. Hyderabad comprising Hyderabad, Berar and Karnatak (Madras and Orissa).

Population — 2,90,65,098
Muslims — 21,44,010; 7.4 per cent

(a) Delhi Province including Delhi, Meerut Division, Rohilkhand division and the district of Aligarh (Agra division)

Population — 1,26,60,000
Muslims — 35,20,000; 28.0 per cent

(b) Malabar Province consisting of Malabar and adjoining areas, i.e., Malabar and South Kanara.

Population — 49,00,000
Muslims — 14,40,000; 27.0 per cent

The author of this scheme also desired that the three States of Pakistan, Bengal and Hindustan should enter into a defensive and offensive alliance on the following basis:

1. Mutual recognition and reciprocity.

2. That Pakistan and Bengal be recognized as the homeland of Muslims and Hindustan as the homeland of Hindus to which they could migrate respectively if and when they wanted to.

3. In Hindustan the Muslims were to be recognized as a nation in minority and part of a larger nation inhabiting Pakistan and Bengal.

4. The Muslim minority in Hindustan and the non-Muslim minority in Pakistan and Bengal would have (i) representation according to population, and (ii) separate electorates together with effective safeguards guaranteed by all the three States. Separate representation according to population might be

granted to all considerable minorities in the the three states, e.g., Sikhs, non-caste Hindus, etc.

5. An accredited Muslim political organization would be the sole official representative body of the Muslims in Hindustan.

Each of the three independent states of Pakistan, Hindustan and Bengal was to have separate treaties of alliance with great Britain and separate Crown representation. There would be a joint court of arbitration to settle any dispute that might arise between the different states or between them and the Crown. Unlike the other schemes which treated Hyderabad also as one one of the Indian states, it claimed for it a sovereign status.[59]

While the schemes of Sikandar Hayat Khan and Abdul Latif proceeded upon the assumption that India was not a country but a subcontinent consisting of several countries which should enter into a confederacy, with each unit in the confederation functioning as a federation of several units within itself comprising both British-Indian Provinces and States, the schemes propounded by Rahmat Ali, 'A Punjabi' and the two Aligarh gentlemen laid more emphasis on Hindus and Muslims being two different nations with nothing in common between them. Therefore, according to them the only solution of the problem was separation of the Muslim majority areas from India.

Among the schemes discussed here, the most important was, of course, the one devised by Rahmat Ali. When he had come forward with his partition scheme in 1933 it failed to receive support from any important section of Muslim leadership but as shown in this and the preceding chapter, a lot happened between 1937 and 1940 to bring about a dramatic change in the situation. The Muslim League evidently based its partition scheme essentially on the plan devised by Rahmat Ali and only modified it by also asking for the separation of the North-eastern region from India. In his presidential address to the League's session which adopted the partition demand Jinnah mainly echoed the sentiments voiced several years earlier by Rahmat Ali. Even the words used were not very much different.

59. Rajendra Prasad, *Pakistan* (Bombay and Calcutta, 1940), pp. 38-41.

7
Conclusion

As we have seen in the previous chapters Muslim politics in India underwent a dramatic change between 1928 and 1940. In 1928 a majority of top Muslim leaders, including those of the Muslim League (Jinnah Group) were even prepared to give up separate electorates provided their other demands were met. These demands included such items as the introduction of constitutional reforms in the North-West Frontier Province and Baluchistan, separation of Sind, statutory Muslim majority in the Punjab and Bengal, a federal constitution with residuary powers vested in the provinces, and one-third Muslim representation in the central legislature. It is evident that none of these demand posed any threat to the unity of India. By 1940 by and large the same Muslim leaders, acting under the same leadership openly announced that the Muslims of India were a separate nation and needed their own separate homeland which could be only carved out by partitioning the country. How to account for this change?

This change cannot be explained by pointing out to an ever present antagonism between Hindus and Muslims as some scholars tend to do. There were certainly occasions when antagonism between the two communities surfaced itself, but this cannot be described as having been always present. Nor can the change in the nature of Muslim politics be described as an inevitable manifestation of a separate Muslim nationalism.

It is, of course, true that ever since organized political activity on an all-India basis began with the foundation of the Indian National Congress in 1885, a section of Muslim leadership showed a marked awareness of a separate Muslim identity and refused to co-operate with the Congress. This found expression in the activities and utterances of Sir Syed Ahmad Khan and later provided the background of the Simla Deputation and the foundation of the Muslim League in 1906. The introduction of separate electorates in 1909 gave official recognition to this separate political consciousness. But such a consciousness did not always work in opposition to the mainstream of the Indian national consciousness.

Many developments in India and abroad soon brought the Congress and the League together and in 1916 they prepared a joint scheme of constitutional reforms which became famous as the Congress-League scheme. During the non-cooperation movement (1920-22) the Hindus and Muslims fought shoulder to shoulder under a common leadership and their relations were marked by unprecedented cordiality. Yet even while the movement was going on the Moplah outbreak created considerable suspicion and distrust between the two communities. After the initial suspension of that movement in 1922 and the abolition of the Caliphate in 1924 this suspicion and distrust further increased. There was now a reaction among both the Hindus and the Muslims and communalism took the place of nationalism as the dominant feeling among them. This heightened communal consciousness resulted in the outbreak of communal riots in many parts of India which further spoiled the relations between the two communities. Yet when the Gauhati Congress (1926) gave a call for renewed efforts for a settlement of the communal problem, thirty Muslim leaders met in Delhi (1927) and came forward with demands (mentioned above), which, if fulfilled, would lead them to give up separate electorates and co-operate with other leaders in taking the country further towards self-government.

The emergence of the demand for India's partition, therefore, was not inherent in the situation from the very beginning, but was primarily the result of developments between 1928 and 1940, though, of course, it cannot be fully understood without referring also to some of the development of the earlier period. The chief among the developments between 1928 and 1940 were the general Muslim dissatisfaction with the Nehru Report, the failure of the efforts to settle the communal problem at the Round Table Conference, the non-fulfilment of the Muslim League's expectation regarding the establishment of coalition ministries in 1937 and Lord Linlithgow's attitude towards the Congress and the Muslim League in the context of the outbreak of the Second World War in September 1939. All these have been discussed at length in the preceding chapters and need not be dealt with in any detail here. It will suffice to point out that two things stand out most significantly throughout the period between 1928 and 1940: the failure of the Congress leadership to satisfy Muslim aspirations regarding the sharing of power and the use by the British of the resultant dissatisfaction among the Muslims to encourage them in moving further on the road of separatist politics.

The failure of the nationalist leadership began with the Nehru Report. As has been shown earlier, Motilal Nehru, the Chairman of the Nehru Committee, had nothing against the Muslim demands, but his attitude shows that he was more concerned with placating the Hindu Mahasabha than with giving satisfaction to the Muslims. The main reason was that the lessons of the 1926 elections, when the Swaraj Party had met with a serious challenge from candidates like Madan Mohan Malaviya and Lajpat Rai who were sympathetic to the Mahasabha, were still fresh in his memory. He remained cautious throughout and seemed determined not to give an opportunity to the Mahasabha to increase its following at the cost of the Congress even though this meant losing a chance to satisfy a large section of Muslim leadership. The Nationalist Muslims, of course, gave their whole-hearted support to him. This led him to think that it might be possible to overcome the Muslim opposition by continuing to maintain a stiff attitude. Another reason why he did not take Muslim opposition seriously was that no single Muslim organization in the country could speak authoritatively for Indian Muslims as a whole and take decisions which might be acceptable to the entire community.

There is no doubt that Motilal Nehru's handling of the communal problem in 1928 proved harmful to the national cause. After their failure to get their demands accepted by national convention in Calcutta, the majority of the Muslim leaders not only felt bitter, but also realised that they must bridge the divisions inside their own ranks so that other parties would take them seriously. One result of this was the formation of an All Parties Muslim Conference. Despite Jinnah's initial reluctance to participate in it, the Shafi section succeeded in getting amalgamated with the majority group of the League. Jinnah then came out with his Fourteen Points, which began to be generally considered the charter of the Muslims. To the British the failure of the national convention and its aftermath exposed the hollowness of the Congress claim to speak on behalf of the entire Indian people.

The refusal of the Congress to participate in the first session of the Round Table Conference (1930) consequent on its involvement in the civil disobedience movement strengthened the position of the Hindu Mahasabha there and gave it a further opportunity to maintain its intransigence on the communal problem. Despite the willingness of the Hindu representatives of the Liberal Federation to satisfy some of the demands of the Muslims, it stuck to its guns with the result that no progress could be made towards resolving the communal deadlock.

As a result of the Gandhi-Irwin truce, Gandhi attended the second session of the Round Table Conference (1931) but his presence did not bring a solution of the communal problem any nearer. Of course, he worked most sincerely towards that end, but like the Liberals, he too found it impossible to surmount the opposition of the Hindu Mahasabha leaders. However, since the expectations for a settlement were higher because of Gandhi's presence, their non-fulfilment produced a much greater reaction among the Muslim leaders and made them turn to the Government for the satisfaction of their demands.

The government for its part was not unwilling to oblige the Muslim leadership. The eagerness of Willingdon to tilt the balance in favour of the Muslims led to the Communal Award (1932) which satisfied all their demands. And having got the Award, they were determined to hold on to it and resisted any negotiations which might diminish the solid gains that they had made through it. They were not prepared to surrender anything without adequate recompense.

The urgent necessity of solving the communal problem was felt by the Congress leadership only after the Communal Award had been announced by the Government. It gave up its insistence on unqualified joint electorates, which had been the main plank of its political programme since 1928, and also agreed to statutory reservation of seats for Muslims in the legislatures of Muslim-majority provinces like the Punjab and Bengal. Moreover the Congress did not mind men like Malaviya and Aney seceding from its Parliamentary Board as it had decided to win over the confidence of the Muslims. The provisions of the Communal Award were incorporated in the Government of India Act 1935 and the Muslims had no grievance against the Congress as far as safeguarding of their interests was concerned. There was also a good deal of similarity in the election manifestoes of the Congress and the League and the elections of 1937 were held against this background of mutual trust.

Yet the sequel proved disastrous to the Congress-League relations. While the former had done reasonably well in the elections the latter had made a poor showing in it. This was the most important factor which shaped the attitude of the Congress towards the question of setting up Congress-League coalition ministries in U.P. and Bombay, the only two provinces where the League had acquired any appreciable strength in the legislatures. There is no documentary evidence to prove that there was a prior understanding between the two parties that coalition ministries would be formed after the elections. But the Congress had been unable to win even a single Muslim seat on its own ticket in U.P. and Bombay and at that time it would not have been difficult for it to find men amongst the Muslim League who were prepared to work whole-heartedly with the Congress. Khaliquzzaman broached the question of a coalition ministry in U.P. on his own initiative and in Bombay it was Jinnah who did the spade work. But the Congress was not prepared to accept the idea except on its own terms and these included the dissolution of the Muslim League Party in the legislature and an agreement on the part of the League not to set up candidates in the bye-elections on its own. This attitude on the part of the Congress marked a turning point in the Congress-League relationship. The impression got round that the Congress was trying to annihilate the League. Moreover the Congress move to win over the Muslim masses by direct appeal to them created further alarm and misgivings among Muslim leaders even outside the Muslim League. So much so that this brought other important leaders like Sikandar Hayat Khan and Fazlul Huq of the Muslim-majority provinces of the Punjab and Bengal respectively into the League's fold under the leadership of Jinnah.

Thus strengthened the Muslim League then retaliated by raising the slogan of Islam in danger and by its open opposition to the federal part of the Government of India Act of 1935. Undoubtedly the League's charges against the Congress ministries of committing "atrocities" on Muslims were exaggerated, but they were not totally unfounded. This is borne out by the remarks contained in the letters of such Congress leaders as Jawaharlal Nehru, Rajendra Prasad, Maulana Azad and Syed Mahmud as well as that of the comparatively detached Liberal leader, Tej Bahadur Sapru. The vocal section of the Muslims was never so bitter against the Congress as it was at this time.

Yet the Congress leadership did precious little to retrieve the situation. Nehru maintained a self-complacent attitude for a long time. It is not that he was unaware of the Muslim grievances and at times, when he needed Muslim support, as in course of his effort to forge a united front with the Muslim League to persuade the government to declare its war aims and recognize India's independence, he confessed to Jinnah that the solution of the communal problem had been neglected by the Congress. But otherwise the important factors for him were the international situation, the impending war and alleviation of the economic conditions of the Indian masses. The solution of the communal problem did not receive the top priority that it demanded. It can safely be asserted that his views were far ahead of the times. There was no dearth of Congress leaders (Maulana Azad and Rajendra Prasad may particularly be mentioned here) who were troubled by the widening gulf between the two communities and wanted immediate action to be taken to resolve the communal deadlock. But Nehru retorted that he would not allow anyone to fall into a trap by opening negotiations with Jinnah at that time.

Once again the Muslim League leadership turned to the Government. When Jinnah saw that like Willingdon, Linlithgow too was contemptuous of the Congress and was not interested in any significant constitutional advance in India, he started giving him his cooperation and in return seeking his support in order to strengthen the position of the Muslim League. He now had no qualms about denouncing the democratic system of government for which he had laboured so hard and even confessed to Linlithgow that earlier he had been misled by his patriotic fervour. The latter wanted to use the Muslim League as an effective barrier against the Congress. With the Congress holding out a threat of a civil disobedience movement in case its demand for independence was not fulfilled, the value of Jinnah's cooperation for the British increased still further. Linlithgow now encouraged him to come out with some positive alternative to the federal principle, which might free the Muslims from the prospect of a Hindu majority rule in India.

The Muslim League had, of course, already been considering such an alternative. Even schemes of partition were in the air. One such scheme, for instance, had been suggested by Rahmat Ali as early as in 1933. But the League's leadership was moving cautiously and did not associate itself with any partition scheme until it had some assurance of British sympathetic interest in it. Even before the outbreak of the Second World War, Khaliquzzaman and Abdur Rahman Siddiqui's conversations with the Secretary of State for India in London in 1939 had given them some hope of it. Linlithgow's attitude after the outbreak of the war further confirmed this hope. This was the background of the adoption of what has become famous as the Pakistan resolution by the League, at its Lahore session in 1940, though the word Pakistan was not actually used in the resolution.

Linlithgow was jubilant at the adoption of the Partition Resolution. Obviously he thought that he could use it as a handy tool against the Congress demand for independence.

He had succeeded in his strategy of projecting the widening gulf between the Hindus and the Muslims as the chief hurdle in the way of constitutional advance. He gave his support to Jinnah and his demand for partition by remaining silent and not saying anything against it formally and advised Zetland also to do the same. His chief concern now was to ensure that the Muslim League was not alienated at a time when its support was most essential to the Governmet. This is corroborated by Linlithgow's remarks in his letter to Zetland after the adoption of the Pakistan resolution by the League. "My first reaction is, I confess," he wrote, "that silly as the Muslim scheme for partition is, it would be a pity to throw too much cold water on it at the moment, though clearly we cannot accept it or associate ourselves with it".[1] In his letter to the King-Emperor a little later, Linlithgow was much more positive in his support to the partition scheme and strongly justified it from the Muslim point of view:

> This plan has been adoped by the leaders of the League because it offered the sole means of escape from the dilemma in which the Muslim minority finds itself in face of the introduction of democratic institutions. . . .They refuse to contemplate a future in which they would be in constant subordination to the Hindu majority. They are therefore constrained to suggest the constitutional severance of the country in such a manner as to secure to them political control in those areas in which the Muslim population exceeds the Hindus.[2]

Thus the mistakes made by the Congress leadership, the frustration and bitterness of the League leadership, and the defensive diplomacy of a British Viceroy cumulatively resulted in the adoption of the demand for partition by an organization whose spokesmen had only a few years earlier dismissed it as a "students" scheme' and "a chimera". That indeed was a fateful moment in India's history.

1. Linlithgow to Zetland, 6 April 1940, Linlithgow Papers.
2. Linlithgow to King-Emperor, 4 June 1940, Linlithgow Papers.

Appendix I

Proposals for Hindu-Muslim settlement popularly known as Delhi Muslim Proposals evolved at a conference of Muslim leaders of different shades of opinion, held at Delhi under the presidentship of M.A. Jinnah, 20 March, 1927.*

Whether the forthcoming revision of the Indian constitution, elections to legislative bodies should be through joint or separate electorates has been the subject of anxious discussion among Hindu and Mussalman leaders in Delhi. The Hindu members of the Congress Party and the Nationalist Party, having already decided in favour of only a joint electorate with the reservation of seats to Mohammedans, either on the basis of the Lucknow Pact or the existing population of each province, the Mussalmans met in informal conference today under the Presidentship of Mr. Jinnah, who had issued invitations to representative Mussalmans in all parts of India.

After a protracted discussion, the conference agreed to the institution of joint electorates under certain conditions. It was unanimously resolved that the Mohammedans should accept a settlement on the basis of the following, so far as representation in the various legislatures in any future scheme of constitution is concerned.

(1) Sind should be separated from the Bombay Presidency and constituted into a separate province.

(2) Reforms should be introduced in the North-West Frontier Province and in Baluchistan on the same footing as in any other province.

*Source: Jamil-ud-Din Ahmed, *Historic Documents of the Muslim Freedom Movement*, (Lahore, 1970) pp. 86-87,

If this is agreed to, Mussalmans are prepared to accept a joint electorate in all provinces so constituted and are further willing to make to Hindu minorities in Sind, Baluchistan and the North-West Frontier Province, the same concessions that Hindu majorities in other provinces are prepared to make to Muslim minorities.

In the Punjab and Bengal the proportion of representation should be in accordance with population.

In the Central Legislature, Muslim representation shall not be less than one-third, and that also by a mixed electorate.

These proposals are subject to ratification by the Muslim organizations concerned, but it was hoped by those present at the conference that the Hindus would accept and the Mussalmans would ratify them.

The question of the Services and other questions with regard to safeguards concerning any bill or resolution which might affect the religion, or the customs or the usages of either community, or affecting inter-communal interests were also discussed by the meeting, but postponed for further consideration and will be taken up, if on the main proposition there can be unanimity of opinion.

Appendix II

M. A. Jinnah's speech on the Nehru Committee's recommendations regarding the future constitution and Hindu-Muslim problem at the All-Parties Convention. Calcutta, December, 1928.*

Mr Chairman and Delegates,

The Report of the Committee which you appointed has already been read out and placed before you. I am exceedingly sorry that the Report of the Committee is neither helpful nor fruitful in any way whatsoever. I am sure, gentlemen, that you all realise that the present moment is very critical and vital to the interest not only of the Mussalmans, but to the whole of India. I think it will be recognised that it is absolutely essential to our progress that Hindu-Muslim settlement should be reached, and that all communities should live in a friendly and harmonious spirit in this vast country of ours. No country has succeeded in either wresting a democratic constitution from the domination of another nation or establishing representative institutions from within without giving guarantees for the security of the minorities, wherever such a problem has arisen. Majorities are apt to be oppressive and tyrannical and minorities always dread and fear that their interests and rights, unless clearly and definitely safeguarded by statutory provisions, would suffer and be prejudiced, but this apprehension is enhanced all the more when we have to deal with communal majority. I am sure, you will, therefore, consider the present situation in which we are working and struggling for freedom and record your vote in favour of modifications

**Ibid.*, pp. 92-98.

proposed, which, as I have said before, are fair and reasonable and thus enable us to triumph in our cause.

The first point that I want to place before you, is a point with regard to our proposal that there should be no less than 1/3rd Muslim representation in the Central Legislature. We propose that 1/3rd of the elected members of the Central Legislature should be the Mussalmans, and that the seats should be reserved for them to that extent in the joint electorates of the country. Now the Nehru Report has stated that according to the scheme which they have formulated, the Mussalmans are likely to get 1/3rd in the Central Legislature and more. It is argued there that the Punjab and Bengal will get many more seats over and above their population and the other minorities Provinces in India will get the representation of the Mussalmans according to their population under the scheme propounded by the Nehru Report. What we feel is this: If it is conceded that Mussalmans should be enabled to secure one-third of the representation in the Central Legislature, the method which is adopted is neither quite fair to the provinces where the Mussalmans are in minority, nor does it guarantee that we shall obtain 1/3rd representation in the Central Legislature. Therefore, the two Mussalman majority provinces—Punjab and Bengal—will get more than their population, which means you are giving more to the rich who will, under normal conditions, get the largest number of Muslim representatives and you are depriving the Muslim minority Provinces of great importance, and restricting them to get no more than their population, whereas we wish to restrict the Punjab and Bengal according to their population and desire that the excess should be distributed amongst the minority Muslim Provinces. In other words, we propose that let us carve out of this 1/3rd as the Mussalmans wish. Take the case of Madras and Bombay—it is not always the only criterion, viz., counting of heads, but the importance of those two provinces. Take the case of the United Provinces again, it is centre of the Mussalman culture and heart and it will be unfair that they should be restricted according to the number of their population in their representation in the Central Legislature. These three Provinces, Sind being separated, will then, so far as the population goes, be in this position, the

United Provinces with the 14 per cent. The method that we want to be adopted is that the excess between 1/3rd and 1/4th should be distributed amongst the other Provinces according to the relative position of their importance to the Mussalmans, and not according to population. I am sure indeed that besides counting of heads, there are other weighty and important considerations, which must not be lost sight of. It is not only a question of getting votes in the Legislature, but it is also essential that various parts of the Provinces which are themselves vast, should be represented, so that, questions affecting the people of their grievances may be ventilated properly and thoroughly on the floor of the Legislature. Very often when proper facts and arguments are placed by one single representative which, when they are convincing, sway the entire legislature. It really comes to this that the Nehru Report makes a gift of the extra seats over and above the population basis to the Punjab and Bengal, whereas, we propose that this extra 7 or 8 per cent seats should be distributed amongst the minority Muslim Provinces.

Our next proposal is that in the event of the adult suffrage not being established, Punjab and Bengal also should have seats reserved on population basis for the Mussalmans. But they should not have the right to contest for more, of course, subject to re-examination of the question at the end of ten years. I am not sure that the establishment of adult suffrage is within the range of practical politics in the near future. You remember, originally the proposal emanated from certain Muslim Leaders in March 1927, known as the Delhi Muslim Proposals. That was dealt with by the All-India Congress Committee in Bombay and in the open session of the Madras Congress and endorsed by them. The Muslim League at its Calcutta Session in December 1927, also confirmed the proposals. I am not going to enter into the pros and cons, but it is an admitted fact that although the Mussalmans in the Punjab and Bengal are numerically in the majority, their voting strength is far below in proportion to their population, and they, therefore, would not secure sufficient representation which will be far below their population. It is now devised to meet this undoubted fact by the Nehru proposals and the Report proposes the substitute of adult franchise and from those premises, it is argued that there is no need for reservation in the Punjab and Bengal, but we wish to provide for the contingency which is most patent and probable that in the event of the adult suffrage not being established, there should be reservation for Mussalmans in the Punjab and Bengal according to their population, but they should not be entitled to additional seats. And we, therefore, attach very great importance to this modification.

Our next proposal is that the form of the constitution should be federal with residuary powers vesting in the Provinces and Clause 13A in the Supplementary Nehru Report is most pernicious and should be deleted and the whole constitution should be revised on the basis of Provincial Governments having the residuary powers vested in them, and subject to that there should be revision of the schedules laying down central and provincial subjects as embodied in the Nehru Report. This question is by far the most important from the constitutional point of view and the future development of India and has very little to do with the communal aspect. If this question is examined carefully, it has much less of communal bearing and far graver of general interest of India and the future constitutional progress of the people of India.

This is hardly a place or an occasion when you would expect me to enter into a debate which might be held between two jurists. We have carefully considered the matter and we have come to the conclusion that a system which will give residuary powers to the Provinces, is the most suited for the Federation of India.

With regard to the question of separation of Sind and the N.W.F. Province, we cannot agree that they should wait until the Nehru Constitution is established with adult suffrage. Do you expect the Mussalmans to oppose the reform being introduced in the N.W.F. Province until the Nehru Constitution is established? I am somewhat amazed that the Committee appointed by the Convention has rejected these proposals on the ground that a resolution was passed at Lucknow which recorded an agreement and signed it and, therefore, they cannot reopen the question. The All-India Muslim League was not a party to any such resolution and was not represented at that meeting. I say with the utmost deference to the Members of the Committee that this is not a valid ground or answer. There are many organizations present here in the Convention today, none of them is bound by any such agreements arrived at between individuals or groups. I venture to say that this Convention is not bound and it is wholly untenable to advance any such reason before this Convention. This Convention is entitled to make any change, or alteration or modification in the proposals now before it, and I ask the Convention whether the separation of Sind and the introduction of reforms in the N.W.F. Province are only to be accepted when the Nehru Constitution with adult suffrage is brought into full effect and operation in this country. Mussalmans feel that it is shelving the issues and postponing their insistent demand till doomsday and cannot agree to it. I, therefore, appeal to the Convention to take all these matters into their careful consideration.

Replying to the debate Mr Jinnah said:
Sir,

The reason why no other delegate from the Muslim League was going to take part in the debate is that we have come to the Convention, which is composed of something like 1,200 delegates not with a purpose of raising controversies which would lead to bad feelings. We have already placed our proposals before the Convention and our grounds for supporting them and on the hypothesis which must be admitted on all hands that communalism exists in this country. We have not come here to apportion blame for it. The offensive remarks or insinuations serve no good purpose and I will not follow the style or the manner of the speech delivered by my friend, Mr Jayakar. Nor will I on this occasion permit myself to deal with specious arguments and pleadings which he has advanced. In short, his position is an ultimatum and with that ultimatum we were made aware from the very start on behalf of the Hindu Mahasabha. If a single word with regard to the communal settlement is changed in the report, they will withdraw their support to it. With regard to the remarks of my friend, Sir Tej Bahadur Sapru, I am afraid some of the speakers have misunderstood them. He called me a spoilt child. I know the spirit in which he meant it and others have put a childish interpretation upon it. But I think, it cannot be denied and I hope that Mr Jayakar and others will agree with me that every country struggling for freedom and desirous of establishing a democratic system of Government has had to face the problem of minorities wherever they existed and no constitution, however idealistic it may be, and, however perfect from theoretical point of view it may seem, will ever receive the support of the minorities, unless they can feel that they, as an entity, are secured under the proposed constitution and government, and whether a constitution will succeed or not must necessarily depend as a matter of acid test whether the minorities are in fact secure. Otherwise no proper constitution will last, but result in a revolution and civil war. I must here point out that it is not correct to say that the Muslim League did not take part at all in the All-Parties Conference. The Council of the League had appointed a Committee in February 1928 and it attended the All-Parties Conference till the 11th of March and the Committee had express instructions not to proceed with the framing of any constitution until the Hindu-Muslim differences were adjusted and agreed upon. It is true that no settlement was reached and as the Committee felt that it was not possible to arrive at any agreement, they ceased to take further part in the All-Parties Conference which is responsible for producing the Nehru Report. I am not here today to express my opinion as to whether a constitution ought to be framed or not, but I would ask Mr Jayakar to consider whether he wants what he calls the greatest common measure of agreement to be still greater or not. We are engaged today in a very serious and solemn transaction. It is not merely for the various organizations to come here and say, we agree to it, and retire. We are here, as I understand, for the purpose of entering into solemn contract and all parties who enter into it will have to work for it and fight for it together. What we want, is that the Hindus and Mussalmans should march together until our object is obtained. Therefore, it is essential that you must get not only the Muslim League but the Mussalmans of India and here I am not speaking as a Mussalman but as an Indian. And it is my desire to see that we get 7 crores of Mussalman to march along with us in the struggle for freedom. Would you be content with a few? Would you be content if I were to say, I am with you? Do you want or do you not want Muslim India to go along with you? You must remember two major communities in India—I say this without the slightest disrespect to other communities like Sikhs, Christians and Parsis—are the Hindus and Mussalmans and naturally, therefore, these two communities have got to be reconciled and united and made to feel that their interests are common and they are marching together for a common goal. I want you, therefore, to rise to that statesmanship which Sir Tej Bahadur Sapru describes, Minorities cannot give anything to the majority. It is, therefore, no use asking me for these modifications because I am a naughty child. If they are small points why not concede? It is up to the majority and the majority alone can give. I am asking you for this adjustment, because I think it is the best and fair to the Mussalmans. Look at the constitutional history of Canada and Egypt. The minorities are always afraid of majorities. The majorities are apt to be tyrannical and oppressive and particularly religious majorities and the minorities, therefore, have a right to be absolutely secured. Was the adjustment between the Copts, Christians and Mussalmans in Egypt regulated by such considerations? We are dealing with politics. We are not in a Court of Law and, therefore, it is no use resorting to hair-spliting and petty squabbles. These are big questions and they can be settled only by the exercise of the highest order of statesmanship and political wisdom. I, therefore, ask you once more to consider this question most carefully before you decide. Please don't think that in anything that I have said, I am threatening any party and I hope that I shall not be misunderstood. If you do not settle this question today, we shall have to settle it tomorrow, but in the meantime our national interests are bound to suffer. We are all sons of this land. We have to live together. We have to work together and whatever our differences may be, let us at any rate not create more bad blood. If we cannot agree, let us at any rate agree to differ, but let us part as friends. I once more repeat. Believe me, there is no progress for India until the Mussalmans and Hindus are united and let no logic, philosophy or squabble stand in the way of our coming to a compromise and nothing will make me more happy than to see the Hindu-Muslim Union.

Appendix III

Draft Resolution (popularly known as Fourteen Points) prepared by M. A. Jinnah representing consensus of opinion between different schools of Muslim political thought.*

The League after anxious and careful consideration, most earnestly and emphatically lays down that no scheme for the future constitution of the government of India will be acceptable to Mussalmans of India until and unless the following basic principles are given effect to and provisions are embodied therein to safeguard their rights and interests.

(1) The form of the future constitution should be federal, with the residuary powers vested in the provinces.

(2) A uniform measure of autonomy shall be granted to all provinces.

(3) All legislatures in the country and other elected bodies shall be constituted on the definite principle of adequate and effective representation of minorities in every Province without reducing the majority in any Province to a minority or even equality.

(4) In the Central Legislature, Mussalman representation shall not be less than one-third.

(5) Representation of communal groups shall continue to be, by means of separate electorates as at present, provided that it shall be open to any community, at any time, to abandon its separate eleectorate in favour of joint electorate.

(6) Any territorial redistribution that might at any time be necessary shall not in any way, affect the Muslim majority in Punjab, Bengal and N.W.F. Province.

**Ibid*, pp. 98-100.

(7) Full religious liberty, i.e. liberty of belief, worship and observance, propaganda, association and education, shall be guaranteed to all communities.

(8) No bill or resolution or any part thereof shall be passed in any legislature or any other elected body if three-fourths of the members of any community in that particular body oppose such a bill, resolution or part thereof, on the ground that it would be injurious to the interests of that community or in the alternative, such other method is devised as may be found feasible and practicable to deal with such cases.

(9) Sind should be separated from the Bombay Presidency.

(10) Reforms should be introduced in the N.W.F. Province and Baluchistan on the same footing as in other provinces.

(11) Provision should be made in the constitution giving Moslems an adequate share along with the other Indians, in all the services of the State and in local self-governing bodies having due regard to the requirements of efficiency.

(12) The Constitution should embody adequate safeguards for the protection of Moslem culture and for the protection and promotion of Moslem education, language, religion, personal laws and Moslem charitable institutions and for their due share in the grants-in-aid given by the State and by local self-governing bodies.

(13) No cabinet, either Central or Provincial, should be formed without there being a proportion of at least one-third Moslem Ministers.

(14) No change shall be made in the constitution by the Central Legislature except with the concurrence of the states constituting the Indian Federation.

The draft resolution also mentioned an alternative to the above provision in the following terms :

That, in the present circumstances, representation of Mussalmans in the different legislatures of the country and other elected bodies through the separate electorates is inevitable and further, the Government being pledged over and over again not to disturb this franchise so granted to the Moslem community since 1909 till such time as the Mussalmans choose to abandon it, the Mussalmans will not consent to joint electorates, unless Sind is actually constituted into a separate province and reforms in fact are introduced in the

N.W.F. Province and Baluchistan on the same footing as in other provinces.

Further, it is provided that there shall be reservation of seats according to the Moslem population in the various provinces; but where Mussalmans are in a majority they shall not contest more seats than their population warrants.

The question of excess representation of Mussalmans over and above their population in provinces where they are in a minority, is to be considered hereafter.

(After the Muslim League Delegation's failure to secure some amendments in the Nehru Committee's draft constitutional scheme at the All-parties Convention at Calcutta, December 1928, the Muslim League session was adjourned to meet again at Delhi. This draft resolution, prepared by Mr. Jinnah, was to be moved at the session reconvened at Delhi in March 1929, but the session had to be adjourned *sine die* owing to disturbances created by a group of Nationalist Muslims.)

Appendix IV

M.A. Jinnah's presidential address at the twenty-fifth session of All-India Muslim League, Lucknow, October, 1937.*

This Session of the All-India Muslim League is one of the most critical that have ever taken place during its existence for more than the last thirty years.

The Policy and Programme that you are called upon to formulate and lay down involves the fate and the future of the Mussalmans of India and the country at large. On April 12, 1936, the Muslim League at its Twenty-fourth Session, for the first time in its history, undertook the policy and programme of mass contact. The League considered the prevailing conditions and surveyed the situation as we had to face the forthcoming elections on the eve of the inauguration of the new Provincial Constitution embodied in the Government of India Act, 1935, and had no alternative but to enter the field and contest the elections to the Provincial Legislatures. It was also felt that there was no alternative but to utilise the provincial Constitution for what it was worth, although it was far from being satisfactory. I may here reproduce the resolution that was passed on April 12, 1936 :

"Whereas the Parliamentary system of Government which is being introduced in this country with the inauguration of the new Constitution presupposes the formation of parties with a well-defined policy and programme which facilitate the education of the electorate, and cooperation between groups with approximate aims and ideals and ensures the working of the Constitution to the best advantage; and, whereas, in order to strengthen the solidarity of the Muslim community and to

**Ibid*, pp, 221-30.

secure for the Muslims their proper and effective share in the Provincial Governments, it is essential that the Muslims should organise themselves as one party, with an advanced and progressive programme, it is hereby resolved that the All-India Muslim League do take steps to contest the approaching Provincial Elections, and for this purpose appoint Mr. Jinnah to form a Central Election Board under his presidentship, consisting of not less than 35 members, with powers to constitute and affiliate Provincial Election Boards in various Provinces, having regard to the conditions of each province and devise ways and means for carrying out the aforesaid objects."

In pursuance of that decision, the Muslim League Central Parliamentary Board was established in June 1936, and also in various provinces Provincial Boards were established to give effect to the resolution and the instructions of the League. It was not without difficulty and it was no small task to be performed, in the absence of any previous preparations or any existing sufficient organisation and machinery. It was a stupendous undertaking to contest elections in all the provinces especially as Mussalmans all over India are numerically in a minority and weak, educationally backward, and economically nowhere. There never had been made any systematic effort for their social and economic uplift, whereas our sister communities have gone far ahead with their organisations and systematic programme supported by a large bulk of people, especially the Hindus, who are not only in a majority but better trained, more disciplined and far better equipped educationally, economically and financially.

But here I may mention that within a short time of about six months work, before the elections were over, the results were very hopeful, and there is no need for us to despair. In each and every provinces where League Parliamentary Board was established and the League Parties were constituted were carried away about 60 and 70 per cent of the seats that were contested by the League candidates, and since the elections (were over), I find that hundreds of District Leagues have been established in almost every province from the fatherest corner of Madras to the North-West Frontier Province. Since April last, the Mussalmans of India have rallied round the League more and more and I feel confident that once they understand

and realise the policy and programme of Muslim League, the entire Mussalman population of India will rally round its platform and under its flag. The Muslim League stands for full national democratic self-government for India. A great deal of capital is made out of phrases more for the consumption of the ignorant and illiterate masses. Various phrases are used such as *Purna Swaraj*, self-government, complete independence, responsible government, substance of independence and dominion status. There are some who talk of complete independence. But it is no use having complete independence on your lips and the Government of India Act, 1935 in your hands! Those who talk of complete independence the most, mean the least what it means. Was the Gandhi-Irwin Pact in consonance with complete independence? Were the assurances that were required before the offices would be accepted and the Provincial Constitution could be worked consistent with *Purna Swaraj*, and was the resolution after assurances were refused accepting offices and working the Provincial Constitution enacted by the British Parliament and forced upon the people of India by the imperialistic power in keeping with the policy and programme and the declarations of the Congress Party? Does wrecking mean working? These paper declarations, slogans and shibboleths are not going to carry us anywhere. What India requires is a complete united front and honesty of purpose and then by whatever name you may call your government is a matter of no consequence so long as it is a government of the people, by the people, for the people.

The preesent leadership of the Congress, especially during the last ten years, has been responsible for alienating the Mussalmans of India more and more by pursuing a policy which is exclusively Hindu, and since they have formed the Governments in six provinces where they are in a majority they have by their words, deeds and programme shown more and more that the Mussalmans cannot expect any justice or fair-play at their hands. Wherever they are in a majority and wherever it suited them, they refused to cooperate with the Muslim League parties and demanded unconditional surrender and signing of their pledges.

The demand was insistent : abjure your party and forswear your policy and programme and liquidate Muslim League;

where they found that they did not a have majority, like the North-West Frontier Province, their sacred principle of collective responsibility disappeared, and promptly the Congress party in that Province was allowed to coalesce with any other group. Any individual Mussalman member who was willing to unconditionally surrender and sign that pledge was offered a job as a minister and was passed off as a Mussalman minister although he did not command the confidence or the respect of an overwhelming majority of the Mussalman representatives in the legislature. These men are allowed to move about and pass off as Muslim ministers for the "loyal" services they have rendered to the Congress, by surrendering and signing the pledge unconditionally and the degree of their reward is the extent of their perfidy. Hindi is to be the national language of all India, and *Bande Matram* is to be the national song, and is to be forced upon all. The Congress flag is to be obeyed and revered by all and sundry. On the very threshold of what little power and responsibility is given, the majority community have clearly shown their hand that Hindustan is for the Hindus; only the Congress masquerades under the name of nationalism, whereas the Hindu Mahasabha does not mince words. The result of the present Congress Party policy will be, I venture to say, class bitterness, communal war and strengthening of the imperialistic hold as a consequence. I dare say that the British Government will give the Congress a free hand in this direction, and it matters very little to them, nay, on the contrary, it is all to the good, so long as their interests, imperial or otherwise, are not touched and the defence remains intact, but I feel that a fearful reaction will set in when the Congress has created more and more divisions amongst Indians themselves, and made a united front impossible.

Here it will not be out of place to state that the responsibility of the British Government is no less in the disastrous consequences which may ensue. It has been clearly demonstrated that the Governors and the Governor-General who have been given the powers and special responsibility to safeguard and protect the minorities under the Constitution which was made so much of by Lord Zetland, the Secretary of State for India, during the controversy of the assurances demanded by the Congress Party, have failed to use them and have thereby been a party to the flagrant breach of the spirit of the Constitution and the instrument of instructions in the matter of appointment of Muslim ministers. On the contrary, they have been a party to passing off men as Muslim ministers by appointing them as such, although they know fully well that they do not command the confidence of the Muslim representatives or the public outside. If, in a matter like this, the Governors have shown their utter helplessness and disregard for their sacred obligations which were assumed by the British Government for the protection of minorities, could they or would they be able to afford protection in hundred and one other matters which may not come up to the surface to be known in the day-to-day working of the Legislatures and the administrative machinery? These are very serious and noteworthy signs of the times. The one wholesome lesson that I ask the Mussalmans to learn, before it is too late, is that the path before the Mussalmans is, therefore, plain. They must realise that the time has come when they should concentrate and devote their energies to self organisation and full development of their power to the exclusion of every other consideration. I have pointed out before that a section of Mussalmans is divided, that there is a group that stands with face turned towards the British. If they have not learnt by now of the bitter consequences they will never learn. God only helps those who help themselves. There is another group which turns towards the Congress and they do so because they have lost faith in themselves. I want the Mussalmans to believe in themselves and take their destiny in their own hands. We want men of faith and resolution, who have courage and determination and who would fight singlehanded for their convictions, although at the moment the whole world may be against them. We must develop power and strength, till the Mussalmans are fully organised and have acquired that power and strength which must come from the solidarity and the unity of people.

No settlement with the majority is possible, as no Hindu leader speaking with any authority shows any concern or genuine desire for it. Honourable settlement can only be achieved between equals, and unless the two parties learn to respect and fear each other there is no solid ground for any settlement. Offers of peace by the weaker party always mean confession of weakness, and invitation to aggression. Appeals to patriotism, justice and fairplay and for the goodwill fall flat. It does not require political wisdom to realize that all safeguards and settlements would be a scrap of paper unless they were backed up by power. Politics mean power and not relying only on cries of justice or fair-play or goodwill. Look at the nations of the world, and look at what is happening every day. See what has happened to Abyssinia, look what is happening to China and Spain, and not to say of the tragedy of Palestine, to which I shall refer later.

The Congress High Command speaks in different voices. One opinion is that there is no such thing as Hindu-Muslim question, and there is no such thing as Minorities' question in the country. The other high opinion is that if a few crumbs are thrown to the Mussalmans in their present disorganised and helpless state, you could manage them. They are sadly mistaken if they think that the Mussalmans can be imposed upon. The All India Muslim League has now come to live, and play its just part in the world of Indian politics, and sooner it is realised and reckoned with, the better it will be for all interests concerned. The third opinion is that there is no light to be seen through the impenetrable darkness, but as the Congress goes on acquiring strength and power, so that past promises of blank-cheques remain unfilled and unsigned.

I want the Mussalmans to ponder over the situation and decide their own fate by having one single, definite, uniform policy which should be loyally followed throughout India. The Congressite Mussalmans are making a great mistake when they preach unconditional surrender. It is the height of a defeatist mentality to throw ourselves on the mercy and goodwill of others, and the highest act of prefidy to the Mussalman community, and if that policy is adopted, let me tell you, the community will seal its doom and will cease to play its rightful part in the national life of the country and the Government. Only one thing can save the Mussalmans and energise them to regain their lost ground. They must first recapture their own souls and stand by their lofty position and principles which form the basis of their great unity and which bind them in one body-politic. Do not be disturbed by the slogans and the taunts such as are used against the

Mussalmans, "communalists", "toadies" and "reactionaries". The worst "toady" on earth, the most wicked "communalist" today amongst Muslims when he surrenders unconditionally to the Congress and abuses his own community becomes the nationalist of nationalists tomorrow! These terms and words and abuses are intended to create an inferiority complex amongst the Mussalmans, and to demoralise them; and are intended to sow discord in our midst and give us a bad name in the world abroad. This is the standard of propaganda which can only be treated with contempt.

The All-India Muslim League certainly and definitely stands to safeguard the rights and interests of the Mussalmans and other minorities effectively. That is its basic and cardinal principle. That is the *Casus Beli.* That is why the Muslim League and those who stand by it have incurred the displeasure of the Congress for what else are we doing which the Congress object to? Congress is doing exactly what we decided two years ago. The League is not going to allow Mussalmans to be exploited either by the British Government or any other party or group inside the legislature or outside. The Congress with all its boasts has done nothing in the past for the Mussalmans. It has failed to inspire confidence and to create a sense of security amongst the Mussalmans and other minorities. The Congress attempt under the guise of establishing mass contact with the Mussalmans is calculated to divide and weaken and break the Mussalmans and is an effort to detach them from their accredited leaders. It is a dangerous move but it cannot mislead any one. All such manoeuvres will not succeed notwithstanding the various blandishments, catchwords and slogans. The only honest and straight-forward course is to give the minorities a fair deal. All the talk of hunger and poverty is intended to lead the people towards socialistic and communistic ideas for which India is far from prepared. The Muslim League, in the present conditions, considers the policy of Direct Action as suicidal and futile. Two such attempts have hitherto failed and have entailed untold misery and suffering to the people, and it had to be wound up after two decades of persistent efforts in the direction, with the result that a more reactionary Constitution is forced upon the people,—and the Congress is working it now!

To ask through a resolution, that the Governor-General convey to the Secretary of State for India to call a Constituent Assembly on the basis of adult franchise is the height of all ignorance. It shows lack of any sense of proportion. A Constituent Assembly can only be called by a sovereign authority and from the seat of power—a special body of men chosen as the representatives with the authority of the sovereign people to frame such a constitution of the government of the country as they may think proper, where function then ceases. The constitution so framed by them would automatically take its place and function as the constitution of the Government of the country. Who is to constitute the electorates on the basis of adult franchise, and how many representatives will be chosen by these electorates constituted on the basis of adult franchise, and what will happen to the minorities in such constituencies, and what will the electorates understand by and how will they make their choice of this special body of men with final authority and power to frame the Constitution of this great sub-continent? Who will direct the machinery to choose the special body of men with representative authority to frame such Constitution as they may think proper? Who will set in motion the machinery? And above all what will happen to the minorities in such a body? Is the Congress really serious that the Secretary of State is going to carry out all these requirements, when, only a few days ago, the representative of the British Government speaking with the highest authority, His Excellency the Viceroy, said that he was full of hope that they might succeed in securing the Federation of India in the near future, that when he came out to Indla he had expressed the hope that scheme of Federation was, on the whole, one calculated to secure, Federation within a reasonable time after the inaguration of provincial autonomy, and that his experience of the last 18 months had confirmed him in that view regarding the establishment of Federation within a reasonable time.

Taking the country as a whole, the Congress is still far from occupying the seat of authoritp; and it is a travesty of realities to think of British Government calling a constituent assembly, and as for the ability of the Congress to do so, that is pure moonshine. Let the Congress first bring all principal communities in the country and all principal classes of interest under its leadership. To ask the foreign Government who is the ruling and sovereign authority in this country to convene such a body before even the communal problem has been solved and before all important communities in India have accepted the leadership of the Congress is like putting the cart before the horse, and to forget that 1/3rd of Indian. India stands on a very special footing, constituting Indian States and Ruling Princes.

Instead of ploughing the sands, let the Congress at least concentrate and see that the All-India Federation scheme embodied in the Government of India Act, 1935, which is more reactionary than even the present central constitution, is not brought into being, for now it is emphatically and confidently asserted by those who speak with authority on behalf of the British Government that it is soon going to be inaugurated. What is the Congress going to do? Do they think that they can single-handed as a party, prevent it? Or will some other formula be evolved, and the Congress quietly accept it as a *fait accompli* as it has done the provincial constitution in spite of all the rantings of some of the foremost leaders of the Congress against it.

To the Mussalmans of India in every province, in every district, in every tehsil, in every town I say: your foremost duty is to formulate a constructive and ameliorative programme of work for the people's welfare and to devise ways and means of social, economic and political uplift of the Mussalmans. We shall not hesitate to cooperate with any party or group in any practical and constructive programme for the welfare and advance of the province or the country. I entreat and implore that every man, woman and child should rally round the common platform and flag of the All-India Muslim League. Enlist yourself by hundreds and thousands as quickly as you can as members of the All-India Muslim League, Provincial Leagues and District Leagues. Organise yourself, establish your solidarity and complete unity. Equip yourself as trained and disciplined soldiers, create the feeling of *esprit de corps*, and of comradeship amongst yourselves. Work loyally, honestly and for the cause of your people and your country. No individual or people can achieve anything without industry, suffering and sacrifice. There are forces which may bully you, tyrannise over you and intimidate you, and you may even have to suffer. But it is by going through this crucible of fire of persecution which may be levelled against you, tyranny that may be exercised, threats and intimidations may un-nerve you, but it is by resisting, by overcoming, by facing these disadvantages, hardships, and suffering and maintaining your true convictions and loyalty that a nation will emerge worthy of its past glory and history and will live to make the future history greater and more glorious not only of India, but in the annals of the world. Eighty millions of Mussalmans in India have nothing to fear. They have their destiny in their hands, and as a well-knit, solid, organized, united force can face any danger, and withstand any opposition to its united front and wishes. There is the magic power in your own hands. Take your vital decisions—they may be grave and momentous and far-reaching in their consequences. Think hundred times before you take any decision, but once a decision is taken, stand by it as one man. Be true and loyal, and I feel confident that success is with you.

Appendix V

Extracts from M. A. Jinnah's Presidential Address at the Twenty-seventh Annual Session of the All-India Muslim League, Lahore, 22-24 March, 1940.*

The problem in India is not of an intercommunal character but manifestly of an international one, and it must be treated as such. So long as this basic and fundamental truth is not realised, any constitution that may be built will result in disaster and will prove destructive and harmful not only to the Mussalmans, but also to the British and Hindus. If the British Government are really in earnest and sincere to secure peace and happiness of the people of this sub-continent, the only course open to us all is to allow the major nations separate homelands by dividing India into "autonomous national states". There is no reason why these states should be antagonistic to each other. On the other hand the rivalry and the natural desire and efforts on the part of one to dominate the social order and establish political supremacy over the other in the government of the country will disappear. It will lead more towards natural goodwill by international pacts between them, and they can live in complete harmony with their neighbours. This will lead further to a friendly settlement all the more easily with regard to minorities by reciprocal arrangements and adjustments between Muslim India and Hindu India, which will far more adequately and effectively safeguard the rights and interests of Muslim and various other communities.

It is extremely difficult to appreciate why our Hindu friends fail to understand the real nature of Islam and Hinduism. They

* *Ibid*, pp. 379-81.

are not religions in the strict sense of the world, but are, in fact, different and distinct social orders and it is a dream that the Hindus and Muslims can ever evolve a common nationality, and this misconception of one Indian nation has gone far beyond the limits and is the cause of more of our troubles and will lead India to destruction if we fail to revise our notions in time. The Hindus and the Muslims belong to two different religious philosophies, social customs, literatures. They neither intermarry, nor interdine together and, indeed, they belong to two different civilisations which are based mainly on conflicting ideas and conceptions. Their aspects on life and of life are different. It is quite clear that Hindus and Mussalmans derive their inspiration from different sources of history. They have different epics, their heroes are different, and they have different episodes. Very often the hero of one is a foe of the other and, likewise their victories and defeats overlap. To yoke together two such nations under a single state, one as a numerical minority and the other as a majority, must lead to growing discontent and final destruction of any fabric that may be so built up for the government of such a state.

History has presented to us many examples such as the Union of Great Britain and Ireland, Czechoslovakia and Poland. History has also shown to us many geographical tracts much smaller than the sub-continent of India, which otherwise might have been called one country but which have been divided into as many states as there are nations inhabiting them. Balkan Peninsula comprises as many as 7 or 8 sovereign states. Likewise, the Portuguese and the Spanish stand divided in the Iberian Peninsula. Whereas under the plea of unity of India and one nation, which does not exist, it is sought to pursue here the line of one central government when we know that the history of the last 12 hundred years has failed to achieve unity and has witnessed, during these ages, India always divided into Hindu India and Muslim India. The present artificial unity of India dates back only to the British conquest and is maintained by the British bayonet, but the termination of the British regime, which is implicit in the recent declaration of His Majesty's Government, will be the herald of the entire break up with worse disaster than have ever taken place during the last one thousand years under the Muslims. Surely that is not the legacy which Britain would bequeath to India after 150 years of her rule, nor would Hindu and Muslim India risk such a sure catastrophe.

Muslim India cannot accept any constitution which must necessarily result in a Hindu majority government. Hindus and Muslims brought together under a democratic system forced upon the minorities can only mean Hindu Raj. Democracy of the kind of which the Congress High Command is enamoured would mean the complete destruction of what is most precious in Islam. We have had ample experience of the working of the provincial constitutions during the last two and a half years and any repetition of such a government must lead to civil war and raising private armies, as recommended by Mr Gandhi to Hindus of Sukkur when he said that they must defend themselves violently or nonviolently, blow for blow, and if they could not they must emigrate.

Mussalmans are not a minority as it is commonly known and understood. One has only got to look round. Even today according to the British map of India, out of 11 provinces 4 provinces, where the Muslims dominate more or less, are functioning notwithstanding the decision of the Hindu Congress High Command to non-cooperate and prepare for civil disobedience. Mussalmans are a nation according to any definition of a nation and they must have their homeland, their territory and their state. We wish to live in peace and harmony with our neighbours as a free and independent people. We wish our people to develop to the fullest our spiritual, cultural, economic, social and political life in a way that we think best, and in consonance with our own ideals and according to the genius of our people. Honesty demands—and the vital interests of millions of our people impose a sacred duty upon us to find—an honourable and peaceful solution, which would be just and fair to all. But at the same time we cannot be moved or diverted from our purpose and objective by threats or intimidations. We must be prepared to face all difficulties and consequences, make all the sacrifices that may be required of us to achieve the goal we have set in front of us.

Appendix VI

True Copy of a circular letter (original in the Hindu Mahasabha Head Office, New Delhi)

16, MONTAGUE ROAD,
CAMBRIDGE,
8th July, 1935

Dear Sir,

May I venture to address this appeal to you on behalf of the people of PAKISTAN at this critical hour, when Parliament is giving final shape to the Government of India Bill, for your valued sympathy and support in our fateful struggle against the ruthless coercion of PAKISTAN into the proposed Indian Federation. The Government of India Bill, based on the Indian Federal Scheme, has created an acute crisis in the national life of PAKISTAN, and has raised a supreme issue—an issue of life or death—for its national future.

Deeply interested as you are in the just and equitable solution of the INDO-PAKISTAN problem, raised by the Government of India Bill, I earnestly hope that you kindly will lend your fullest support to the inexorable demand of PAKISTAN—a demand based on justice and equity—for the recognition of its sacred right to a separate national existence as distinct from HINDOOSTAN.

It is, therefore, most essential for me to restate before you, as before the People and Parliament of Great Britain, the fundamental importance of the INDO-PAKISTAN problem,

Source : C. Rahmat Ali to [name of the person not given], 8 July 1935 enclosed in M. R. Jayakar Papers, File No. 752/1941-45.

and the vital difference between the two nations living in PAKISTAN and HINDOOSTAN the two countries which comprise the British Indian Empire. Unless the basic distinction is fully realised and firmly grasped, the full appreciation of our demand for a Federal Constitution for PAKISTAN, as separate from HINDOOSTAN, on social, cultural, religious, and historical grounds, is impossible.

PAKISTAN is not Hindoo soil, nor are its people Hindoostani citizens. It has always possessed a historical spiritual, territorial, and national individuality of its own. It has been our national home from the very dawn of history as it has remained the stronghold of our civilisation from very early ages. It was the cradle of our past, as it is the hope of our future. While Hindustanis claim HINDOOSTAN as their mother country by birth, we claim PAKISTAN as our fatherland by the same right. If HINDOOSTAN is theirs because they form three-fourths of its inhabitants, PAKISTAN is ours because we constitute four-fifths of its total population.

We, the Pakistanians, have lived, from time immemorial, our own life, and sought our national salvation along our own lines. PAKISTAN has retained, during the whole of its existence, its own laws, and has cherished its own religious, spiritual, and cultural ideals which are basically different from those of HINDOOSTAN. We have, as a nation, nothing in common with them; nor they with us. In individual habits as in national life, we differ from them as fundamentally as from any other civilised nation in the world. The very basis and content of our national life is founded on fundaments essentially different from those on which Hindooism lives and prospers. Our age-long social system and our ancient national tradition have given us a civilisation with a philosophy, a culture, a language, a literature and an art basically and fundamentally different from that of Hindoostan. That is not all. "We do not interdine: we do not intermarry. Our national customs and calendars, even our diet and dress are different." There is no dispute about these hard facts. They remain to-day, as they have ever been, unchangeable realities. This supreme distinction between PAKISTAN and HINDOOSTAN is ineffacable, as it is based on eternal truths.

Our constitution-makers must reckon with Nature's decrees. It is, therefore, most important that we should call attention —reiterated attention—to this vital distinction—the attention of the British people and Parliament, the attention of HINDOOSTAN as well as the attention of the whole world.

The Joint Select Committee on Indian Constitutional Reform, on the very first page of its Report (Session 1933-35; Vol. I, Part I), confirms our irrefutable contention in the following words :

> "India is inhabited by many races . . . often as distinct from one another in origin, tradition and manner of life as are the nations of Europe. Two-thirds of its inhabitants profess Hindooism in one form or another as their religion; over seventy-seven millions are followers of Islam; and the difference between the two is not only one of religion in the stricter sense, but also of law and culture. They may be said indeed to represent two distinct and separate civilisations. Hindooism is distinguished by the phenomenon of caste which is the basis of its religious and social system, and save in a very restricted field remains unaffected by contact with philosophies of the West; the religion of Islam, on the other hand, is based upon the conception of the equality of man."

Not only that. Geographically also, the lands comprising PAKISTAN form a separate and distinct unit. That nature herself decreed that PAKISTAN should remain a separate entity, and that the Jumna should flow as a boundary river between PAKISTAN and HINDOOSTAN, is revealed by the fact that it is connected with HINDOOSTAN only by the narrow strip of land which comprises the historic plain of Panipat.

This great cleavage, which distinguishes PAKISTAN from HINDOOSTAN, is the most natural and, therefore, the most permanent and most eternal. It has existed from time immemorial and shall exist for ever. It represents our body and soul, as it stamps our separate national entity, and gives us an unchallengeable right to demand its recognition. It constitutes our ancient heritage—of Fatherland—and we are firmly resolved to preserve it.

The PAKISTAN NATIONAL MOVEMENT stands, on these eternal truths, for the right of PAKISTAN for equal status and identical position with HINDOOSTAN in the British Commonwealth of Nations. We demand the creation of a PAKISTAN FEDERATION, as our full national development would become utterly impossible after amalgamation with HINDOOSTAN as aimed at by the proposed Indian Federal Constitution. We ask for nothing more than the elementary right of national status—a right claimed by, and conceded to, HINDOOSTAN herself. We, the Pakistanians, have emphatically repudiated, more than once, the most shameful surrender of our national future made by the State-nominated Muslim delegates to the Round Table Conference in agreeing to the Indian Federal Scheme. They were neither the delegates of PAKISTAN, nor the representatives of the Pakistanian people. They had neither mandate nor authority from the nation to accept the proposed Federal Constitution. These distinguished exponents of the art of surrender, in complete disregard of the warnings of history, sold our nationality and sacrificed our posterity. They shall have to answer for this—the most contemptible betrayal of Pakistan—before History.

I hope, it is clear that in demanding the creation of a PAKISTAN Federation, we are not, in any way, moved by a feeling of hostility towards either the British or the Hindoostanis. The demand springs from the motives of self-defence and self-preservation alone. We, the Pakistanians, are neither anti-British nor anti-Hindoostani, but we are, and will ever remain, pro-Pakistani. We are neither opposed to nor to an understanding with Hindoostan. We are opposed to the glaring iniquity and gross injustice done to our Fatherland by means of the proposed Indian Federal Scheme. Our acceptance of Hindoostani nationality and amalgamation with Hindoostan is not only impossible, but unthinkable, and from the highest interests of humanity, undesirable. We are, therefore, unflinchingly determined to protect the purity of Pakistanian principle, practice and philosophy; and we are content, and will ever be content, to remain Pakistani. We have, therefore, a moral and legal duty to oppose, by all constitutional means, the proposed Indian Federal Scheme, which is fatal for our future national being and well-being.

It is a tragedy of the first magnitude that the framers of the Government of India Bill, whilst realising the eternal differences between the two nations, failed to lay before Parliament the one and only just and equitable solution of the INDO-PAKISTANIAN problem by the grant of separate constitutions for the nations living in PAKISTAN and HINDOOSTAN. The INDO-PAKISTANIAN problem is not an inter-communal issue, and will never be solved on inter-communal lines. It is an inter-national problem and, therefore, will submit itself to a permanent solution on that basis alone. Any constitution—Federal or Unitary—which disregards this vital fact, while destructive for the Pakistanians, cannot but be disadvantageous to the British and Hindoostanis as well.

It is my solemn duty, as founder of the PAKISTAN NATIONAL MOVEMENT, to submit that for us, the Pakistanians, it is impossible to blink at the gravity of the situation created by the proposed Federal Constitution. There can be for us no sense of security unless the right of PAKISTAN to a separate constitution, as distinct from HINDOOSTAN is recognised. While BURMA is being separated from HINDOOSTAN with a distinct national status, it remains a mystery to us why PAKISTAN, in utter disregard of the fervent appeals of its people, is to be forced into the Indian Federation.

This denial of justice to the national demand of PAKISTAN has caused bitter disappointment and sent a current of discontent from one end of the country to the other. It has stirred the social conscience to its very depths and roused the nation to the sense of utter wrong and irreparable injustice done to it by forcing it into a position of permanent serfdom and perpetual slavery. There is a deep and passionate resentment in the country at the proposed dismemberment of its separate national existence; and we, the Pakistanians, fully realise that to accept the proposed Indian Federal Constitution will be for us the permanent surrender of our national life, and an unqualified renunciation of our national future.

If the supporters of the Government of India Bill think

that with the passage of the legislation we shall submit to it, they are mistaken. They can pass legislation, but they cannot command Pakistanian co-operation to work it. They cannot impose a constitution unless they also impose justice. The proposed Federal Constitution denies sacred justice to Pakistan and therefore, will never satisfy the soul of the nation, and will never secure its sentiment and sympathy for the Government of India Bill.

So far as the PAKISTAN NATIONAL MOVEMENT is concerned, we will never look upon the Federal Act as a permanent solution of the INDO-PAKISTAN problem, nor can we ever induce ourselves to play the suicidal part allotted to us under Indian Federal Scheme. We cannot give up what we have inherited from our forefathers; nor can we surrender what has been bequeathed to us by our heroes and martyrs. We can sacrifice all but we cannot commit an act of self-strangulation by joining the Indian Federation to please the British, or to satisfy the Hindoos. That fate of serfdom, and that future of servitude—PAKISTAN as a mere administrative district subordinated to the authority of HINDOOSTAN, we will never accept. We have a sacred duty to maintain our national entity and keep our territorial integrity intact, and, with a complete fixity of purpose, we are determined to discharge that duty.

It is no exaggeration to say that this cataclysm threatens to involve our very existence and our most precious spiritual treasures. It has, therefore, forced upon us the fateful struggle for the life and honour of PAKISTAN. We have the fullest faith in the justice of our national demand, and an unshakable belief in the destiny of our Fatherland. We will, therefore, enter upon this grim struggle with a clear conscience and clean hands and continue it, with all the Constitutional weapons at our disposal, until justice is meted out to PAKISTAN and the wanton wrong done to its people is righted. The struggle may be long and trying, it may entail suffering and sacrifice: but no trial can be too severe, and no sacrifice too great in this noble cause. We are sure that in our fight for the eternal truths of Faith and Fatherland, our God will help us and the inspiring example of our heroes will sustain us.

Yours truly,
C. RAHMAT ALI
(President, Pakistan National Movement)

Bibliography

A. Private Papers

1. India Office Library

(a) Templewood Collection, MSS. EUR. E240
(b) Linlithgow Collection, MSS. EUR. F125
(c) Zetland Collection, MSS. EUR. E609
(d) Hailey Collection, MSS. EUR. E220
(e) Brabourne Collection, MSS. EUR. F97
(f) Reading Collection, MSS. EUR. E238
(g) Halifax Collection. MSS. EUR. C152
(h) A. P. Hume Collection, MSS. EUR. D724

2, Jamia Millia Library

Muhammad Ali Papers

3. Nehru Memorial Museum and Library

(a) Motilal Nehru Papers
(b) Jawaharlal Nehru Papers
(c) Purshotamdas Thakurdas Papers
(d) M. A. Ansari Papers (microfilm copy)
(e) Tej Bahadur Sapru Papers (microfilm copy)
(f) Hindu Mahasabha Papers
(g) Diaries of B. R. Moonje
(h) Syed Mahmud Papers
(i) S. A. Brelvi Papers

(j) Nawab of Chhatari Papers
(k) A. M. Khwaja Papers
(l) M. C. Chagla Papers
(m) M. S. Aney Papers
(n) Oral History Transcripts of Sri Prakasa and K.M. Munshi

4. National Archives of India, New Delhi

(a) Rajendra Prasad Papers
(b) M. R. Jayakar Papers

5. Gandhi Smarak Nidhi, New Delhi

Gandhi Collection, Correspondence

B. Other Unpublished Sources

(a) The Official Records of the Government of India, deposited at the National Archives of India esp. Foreign and Political Department (F and P.D.) files and Home Dept., Political Branch Proceedings., 1928-40.
(b) Private Office Records files available at India Office Library in London, 1928-40.
(c) The All India Congress Committee files available at Nehru Memorial Museum and Library.
(d) Political and Secret Department (L/P&S) files available at India Office Library.
(e) Public and Judicial Department (L/P&J) files, Governor's Reports 1936-40, available at India Office Library.

C. Official Records

(a) Act of Parliament.
The Government of India Act, 2 August 1935.
(b) Parliamentary Debates, 1935-40.
(c) Minutes and Debates of the Legislative Council of India and its successors, 1928-1940.

D. Parliamentary Papers

Cmd. 3978 (1931). Proceedings of the Indian Round Table Conference, First Session, 12 November 1930-19 January 1931.

Cmd. 3997 (1932). Proceedings of the Indian Round Table Conference, Second Session, 7 September 1931-1 December 1931.

Indian Round Table Conference, Second Session: Proceedings of the Federal Structure Committee and Minorities Committee, 1932 (H.M.S.O., 1932), 3 vols.

Cmd. 4147 (1932). East India (Constitutional Reforms): Communal Decision.

Cmd. 4238 (1933). Reports and Proceedings of the Indian Round Table Conference, Third Session, 17 November 1932-24 December 1932.

Joint Committee on Indian Constitutional Reform Session (1932-33): Report with Minutes of Evidence and Records, 6 vols, (H.M.S.O., 1933-34).

Return showing the Results of the Election in India, 1937 (1937).

Cmd. 6121 (1939). India and the War: Announcement Published by the Governor-General of India on 17 October 1939 with Appendices.

Cmd. 6129 (1939). India and the War: Announcement Published by the Governor-General of India on 6 November 1939, and correspondence connected therewith.

Cmd. 6196 (1939-40). India and the War: Communique issued by the Governor-General and Resolution by the Indian National Congress, the All-India Moslem League and the Chamber of Princes.

Cmd. 6219 (1939-40). India and the War. Statement by the Governor-General, 8 August 1940.

Cmd. 6235 (1940). India and the War: Statement by the Governor-General, 20 November 1940.

2. Indian National Congress Proceedings, Reports, etc.

Indian National Congress Publications. Reports (Annual), 1928-1940.

Resolutions of the Indian National Congress, 1928-40.
Twenty-seven Months of Service; Being a Brief Account of What the Congress Ministries did from July 1937-October 1939 (Bombay, 1939).
The War Crisis; Statement issued by the Congress Working Committee at Wardha on September 14, 1939, in regard to the war crisis and India (Allahabad, 1939).
Congress and the War Crisis (Allahabad, 1940).

3. All-India Muslim League Publications

The Constitution and Rules of the All-India Muslim League (Delhi)
List of the Members of the Council of the All-India League (Delhi).
Resolutions of the All-India Muslim League, May 1928-December 1940. Compiled by Liaquat Ali Khan. 6 vols. (Delhi, n.d.).
Presidential Address of Dr. Sir Muhammad Iqbal delivered at the Allahabad Session of the All-India Muslim League, December 1930.
Presidential Addresses of Qaid-e-Azam M. A. Jinnah delivered at the session of the All-India Muslim League [1937-40] (Delhi, 1946).
Re. Hindu-Muslim Settlement: Correspondence between Gandhi and Jinnah, Pundit Nehru and Jinnah and between S. Bose and Jinnah (Delhi, 1938).
Report of the Enquiry Committee appointed by the Council of the All-India Muslim League to enquire into Muslim Grievances in Congress Provinces, 15 November 1938 (Pirpur Report) (Delhi, 1938).
All-India Muslim League (Bihar Province) Publicity Committee: Report . . . on some Grievances of the Muslims 1938-39. President S. M. Shareef (Shareef Report). 2 vols. (Patna, 1940).
Report of the Committee appointed by the Council of the All-India Muslim League to examine the Wardha Scheme, (Lucknow, n.d.).
The War! Problem of India's Future Constitution: What

Muslim India and its leader Mr M.A. Jinnah think (Delhi, 1940).

4. All-Parties Conference Publications

Report of the Committee appointed by the Conference to determine the Principles of the Constitution for India (Nehru Report) (Allahabad, 1928).
Proceedings of the All-Parties Convention, 22 December 1928-1 January 1929 (Allahabad, 1929).

E. Newspapers and Journals

1. In Britain

The Times (*London*)
The Daily Telegraph and Morning Post (*London*)
The Guardian (*Manchester*)
The Daily Mail (*London*)
The New Statesman and Nation (*London*)

2. In India (English language only)

Amrita Bazar Patrika (*Calcutta*)
Civil and Military Gazette (*Lahore*)
Harijan (*Ahmedabad*)
The Hindustan Times (*Delhi*)
The Leader (*Allahabad*)
The Modern Review (*Calcutta*)
The Pioneer (*Allahabad*)
The Times of India (*Bombay*)
The Tribune (*Lahore*)
Young India (*Ahmedabad*)

F. Other Contemporary Materials

1. The Indian Annual Register

An annual digest of public affairs in India 1919-40, ed. by N. N. Mitra (Calcutta).

2. Section of Documents

Banerjee, A.C., ed., *Indian Constitutional Documents, 1917-39*, Vol. III (Calcutta, 1949).

Gwyer, M. & Appadorai, A. eds., *Speeches and Documents on the Indian Constitution, 1921-47*, 2 vols. (London, 1957).

Philips, C.H., ed., *The Evolution of India and Pakistan, 1858-1947* (London, 1962).

3. Collected Writings—Correspondence and Speeches

Afzal, M. R., ed., *Selected Speechcs and Statements of the Qaid-e-Azam Mohammad Ali Jinnah* (1911-34 and 1947-48) (Lahore, 1966).

Ahmad, Jamil-ud-din, ed., *Some Recent Speeches and Writings of Mr Jinnah*, Vol I (Lahore, 1948; 6th edn., 1960); Vol. II (Lahore, 1947; 6th edn., 1964).

Bose, S. C., *Crossroads: Being Works, 1938-40*, comp. by the Netaji Research Bureau, Calcutta.

Bright, J. S., ed., *Important Speeches of Jawaharlal Nehru . . . , 1922-46*, 2nd edn. (Lahore, n.d.).

Gandhi, M. K., *Collected Works of Mahatma Gandhi*, Vols. 1-50 (Government of India, New Delhi).

———*Letters to Sardar Patel* (Ahmedabad, 1957).

Iqbal, A., ed., *Selected Writings and Speeches of Maulana Mohamed Ali* (Lahore, 1936).

Iqbal, M., *Letters of Iqbal to Jinnah . . . Conveying his Views on the Political Future of Muslim India* (Lahore, 1943).

Jinnah, M. A., *Writings*, 2 vols. (Ahmedabad, 1947).

Jung, N. Y., ed., *The Pakistan Issue, being the correspondence between Sayyid Abdul Latif and M.A. Jinnah on the one hand and between him and Maulana Abul Kalam Azad, Rajendra Prasad and Jawaharlal Nehru on the other and connected papers on . . . Pakistan* (Lahore, 1943).

Linlithgow, Marquess of, *Speeches and Statements, 1936-43* (New Delhi, 1945).

Mohamed Ali Jinnah: Ambassador of Unity: His Speeches and Writings 1912-17. With a Biographical Appreciation by Sarojini Naidu (Madras, n.d.).
Nehru, J., *Recent Essays and Writings on the Future of Indian Communism. Labour and other Subjects* (Allahabad, 1937).
——*Selected Works of Nehru,* Vols. 1-8. edited by S. Gopal. (New Delhi)
The Unity of India, Collected Writings 1937-40 (London, 1941).
——*Nehru-Jinnah Correspondence, including Gandhi-Jinnah and Nehru-Nawab Ismail Correspondence* (Allahabad, 1938).
——*A Bunch of Old Letters* (Bombay, 1958).
Norman, Dorothy, *Nehru : The First Sixty Years* [A Selection of Nehru's Political Writings], 2 vols. (London, 1965).
Panikkar, K.M., and Pershad, A., eds., *The Voice of Freedom: Selected Speeches of Pandit Motilal Nehru* (Bombay, 1971).
Pirzada, S. S., ed., *Leaders' Correspondence with Mr Jinnah* (Bombay, 1944).
Qaid-e-Azam Jinnah's Correspondence (Karachi, 1966).
'Shamloo', ed., *Speeches and Statements of Iqbal,* 2nd edn. (Lahore, 1948).
Singh, Durlab, *A Complete Record of Unity Talks* (Lahore, 1945)
Willingdon, Lord, *Speeches* (Simla, 1935-37).

G. Memoirs and Autobiographies

Aga Khan, *The Memoirs* (London, 1954).
Ali, Chaudhuri Muhammad, *The Emergence of Pakistan* (New York, 1967).
Azad, A. K., *India Wins Freedom* (Bombay, 1959).
Birla, G. D., *In the Shadow of the Mahatma: A Personal Memoir* (Bombay, 1953).
Chaudhury, Nirad C., *An Autobiography of an Unknown Indian* (London, 1951).
Ispahani, M.A.H., *Qaid-e-Azam Jinnah As I Knew Him* (Karachi, 1966).

Jayakar, M. R., *The Story of My Life*, 2 vols. (Bombay, 1958-59).

Khaliquzzaman, C., *Pathway to Pakistan* (Lahore, 1961).

Nehru, J., *An Autobiography* (London, 1936).

Reed, S., *The India I Knew, 1897-1947* (London 1952).

Sayeed, K. B., *Pakistan: The Formative Phase*, 2nd edn. (Lahore, 1968).

Sinha, S., *Indian Independence in Perspective* (London, 1964).

Stephens, I., *Pakistan* (London, 1963).

William, L. F. Rushbrook, *The State of Pakistan*, rev. edn. (London, 1966).

H. Contemporary Books and Pamphlets

Adhikari, G. M., *Pakistan and Indian National Unity* (London, 1943).

———, *Pakistan and National Unity: The Communist Solution*, 2nd edn. (1944).

Ahmad, Jamil-ud-din, *Muslim India and Its Goal* (Aligarh, 1941).

———, *Some Aspects of Pakistan* (Lahore, 1947).

Ahmad, K. S. *The Communal Pattern of India* (Lahore, 1947).

Ahmad, Sir A., *The Indian Minorities Problem* (1952).

Aiyangar, N. R., *The Government of India Act 1935* (Madras, 1937).

Ambedkar, B. R., *Thoughts on Pakistan* (Bombay, 1944).

———, *Ranade, Gandhi and Jinnah* (Bombay, 1943).

———, *Pakistan or the Partition of India*, 3rd edn. (Bombay, 1946).

Bapat, N. S., *Nationalism versus Communalism* (An Essay on Hindu-Muslim Unity), 3rd edn. (Poona, 1943).

Bose, S. C., *The Indian Struggle* (London, 1935).

Chaudhuri, B. M., *Muslim Politics in India* (Calcutta, 1946).

Confederacy of India by 'A Punjabi' (Lahore, 1939).

Fazl-ul-Huq, A.K., *Muslim Sufferings Under Congress Rule* (Calcutta, 1939).

Jinnah, M. A., "Two Nations in India", *Time and Tide*, Vol. XXI, 1940, p. 10.

Graham, G. F. I., *The Life and Work of Syed Ahmed Khan* (Edinburgh, 1885).

India's Problem of her Future Constitution. All India Muslim League's Lahore Resolution, popularly known as 'Pakistan' Resolution; an unbiased scientific and analytical study, being a collection of essays by various authors. Preface by M. A. Jinnah (Bombay, 1948).

Kabir, H., *Muslim Politics 1906-1942* (Calcutta, 1943).

Kanji, Dwarkadas, *India's Fight for Freedom* (Bombay, 1966).

Kaushik, B. G., *The House that Jinnah Built* (Bombay, 1944).

Khan, A. M., *The Communalism in India: Its Origin and Growth* (Lahore, 1944).

Kheiri, M. A. S., *National States and National Minorities* (Lahore, 1947).

Krishna, J. B., *The Problem of Minorities* (London, 1939).

Manshardt, C., *The Hindu-Muslim Problem of India* (London, 1936).

Maudoodi, A. A., *Nationalism and India*, 2nd edn. (Pathankot, 1947).

Mehta, A. and Patwardhan, A., *The Communal Triangle in India* (Allahabad, 1942).

Moon, P., *Strangers in India* (New York, 1945).

Nehru, J., "The Solidarity of Islam", *Modern Review*, November 1935.

———, "His Highness the Aga Khan", *Modern Review*, November 1935.

———, "The Orthodox of All Regions Unite", *Modern Review*, December 1935.

———, *Eighteen Months in India, 1936-37* (Allahabad, 1938).

Noman, M., *Muslim India: Rise and Growth of the All-India Muslim League* (Allahabad, 1949).

'Pakistan' in Encyclopaedia of Islam (Leiden, 1937).

Prasad, R., *India Divided* (Bombay, 1947).

Rajput, A. B., *Muslim League, Yesterday and Today* (Lahore, 1946).

Rahmat Ali, C., *Pakistan, the Fatherland of the Pak Nation*, 3rd edn. (Cambridge, 1947).

Russell, W. W., *Indian Summer* (Bombay, 1961).

Smith, W. C., *Modern Islam in India: A Social Analysis* (London, 1946).

Suleri, Z. A., *My Leader*, 3rd edn. (Lahore, 1946).

Zetland, 2nd Marquess of "*Essayez*" (London, 1956).

I Other Books and Pamphlets

Agarwalla, N., *The Hindu-Muslim Question* (Calcutta, 1951).
Ahmad, A., *Islamic Modernism in India and Pakistan 1857-64* (London, 1967).
Ahmad, Jamil-ud-din, *Final Phase of Struggle for Pakistan* (Karachi, 1964).
Ahmed, Abdulla, *The Historical Background of Pakistan and its People* (Karachi, 1973)
Ashe, G., *Gandhi: A Study in Revolution* (London, 1968).
Aziz, K. K., *Britain and Muslim India, 1857-1947* (London, 1963).
———, *The Making of Pakistan: A Study in Nationalism* (London, 1967).
———, *All India Muslim Conferences 1928-1935: A Documentary Record* (Karachi, 1972).
Bahadur, L., *The Muslim League, Its History, Activities and Achievements* (Agra, 1954).
Baig, M. R. A., *The Muslim Dilemma in India* (Delhi, 1974).
Bamford, P. C., *Histories of the Non-Cooperation and Khilafat Movements* (Delhi, 1974) First Published 1925.
Basu, Aparna, *Growth of Education and Political Development in India, 1898-1920* (Delhi, 1974).
Bolitho, H., *Jinnah: Creator of Pakistan* (London, 1937).
Brass, Paul R., "Muslim Separation in U. P.: Social Context and Political Strategy before Partition", *Economic and Political Weekly*, Vol. 5, Jan-May 1970.
Broomfield, J. H., *Elite Conflict in a Plural Society: Twentieth Century Bengal* (Berkeley, 1968).
Callard, K., *Pakistan: Political Study* (London, 1951).
Davis, K., "India and Pakistan : The Demography of Partition", *Pacific Affairs*, Vol. XXIII, September 1949.
Dalwai, Hamid, *Muslim Politics in India* (Bombay, 1968).
Dixit Prabha, *Communalism in India: A Struggle for Power* (Delhi, 1974).
Faruqi, Z. H., *The Deoband School and the Demand for Pakistan* (Bombay, 1963).

Gallagher, John, *et. el.*, ed., *Locality, Province and Nation: Essays on Indian Politics* (London, 1973).

Gopal Krishna, "Religion in Politics", *Indian Economic and Social History Review*, Vol. 8, 1971, pp. 392-94.

Gopal, R., *Indian Muslims: A Political History* (Bombay, 1959).

Gopal, S., *The Viceroyalty of Lord Irwin, 1926-31* (Oxford, 1957).

———, *Jawaharlal Nehru, A Biography Vol. 1, 1889-1947* (New Delhi, 1976).

Griffiths, P. J., *The British Impact on India*, 2nd edn. (London, 1965).

Ghurye, G. S., *Social Tensions in India* (Bombay, 1968).

Gupta, D. C., *Indian National Movement* (Delhi, 1970).

Gurmukh Nihal Singh, *Landmarks in Indian Constitutional and National Development* (Delhi, 1963).

Hamid, A. A., *A Brief Survey of Muslim Separatism in India* (New Delhi, 1968).

Hardy, Peter, *The Muslims of British India* (London, 1972).

———, *Partners in Freedom and True Muslims : The Political Thought of Some Muslim Scholars in British India* (Sweden, 1971).

Haq, M., *Muslims in India* (Delhi, 1964).

Hodson, H. V., *The Great Divide: Britain, India, Pakistan* (London, 1969).

Humayun Kabir, *Muslim Politics 1906-1947* (Calcutta, 1969).

Humaira Momen, *Muslim Politics in Bengal: A Study of Krishak Praja Party and the Elections of 1937* (Dacca, 1972).

Hunter, W. W., *The Indian Musalmans: Are They Bound in Conscience to Rebel Against the Queen?* (Lahore, 1968). Reprint of 1871 ed.

Husain, S. A., *The Destiny of Indian Muslims* (Bombay, 1965).

Ikram, S. M., *Modern Muslim India and the Birth of Pakistan* (Lahore, 1965).

India and Contemporary Islam: Proceedings of Seminar, ed. by S. T. Lokhandwalla, (Simla, Indian Institute of Advance Study, 1971).

Ishwari Prasad and Subedar, S. K., *Hindu-Muslim Problem* (Allahabad, 1974).

Islam, M. Nurul, *Bengali Muslim Public Opinion as Reflected in the Bengali Press, 1901-1930*. (Dacca, 1973).

Jain, A. P., *Rafi Ahmad Kidwai: A Memoir of His Life and Times* (Bombay, 1965).

Jain, M. S., *The Aligarh Movement: Its Origin and Development* (Agra, 1965).

Jones, K. W., "Communalism in the Punjab: The Arya Samaj Contribution", *Journal of Asian Studies*, Vol. 27, November 1968.

Karandikar, M, A., *Islam in India's Transition to Modernity* (Bombay, 1968).

Karunakaran, K, P., *Religion and Political Awakening in India* (Meerut, 1965).

Khan, M. R., *What Price Freedom: A Historical Survey of the Political Trends and Conditions Leading to Independence and the Birth of Pakistan and After* (Madras, 1969).

Khosla, G. D., *Stern Reckoning : A Survey of the Events Leading upto and Following the Partition of India* (New Delhi, 1949).

Lajpat Rai, *Writings and Speeches,* ed. by V. C. Joshi (Delhi, 1966).

Majumdar, A. K., *Advent of Independence* (Bombay, 1963).

Majumdar, R. C., *History of the Freedom Movement* (Calcutta, 1962 *et seq*).

Majumdar, S. K., *Jinnah and Gandhi: Their Role in India's Quest for Freedom* (Calcutta, 1966).

Malik, H., *Moslem Nationalism in India and Pakistan* (Washington, D. C., 1963).

Matiur Rahman, *From Consultation to Confrontation: A Study of Muslim League in British Indian Politics, 1906-12* (London, 1970).

Menon, V. P., *The Transfer of Power in India* (London, 1957).

Mohammad Ghouse, *Secularism, Society and Law in India* (Delhi, 1973).

Mohibbul Hasan, "Mahatma Gandhi and the Indian Muslims." In Seminar on *Gandhi; Theory and Practice: Social Impact and Contemporary Relevance* (Simla, 1968).

Moin Shakir, *Khilafat to Partition : A Survey of Major Political Trends Among Indian Muslims During 1919-1947* (New Delhi, 1970).

Moon, Penderel, *Divide and Quit* (London, 1961).

Mosley, L., *The Last Days of the British Raj* (London, 1961).
Mujeeb, M., *The Indian Muslims* (London, 1967).
Mushir U. Haq, *Muslim Politics in Modern India, 1857-1947* (Meerut, 1970).
Nanda, B. R., *Mahatma Gandhi* (London, 1958).
———, *The Nehrus, Motilal and Jawaharlal* (London, 1962).
Niemeijer, A. C., *The Khilafat Movement in India, 1919-1924* (The Hague, 1972).
Owen, Hugh, F, "Negotiating the Lucknow Pact", *Journal of Asian Studies*, Vol. XXXI No. 3. May 1972.
Philips, C. H., *The Partition of India, 1947* (Leeds, 1967).
Philips, C. H. and Wainwright, M. D., eds., *The Partition of India: Policies and Perspectives, 1935-1947* (London, 1970).
Pirzada, S.S., *Evolution of Pakistan* (Lahore, 1963).
———, ed., *Foundations of Pakistan: All India Muslim League Documents, 1906-24*, Vol. 1, 1924-47, Vol. II (Karachi, 1969).
Pyarelal, *Mahatma Gandhi: The Last Phase* (Ahmedabad, 1956-58), 2 vols.
Qureshi, I. H., *The Struggle for Pakistan* (Karachi, 1965).
———, *Ulema in Politics: A study relating to the Political Activities of the Ulema in the South Asian Subcontinent 1556-1947* (Karachi, 1972).
———, *The Muslim Community of the Indo-Pakistan Subcontinent* (S-Gravenhage, 1962).
Qureshi, Saleem M. M., *Jinnah and the Making of a Nation* (Karachi, 1969).
Ray, Niharranjan, *Nationalism in India: An Historical Analysis of its Stresses and Strains* (Aligarh, 1973).
Robinson, Francis, *Separatism Among Indian Muslims: The Politics of the United Provinces Muslims, 1860-1923* (New Delhi, 1975)
Saiyid, M. H., *Mohammad Ali Jinnah* (A Political Biography) (Lahore, 1953).
Sayeed, K. B., *Pakistan: The Formative Phase*, 2nd edn. (London, 1969).
Seal Anil, *The Emergence of Indian Nationalism: Competition and Collaboration in the late Nineteenth Century* (London, 1968).

Shah, A. B., Gandhi and Hindu-Muslim Question, *Quest*, No. 64, January-March 1970.

———, "Gandhi, Communalism and National Unity". In Seminar on *Gandhi; Theory and Practice: Social Impact and Contemporary Relevance* (Simla, 1969).

Shan Mohammad, ed., *Writings and Speeches of Syed Ahmad Khan* (Bombay, 1974).

Shelat, J. M., *Secularism : Principles and Application* (Bombay, 1972).

Smith, D. E., *India as a Secular State* (Princeton, 1963).

Stephens, I., *Pakistan* (London, 1963).

Symonds, R., *The Making of Pakistan* (London, 1950).

Tendulkar, D. G., *Mahatma: Life of Mohandas Karamchand Gandhi*, 8 vols. (Bombay, 1951-54).

Tinker, H., *Experiment with Freedom: India and Pakistan 1947* (London, 1967).

Tyabji, H. B., *Badruddin Tyabji: A Biography* (Bombay, 1952).

Waheed Khan, A., *India Wins Freedom: The Other Side* (Karachi, 1961).

Waheed-uz-Zaman, *Towards Pakistan* (Lahore, 1964).

Wasti, Syed Razi, *Lord Minto and Indian Nationalist Movement, 1905 to 1910* (London, 1964).

Zakaria, Rafiq, *Rise of Muslims in Indian Politics* (Bombay, 1970).

Index